Tax Reform in Rural China

Revenue, Resistance, and Authoritarian Rule

How does China maintain authoritarian rule while it is committed to market-oriented economic reforms? This book analyzes this puzzle by offering a systematic analysis of the central-local governmental relationship in rural China, focusing on rural taxation and political participation. Drawing on in-depth interviews with Chinese local officials and villagers, and combining them with game-theoretic analyses, the book argues that the central government uses local governments as a target of blame for the problems that the central government has actually created. The most recent rural tax reforms, which began in 2000, were a conscious trade-off between fiscal crises and rural instability. For the central government, local fiscal crises and the lack of public goods in agricultural areas were less serious concerns than the heavy financial burdens imposed on farmers and the rural unrest that the predatory extractive behavior of local governments had generated in the 1990s, which threatened both economic reforms and authoritarian rule.

Hiroki Takeuchi is Associate Professor of Political Science and Director of the Sun and Star Program on Japan and East Asia in the Tower Center for Political Studies at Southern Methodist University. He previously taught at the University of California, Los Angeles, as Faculty Fellow in the political science department and at Stanford University as Postdoctoral Teaching Fellow in the public policy program. He received his PhD in political science from UCLA, specializing in comparative politics and international relations. His research focuses on Chinese and Japanese politics, comparative political economy of authoritarian regimes, and political economy and international relations in East Asia, as well as game theory applications to political science. His recent articles have been published in the *Journal of Contemporary China*, the *Journal of Chinese Political Science*, the *Japanese Journal of Political Science*, the *Journal of East Asian Studies*, *International Relations of the Asia-Pacific*, and *Modern China*.

Tax Reform in Rural China

Revenue, Resistance, and Authoritarian Rule

HIROKI TAKEUCHI
Southern Methodist University

CAMBRIDGE
UNIVERSITY PRESS

CAMBRIDGE
UNIVERSITY PRESS

Shaftesbury Road, Cambridge CB2 8EA, United Kingdom

One Liberty Plaza, 20th Floor, New York, NY 10006, USA

477 Williamstown Road, Port Melbourne, VIC 3207, Australia

314–321, 3rd Floor, Plot 3, Splendor Forum, Jasola District Centre, New Delhi – 110025, India

103 Penang Road, #05–06/07, Visioncrest Commercial, Singapore 238467

Cambridge University Press is part of Cambridge University Press & Assessment, a department of the University of Cambridge.

We share the University's mission to contribute to society through the pursuit of education, learning and research at the highest international levels of excellence.

www.cambridge.org
Information on this title: www.cambridge.org/9781107056848

First published 2014

A catalogue record for this publication is available from the British Library

Library of Congress Cataloging-in-Publication data
Takeuchi, Hiroki.
Tax reform in rural China : revenue, resistance, and authoritarian rule / Hiroki Takeuchi.
pages cm
Includes bibliographical references and index.
ISBN 978-1-107-05684-8 (hardback)
1. Fiscal policy – China. 2. Taxation – China. 3. Rural population – China 4. Rural development – China. I. Title.
HJ1401.T35 2014
336.2′01451 – dc23 2014009754

ISBN 978-1-107-05684-8 Hardback

For my parents

Contents

Tables

Figures

Acknowledgments

Writing a book is often a lonely journey, but it is also a collective work. I have been fortunate to receive advice, encouragement, and guidance from many people. So it is a great pleasure to acknowledge the many individuals and institutions whose generous support made the writing of this book possible. At UCLA I encountered an extraordinary scholarly community open to diverse ideas and approaches. Although I was in the political science department, I benefited tremendously from various disciplines – including anthropology, economics, geography, history, and sociology – and I thank UCLA for providing me with the environment where I could explore a true multidisciplinary approach.

Within the larger UCLA community, I would first like to express my gratitude to my dissertation committee chair, the late Richard Baum. He was a constant source of encouragement, advice, and support in both the research and writing stages, through the process of transforming an initial idea into a feasible research project and then into a final product. He encouraged me to pursue a topic in which I was really interested, no matter how challenging, gave me timely and right-to-the-point guidance throughout my dissertation research, and patiently pushed me to achieve high academic standards with a perfect sense of when I needed to move faster and when I needed to slow down. I had to answer his tough questions before my dissertation was finished, and they improved the overall argument of this book tremendously. I always admired his ability to capture the big trends in China and explain them using ordinary language, and I have greatly missed him since he passed away. It is my regret that I did not have the opportunity to show him this book.

I would also like to thank Kathy Bawn. I had been disappointed with economics – my undergraduate major – but she showed me how useful game theory and other economics approaches are as tools to analyze political problems. Her guidance formed the methodological ground of my research and her warm encouragement always replenished my diminishing confidence while

I was writing my dissertation. I was fortunate to have Kathy as my adviser, mentor, and friend.

I am also grateful to my other dissertation committee members: Cindy Fan and Jean-Laurent Rosenthal. They provided me with very insightful and constructive suggestions that helped me build ideas for my dissertation. As members outside the political science department, they gave me different angles from which to analyze China's rural politics. Cindy, an economic geographer, constantly reminded me of the uniqueness and innovativeness of combining fieldwork-based empirical research with a game-theory–based theoretical approach. Jean-Laurent, an economist, always helped me keep the rigor of my game-theoretic analysis while thinking about implications of the models' equilibria for the empirical observations from my field research.

Working with Michael Chwe and Barbara Geddes at UCLA was an extremely pleasant and enriching experience. Michael and Barbara helped me tremendously in the building of a rigorous research design. Michael taught me how much a simple formal model could inform us about logical explanations for people's behavior. Barbara encouraged me to focus my efforts on developing good formal models for making convincing arguments. Without their guidance, this book could not develop rich theoretical explanations to support my arguments.

My colleagues at Southern Methodist University (SMU) have enriched the past several years with their advice, conversation, and friendship. I especially want to thank Jim Hollifield, Diana Newton, and Bill Tsutsui. I have been fortunate to have Jim as my colleague, friend, and mentor. With Diana I have shared a fascination for East Asian politics, and she has helped me think about the policy implications of my findings. Bill has always given me encouragement, and his passion for academia has recharged my battery to complete this book whenever its energy level had waned. I also want to thank Michael Lusztig, Steve Wegren, and Matthew Wilson, who gave me incisive suggestions for transforming my project into the publication of this book. Conversations with my colleagues from Chinese studies at SMU, Johan Elverskog and Ling Shiao, have sharpened my understanding of China and improved this book. Dennis Ippolito, Chair of the Political Science Department, has patiently followed and supported my progress. I also thank my other colleagues at SMU – Sabri Ates, Anna Batta, Chelsea Brown, Seyom Brown, Brad Carter, Karisa Cloward, Pam Corley, Liljana Elverskog, Cal Jillson, Jeff Kahn, Joe Kobylka, LaiYee Leong, Steven Lindquist, Luigi Manzetti, Azfar Moin, Steve Rankin, Josh Rovner, Libby Russ, Dennis Simon, and Harold Stanley.

At SMU, I have also been fortunate to be supported by the John Goodwin Tower Center for Political Studies, a policy institute at SMU. In addition to financially supporting my research for the past six years, the Tower Center has given me opportunities to organize many conferences, symposia, and talks, through which I have learned a lot about how to present academic findings to the Dallas/Fort Worth community and beyond, as the Tower Center's mission is bridging academia and a well-informed public. Moreover, participation in numerous events at the Tower Center has expanded and stimulated my interest in politics and public policy, and reminded me of the mission of an intellectual to contribute to society. Such activities are possible thanks to the excellent staff members of the Tower Center, with whom I have made friends, and I thank Luisa del Rosal, Mariko Isozaki, Noëlle McAlpine, Jieun Pyun, Ray Rafidi, Matt Tullman, and Carole Wilson. Furthermore, through the Tower Center's activities I have had opportunities to work with Tom Schieffer, Amanda and David Schnetzer, and Pat Walsh. These opportunities have sharpened my views on international politics and motivated me to think about the implications for U.S. foreign policy. Discussion with them is not only stimulating but also fun, and I thank them for being great friends of mine.

Many people have read my work. I am especially grateful to Melanie Manion. I met her just after I had completed my dissertation, and since then, working with her has been the most stimulating experience. Melanie has always asked me challenging questions and guided me toward not only a better understanding of China and Chinese politics but also a better grasp of the political science discipline. Although I do not think that I have been able to answer all the questions she has raised, my efforts to answer her questions have laid the foundation of this book. Melanie has also encouraged me by focusing on the importance of this book's contribution, especially when I struggled with its progress.

Among many others who have read my work, Steph Haggard and Ralph Thaxton deserve special thanks for their comments on the entire manuscript and substantial suggestions for improvement. I also thank Peter Gries, who provided encouragement, gave me comments on the manuscript, and perhaps most importantly, suggested the title of this book. Without his help, the book's title would have been a much more convoluted one. Conversations with a number of people helped me formulate my ideas. I am grateful to Tomoko Ako, Greg Anderson, Yuen Ang, Tom Bernstein, Lisa Blaydes, Yongshun Cai, Alberto Diaz-Cayeros, Martin Dimitrov, Yusaku Horiuchi, You-Tien Hsing, Lianjiang Li, Phillip Lipscy, Xin Liu, Peter Lorentzen, Dan Lynch, Patti Maclachlan, Barry Naughton, Will Norris, Kevin O'Brien, Jean Oi, Wooyeal Paik, Karen Remner, Ron Rogowski, Michael Ross, Scott Rozelle, Idean Salehyan, Yoshihide Soeya, Heizo Takenaka, Mike Thies, Dan Treisman, Lily Tsai, Jeremy Wallace, Anny Wong, Bin Wong, Stan Wong, Terri Wright, Tatsuo Yamada, Dali Yang, Ka Zeng, Yu Zheng, and Xueguang Zhou.

Since I started my graduate work in the United States more than ten years ago, several scholars have especially influenced me and formed my foundation as a scholar. Although they are from different disciplines and different fields, they are my role models, and without opportunities to meet and work with them I would not have become who I am now as a scholar and a teacher.

I thank Tom Gold, Ryosei Kokubun, Jeff Lewis, Skip Lupia, Liz Perry, Ken Schultz, Beth Simmons, and Andrew Walder for guiding me to the world I am truly enjoying and reminding me of the standard I should follow.

In conducting field research in China's rural villages, I received help from many people. I first thank those who arranged interviews for me: Huang Keyue, Li Changping, Qiu Jiaansheng, Xiao Tangbiao, Xu Jianbo, Yuan Baishun, Zhan Zhengguo, Zhao Shujin, and Zhao Shukai. I also thank the scholars, journalists, and practitioners who have shared their insights with me through discussions: Cao Jinqing, Jing Yuejin, Li Changping, Liu Ya, Tang Shiping, Wang Jiabing, Xiang Jiquan, Xiao Tangbiao, Xu Fuqun, Zhang Jianjun, Zhang Jifeng, Zhao Shukai, and Zhou Li. I am also grateful to Jean Hung and the staff at the Universities Service Centre for China Studies at the Chinese University of Hong Kong for guidance and assistance with my research. Finally, this book would not have been possible without the help of the more than one hundred individuals in rural China who agreed to be interviewed. They taught me how village politics was working. Although I am not able to name them, I thank them for being great teachers of the Chinese rural political economy.

My undergraduate students at SMU have stimulated my interests in rural politics in China and helped me think about why it matters. Discussions with my students have motivated me to think about China's rural problems even further and improved this book. To mention just a few, I am particularly grateful to Rahfin Faruk, Elise Houren, Amber Stubblefield, Jack Swearingen, Julien Teel, and Ryan Wilson. My teaching philosophy is that real teaching should not consist of merely giving lectures, but should give education to individual students. Thus, I treat my students as analysts. The achievements my students have made are my pride.

Some of the material here is revised from "Vote Buying, Village Elections, and Authoritarian Rule in Rural China: A Game Theoretic Analysis," by Hiroki Takeuchi that appeared in *Journal of East Asian Studies*, Volume 13, Number 1 (January–April), 2013, copyright © by the East Asia Institute, and used with permission of Lynne Rienner Publishers, Inc. I would like to thank Lynne Rienner Publishers for this permission. I am also grateful to the Taylor & Francis Group, which provided permission to reprint material revised from "Survival Strategies of Township Governments in Rural China: From Predatory Taxation to Land Trade," by Hiroki Takeuchi that appeared in the *Journal of Contemporary China*, Volume 22, Number 83, 2013, www.tandfonline.com.

At Cambridge University Press, I particularly want to thank Lew Bateman, who has supported my ideas on this research and book from an early stage and whose encouragement and judicious advice have brought this project to fruition. I also want to thank Shaun Vigil, who has patiently dealt with long email exchanges, answering many questions and responding to various requests. They are often tedious, but he has handled them in the utmost professional way. I also thank three anonymous reviewers for the Press, whose comments richly improved the manuscript.

Before the book went to press, Christine Carberry proofread the whole manuscript a few times because this book went through several revisions. Every time she proofread, she did it with an expert eye, saving me from many mistakes, and patiently giving me many helpful suggestions. After the book went to press, she assisted me in transmitting my manuscript for publication. Without her help I would have gotten lost somewhere in the publication process. Even when I was not sure what I was doing, she was sure. Finally, but not least importantly, she prepared the index of this book. I am fortunate to have Chris as my colleague and friend.

Friends, family, and colleagues, from near and far, kept me rooted and sane when I most needed a break (or breaks). I cannot list all those who offered words of encouragement that pulled me out of numerous slumps. To mention just a few, Vivian Zhan, Xin Zhang, and Eric Zusman deserve special credit for providing me with valuable input and selfless help while I went through the PhD program. It was with pleasure that we identified ourselves as the "Gang of Four" while organizing the Chinese Politics Study Group at UCLA. I would also like to express with profound gratitude my debt to Linda Choi Hasunuma, who read and edited an entire draft of my dissertation to suggest corrections and improvements in my writing style. Among other friends, I particularly thank Satoshi Ikeuchi, Tomoki Kamo, Kazuko Kojima, and Kimiko Shiki. My friends have made my work easier and a challenging project again seem possible.

This book grew out of my ongoing journey across three countries. Thus, my greatest debt is to my family, who had to endure during my constant travels. My deepest thanks goes to my wife, Honghong Ma, for her love and support, without which I could not have completed this book. Since we started the journey together, Honghong has listened to me talk enthusiastically about arcane matters of China's rural problems. Her passion and dedication to scholarship have also refreshed my energies for writing this book. In addition to all the support she gives me, I thank her for laughing together with me every day. I am also grateful to my parents-in-law, Anderson Ma and Dang Huu, for being truly supportive for my passion and interest in China.

My parents, Yoshio and Michiko Takeuchi, have always believed in their son and supported my work in diaspora. My parents have encouraged me to pursue whatever I want to pursue, however challenging it is, and have been models of integrity, tenacity, and courage. I am deeply saddened that my father passed away before he could see this book's publication. Conversation with my father was always stimulating and filled with love. He constantly reminded me of the importance of contributing to society through academic work. I hope that his fingerprints are on this book.

Abbreviations

ALL	Administrative Litigation Law (*Xingzheng Susong Fa*)
APCs	agricultural producers' cooperatives (*nongye shengchan hezuoshe*)
CASS	Chinese Academy of Social Sciences
CCP	Chinese Communist Party
CRS	cadre responsibility system
EBFs	extrabudgetary funds (*yusuanwai zijin*)
FERD	State Council's Decision Concerning Fundamental Education Reform and Development (*Guowuyuan Guanyu Jichu Jiaoyu Gaige he Fazhan de Jueding*)
GLF	Great Leap Forward (*Da Yuejin*)
KMT	Nationalist Party (*Kuomintang*)
MATs	mutual aid teams (*huzhuzu*)
MSNE	mixed strategy Nash equilibrium
NPC	National People's Congress
PSNE	pure strategy Nash equilibrium
ROC	Republic of China
SOEs	state-owned enterprises
TVEs	township-and-village enterprises (*xiangzhen qiye*)
VAT	value added tax
VC	villagers' committee (*cunmin weiyuanhui*)
VPB	village party branch (*cun dang zhibu*)
VRA	villagers' representative assembly
VSGA	villagers' small group assembly
WBFs	within-budget funds (*yusuannei zijin*)

Introduction

Why do some tax systems succeed and others fail? In this book, I explore this fundamental question in the field of political economy by studying rural taxation in China. In particular, I examine the motivations and consequences for the Chinese Communist Party's (CCP) introduction of rural tax reforms, asking why the central government adopted the reforms, why local governments implemented them despite potentially negative consequences, and what this analysis contributes to our understanding of authoritarian politics in the world. Few places are better than the Chinese countryside to explore these questions. China's geographic and chronological variation during the political, economic, and social transition of the post-Mao market-oriented reform represents ideal conditions to examine the implementation and enforcement of taxation.

Rural taxation was regressive throughout China's long history, but it worsened in the 1990s. Over the past decades, especially in the 1990s, Chinese villagers were forced to pay a variety of taxes and fees, leading many to complain – and some to protest – that local exactions took up an increasing proportion of their incomes. Students of China's rural issues were stunned by the well-documented cases reported by two sensational Chinese books published at the beginning of this century: *Telling the Premier the Truth*, by Li Changping (2002), a former township party secretary in Jianli County of Hubei Province;[1] and *An Investigation of Chinese Farmers*, by Chen Guidi and Wu Chuntao (2004), writers from Anhui and Hunan Provinces, respectively. Li described, on the basis of his experience as party secretary of poor townships, the difficult livelihood of the villagers and the tense relationship between villagers

[1] *Xiang* is translated as "township" and *zhen* is translated as "town." In this book, I follow this rule to note a specific township or town. When indicating *xiang* or *zhen* as a general administrative level, I use "township."

and local officials in agricultural areas. For example, in Qipan Township of Jianli County in 1999, when Li started serving as party secretary, villagers paid 14 million yuan in taxes and other forms of levies – although only 6 million yuan was considered legitimate – while the total agricultural revenue of the town was less than 10 million yuan (Li C. 2002, 2).[2] Chen and Wu (2004) reported in detail, on the basis of several cases in Anhui, how local officials often employed violent methods to collect taxes and fees and how villagers in agricultural areas, in desperate conditions of poverty, resisted them. Concerned that these signs of discontent would become a source of political instability, the central government initiated a series of rural tax reforms in 2000.

My own experience in two villages at the beginning of my field research in December 2004 confirmed that the Chinese countryside was a good place to explore the issue of taxation. Highland Park Village of Zhejiang Province was, at the time, one of the richest villages in China.[3] The village government had plenty of fiscal revenue to provide public goods.[4] The village cadre I interviewed proudly told me that in 2003 the village government constructed five clean public flush toilets (Interviewee 104).[5] As the village had several factories, 80 percent of its fiscal revenue came from the corporate tax and 20 percent came from the animal husbandry tax. The agricultural tax had been abolished in this village in 1999, before a series of rural tax reforms started in the rest of the nation. Since then, the village government was paying subsidies to villagers who farmed, because no one would be engaged in farming otherwise. Under China's household responsibility system, the village government had to distribute a certain area of land for villagers to farm, regardless of their desire to do so.

Although Long Bridge Village neighbors Highland Park Village, its taxation situation was very different. In 2003, a large part of the revenue of Long Bridge Village still came from the agricultural tax, representing 60 percent of fiscal revenue, while only 30 percent came from the corporate tax (Interviewee 105). The villagers who farmed still had to pay the agricultural tax without receiving any subsidies (Interviewees 106–108). The village did not have flush toilets and villagers were dissatisfied with taxation and the provision of public goods. One of the villagers described: "Last year [in 2003], we not only had to pay the agricultural tax (*nongye shui*) but also had to provide 'compulsory labor' (*yiwu gong*) for repairing an irrigation canal because the village government had not

[2] By "legitimate," I mean the items stipulated by law.

[3] To keep the anonymity of my interviewees, I use fictitious names to describe the localities where I conducted interviews.

[4] The village level is included in my study as a part of the rural governmental structure (even though it is *not* an *official* governmental organization) because officials and villagers both perceive the village level to be part of the local government structure for taxation, the provision of public goods, and the implementation of various policies.

[5] Interviewees are cited by number throughout the book. The list of the interviewees is provided in Appendix A.

repaired it. The village cadres are not helpful. Village elections are useless. The cadres are the same as the officials for the emperor during the imperial period. They are not serving us" (Interviewee 106). In short, in this interviewee's eyes, village cadres did not represent villagers' interests.

The comparison of the two villages was interesting. In richer Highland Park Village, residents did not have to pay the agricultural tax but received subsidies, whereas in poorer Long Bridge Village, residents still paid this tax. Clearly, China's rural financial burdens were regressive. Research on the agricultural tax and other sources of financial burdens in rural areas indeed identifies their regressive character (e.g., X. Li 2003; Lin, Tao, and Liu 2007; Lin et al. 2002a, 2002b). Thus, one of the central questions this book poses is why regressive taxation emerged in the Chinese countryside.

Following decollectivization and subsequent post-Mao reforms, in the 1980s local governments in rural China – including all levels from province to village – gained political authority for tax revenue sources, while the central government lost major fiscal revenue with the decline of state-owned enterprises (Oksenberg and Tong 1991; Wong 1991).[6] However, when the tax-sharing system (*fenshuizhi*) was adopted in 1994, the central government gained back its authority over rural taxation, while local governments – especially at the county (*xian*) and township (*xiang* and *zhen*) levels – lost their revenue sources of easily collected taxes as well as their rights to keep a significant portion of the taxes collected in their locality (Wang 1995; Wang and Hu 2001; White 1998; Zhan 2009a). Local governments – especially at the county and township levels – became increasingly dependent on exactions from local residents to cover budgetary needs. These exactions – informal and sometimes illegal – became a source of villagers' resentment and caused an increase in protests in the Chinese countryside (Bernstein and Lü 2003).

Concerned that these protests would become a source of political instability, the central government initiated the tax-for-fee (*feigaishui*) reform in 2000 and the gradual abolition of the agricultural tax in 2002 (Chen 2003; Li C. 2006; L. Li 2006, 2007; Li and Wu 2005; Oi 2004; Yep 2004).[7] A series of tax reforms beginning in 2000 not only alleviated the villagers' financial burden but also created a new set of problems: local fiscal crises (Chen 2007; Chen and Chen 2004; Huang 2005; Kennedy 2006; Li and Dong 2004; Oi and Zhao 2007; Xiang 2004; Zhao 2010). In areas that relied heavily on the agricultural tax and other ad hoc fees, government officials at the county and township levels

[6] Constitutionally, the structure of China's local governments consists of four levels in rural areas: province (*sheng*), prefecture (municipality or city: *shi*), county (*xian*), and township (*xiang* and *zhen*). Among the four levels, governments at the county and township levels are especially influential on the administration of rural governance, whereas the governments at the provincial and prefectural levels are more influential on the administration of urban governance.

[7] The tax-for-fee reform started with Anhui Province as a test province in 2000 and spread to the whole nation in 2002. Thus, in this book I take 2000 as the year when a series of rural tax reforms started.

found themselves with inadequate revenues and limited incentives to provide public goods. What does the recent experience of rural tax reforms reveal about the evolving logic of power in China's authoritarian regime? And does this experience shed light on the future possibility of China's democratization?

THE ARGUMENT

Although many factors contribute to the explanation of rural tax reforms in China, the argument here places particular emphasis on taxation and state building under authoritarian rule. It fits in the tradition of Margaret Levi's claim: "The history of state revenue production is the history of the evolution of the state" (1988, 1). Previous studies on taxation by political economists and economic historians have suggested that solely relying on the repressive apparatus to collect taxes is inefficient and some institutional mechanism through which taxpayers are willing to cooperate with tax collectors (i.e., the state) is necessary for efficient taxation (e.g., Brewer 1989; Gehlbach 2005; Hoffman and Norberg 1994b; Hoffman and Rosenthal 1997; Mathias and O'Brien 1976; Tilly 1990). Once the state succeeds in establishing efficient taxation based on taxpayers' cooperation, it can invest revenue in building infrastructure to foster further economic development – including the formation of institutions such as wealth-enhancing property rights regimes (Greif 2006; Hoffman and Rosenthal 1997; North 1981, 1990; North and Thomas 1973; North and Weingast 1989). By contrast, if the state fails to establish an institutional mechanism through which it gains taxpayers' cooperation, it not only struggles with collecting tax revenue but also has to expend resources on the repressive apparatus and to create bureaucracies for monitoring coerced compliance by the economic sectors under their control, instead of investing in infrastructure for economic development (Hoffman and Rosenthal 1997, 53).

Empirical findings from preindustrial Europe support this argument. For example, democratic Holland and Britain successfully raised tax revenue while autocratic France and Spain failed miserably to do the same. The British government, because its parliament assured citizens that new impositions would be spent on public goods, created and collected taxes with relative ease (Sacks 1994). Meanwhile, the French government, because it could not credibly commit to similar intentions, ran up sizable deficits on high interest loans (Norberg 1994).

The fact that the most recent rural tax reforms in China were introduced to abolish the agricultural tax suggests that the Chinese state failed to establish a legitimate institution to raise fiscal revenues in order to meet financial needs in its rural areas. In truth, many of the problems confronting rural local governments, which gave the central government an incentive to implement the tax reforms, would not have appeared if villagers had been confident that their money was being spent on public goods. Knowing this, they would have been willing to pay taxes. Why did the state fail to establish a tax system that might give villagers an incentive to pay in rural China?

The major arguments in this book concern the political economy of rural tax reforms between the central government and local governments in contemporary China. I hypothesize that the central government leadership in Beijing designed and constructed the political and economic framework of reforms so that the CCP could maintain authoritarian rule while remaining committed to the post-Mao market-oriented reform. In this book, I discuss how China is ruled by examining the central government's strategies of keeping power, focusing on the intrastate relationship between the central government and local governments. Ultimately, I argue that the central government uses the local government as a scapegoat for problems that the central government has actually created.

Having experienced the disaster of the Great Leap Famine (1958–60) and the Cultural Revolution (1966–76), the CCP leadership reached a consensus that reverting to the planned economy was not a viable option (Baum 1994; Fewsmith 1994; Pye 1986; Thaxton 2008; Yang 1996). Once the post-Mao market-oriented reform started, the central government found it difficult to collect sufficient revenue to finance the expenditures of local governments. This was attributable to reduced revenue from inefficient state-owned enterprises, which had been the major revenue source for the central government under the Maoist planned economy (Naughton 2007, chapter 13; Steinfeld 1998, chapter 3). This difficulty gave the central government a strong incentive for the fiscal reform in 1994, called the tax-sharing system (*fenshuizhi*), which increased the central share of fiscal revenue and significantly decreased the share that local governments could claim (Zhan 2006). Having lost a major revenue source by the introduction of the tax-sharing system, local governments increasingly relied on exactions from local residents in rural areas. Reflecting tensions caused by increased financial burdens, villagers started to express their grievances with greater frequency and intensity in the 1990s. Organized demonstrations, protests, and even riots began to occur on a growing scale and with sporadic but increasing violence. In response, China's authoritarian regime introduced (or revamped old) participatory channels designed to give political voice – albeit a limited, controlled voice – to villagers, hoping to ease rural discontent and reduce the likelihood of political instability (Bernstein and Lü 2003; O'Brien and Li 2006; Unger 2002).

At the same time, reflecting the importance of maintaining political and social stability and an unwillingness to relinquish power, the CCP leadership has retained authoritarian rule instead of being committed to political reforms for establishing a democratic regime based on representative institutions. Political reforms advanced to a certain extent during the post-Mao period; however, the condition of maintaining authoritarian rule limited the CCP leadership's available means to improve the quality of rural governance through effective taxation and the provision of public goods. Note that I do not claim that the CCP's effort to maintain authoritarian rule is the only factor that explains rural tax reforms in contemporary China and (the lack of) the provision of public goods, nor do I claim that if China's political regime is democratized then all the problems concerning taxation and the provision of public goods in the Chinese countryside will be solved. Many factors have contributed to these issues. However, I do argue that the CCP's commitment to maintaining authoritarian rule while advancing market-oriented reform played a crucial and hitherto poorly understood (or misunderstood) role in shaping the consequences of rural tax reforms beginning in 2000.

This argument also has a practical implication for public policy: that is, taxation may give an authoritarian ruling party a possible rational interest to initiate democratization. While there has been a consensus that China's democratization will be elite-led – not mass-oriented – *if* the political regime becomes more democratic (e.g., Baum 1996; Gilley 2004), the issue of how and why the elite may lead democratization remains largely unresolved. On the one hand, because of the rural tax reforms beginning in 2000, the CCP succeeded in defusing popular dissatisfaction over rural taxation without extending popular franchise in the countryside. Perhaps because of this success, the CCP leadership might be less likely to embrace further democratic reforms. On the other hand, this success was achieved at the expense of local governments' administrative capacity and popular legitimacy. The central government managed to rechannel the blame for the lack of public goods on local governments and (perhaps) enhance its own authority. However, blaming the local authorities did not necessarily strengthen the central government's hand. Local people knew that the central government and its clients had appointed the local cadres that plundered from them. Theoretically, democracy may give the regime a way to successfully collect the taxes it needs for financial stability, as well as provide funds needed to provide public goods. In previous studies, some have argued that democracy should be embraced in order to defuse unrest, whereas others have argued that its justification should derive from its normative value (e.g., Barber 1984; Bobbio 1987; Cunningham 1987; Dahl 1989; Dominguez and Shifter 2003; Held 1993; Pateman 1970; Powell 1982; Sartori 1987; Shapiro 1996). I argue instead that democracy is needed – or desirable – for the economic reason of efficient taxation. To prove my argument generally and rigorously would go far beyond the evidence this book can muster. Instead I offer analyses using simple game-theoretic models, supported by interview data, about taxation, political participation and popular resistance, and authoritarian rule based on what has been observed in the Chinese countryside.

RESEARCH DESIGN AND METHODOLOGY

The empirical analysis of this book uses both documentary sources and interviews. Documentary sources in Chinese and English include newspapers, magazines, books, and publicly available governmental and nongovernmental reports. Publicly available academic and media sources, secondary literature, and field notes of other scholars in both Chinese and English were also consulted. I use these sources to discuss rural taxation and tax resistance in the period of 1985–2005, especially in the 1990s, and to document the growing crisis of legitimacy surrounding the issue of rural taxation and fiscal revenue. I especially use Chinese-language sources that have been little referenced in the English-language literature, which give a great wealth of data on this issue.[8] By extensively using Chinese-language sources, I discuss why 2005–06 was the date for abolishing the agricultural tax, whether anti-tax resistance crested when the agricultural tax was abolished, and how the situations varied between poor agricultural villages and richer industrialized villages.

Moreover, interviews with 108 individuals – local cadres and rural residents in the seven provinces of Guangdong, Guizhou, Hebei, Hubei, Hunan, Jiangxi, and Zhejiang during 2004 and 2005 – are a crucial part of the data I use in this book for ascertaining the motivations behind local cadres' and rural residents' behavior. The interviews are not representative, and I reference other studies and reports when discussing the information I obtained from the interviews. I use the interviews to discuss rural tax reform in contemporary China, focusing on how the central government ruled rural areas, while bringing in the established (both Chinese-language and English-language) literature to show how the literature differs from my findings or supports them. In particular, my interviews with local cadres reveal how they saw the central government and how they understood the central government's strategy of ruling the countryside and engaging in rural governance.[9] My interviews with local cadres and villagers show how they viewed the dilemma posed by the central government's dominant power in rural governance.

Semistructured interviews were conducted with both local cadres (county, township, and village) and rural residents. Table 0.1 shows the structure of the pool of interviews. Among the seven provinces where I conducted interviews, a majority of interviewees were from Hebei, Hunan, and Jiangxi, where I stayed longer than the other provinces. The regional variation in political-economic conditions helped me examine how economic levels and other socioeconomic and geographic factors *across* and *within* each province influenced political participation and rural taxation. For example, in two of the five townships

[8] *Taxation without Representation in Contemporary Rural China* by Bernstein and Lü (2003) is the best work in English-language literature on rural taxation and tax resistance in China in the 1990s.

[9] In this way, I see rural tax reform and rural governance from the local cadres' eyes. Thus, I do not directly observe or argue the central government's real intention, which is difficult to determine because the central government's (and any organization's) decision making is collective and each policy outcome often does not meet each policy maker's original intention. On the issue of the gap between the state's or policy maker's intention and the policy outcome, see the book by James Scott (1998).

TABLE 0.1. *Composition of the Informant Pool*

	Local Cadres					
	Prefecture	County	Township	Village	Villagers	Total
Guangdong	–	–	–	1	2	3
Guizhou	–	–	1	–	7	8
Hebei (Baoding)	–	–	–	2	12	14
Hebei (Zhangjiakou)	–	1	8	5	5	19
Hubei	3	1	–	1	2	7
Hunan	–	1	5	17	3	26
Jiangxi	–	–	6	6	13	25
Zhejiang	–	1	–	2	3	6
Total	3	4	20	34	47	108

in Hunan Province where I conducted field research, one consisted of mostly agricultural villages while the other consisted of mostly industrialized villages. The observed variation was useful for discerning which variables influenced local cadres' and villagers' behavior. Being on the ground helped me see how less quantifiable historical and cultural variables influenced political and economic outcomes.

All interview questions were open-ended: respondents answered questions in as many or as few words as they deemed necessary.[10] The questions focused on: (1) conditions of local finance, including sources of revenue and a breakdown of expenditures; (2) decision-making processes of local governance; and (3) execution of village elections.[11] I also gathered basic geographic and demographic information on each locality. During the course of the interviews, I met with local cadres first and then moved to rural residents, so that I could confirm with villagers the information local cadres provided.

My interviews provided me with a nonrepresentative sample based on the snowball sampling method – which means that I was introduced to the respondents rather than employing a random sample. With this method, the sample was suggestive and provided rich details and analyses of how local cadres and villagers saw the rural tax reforms and responded to the policy change. Interviews were arranged through my friends and through the local cadres that I knew. Most of the interviewees were eager to share their experiences with me, although several apparently told me what they had been instructed by

10 In this sense, my interview method is different from the structured interview methods that follow the same questionnaire in every interview (e.g., Guthrie 1999). Instead my interviews are similar to those conducted by William Hurst, which "allowed interviewees to discuss issues and ideas that concerned them" (2009, 9). My interviews are similar to the interview strategy taken by David Wank (1999).

11 Interview questions are provided in Appendix B.

higher authorities to tell me. Just as Kevin O'Brien (1994a, 362) found that his interviewees (i.e., National People's Congress delegates) expressed "personal standpoints and preferences that enabled them to transcend informal pressures and formal demands to reshape their own roles," so also I found in my interviews; local cadres expressed their own views about the reality of rural politics in their locality, transcending formal and informal constraints about what they should tell me about local governance. In most of the interviews it was not possible to tape record responses, so I translated and transcribed answers in every instance as soon as possible after the interviews.

The semistructured interviews were supplemented with what Thomas Gold (1989) called "guerrilla interviewing" – that is, informal conversations with local cadres in a dining room of the local government, chatting with villagers in informal settings, and so forth. Although guerrilla interviewing is not systematic, many previous studies have established that it is a good way to authenticate what is happening on the ground (e.g., Hurst 2009; Kelliher 1992). For example, a town official spoke of informal and quasi-illegal ways of financing his local government when I chatted with him while eating lunch, but he referred only to formal ways of financing when I formally interviewed him in his office. Informants used for guerrilla interviewing only are not included in the 108 interviewees listed in Appendix A. However, when an informant with whom I formally interviewed showed me more reliable information during guerrilla interviewing than during systematic interviewing, I replaced the information from their systematic interview with the information from the guerrilla interview. For example, in the aforementioned case of a town official, I took the information about quasi-illegal financing he gave me when eating lunch, instead of the information about formal ways of financing he gave me during the systematic interview in his office.

In Part II (Chapters 5–7), I use simple game-theoretic formal models to make theoretical arguments that may account for the logic of the behavior of the central government, local officials, and villagers.[12] The formal models are abstract, stylized representations of certain aspects of rural politics in China. One of the benefits of using formal modeling is to "force one to specify all the assumptions that one is making and verify that the logical connections between these assumptions and the subsequent claims is ironclad" (Kydd 2005, 22–23). My arguments are built on the following assumption, which originates in Levi (1988, 3): all the actors are rational and strategic. Here rationality means that the actors can define their preferences based on their own interests and that their preferences are consistent. Thus, the actors calculate costs and benefits

[12] The title of Part II, "Analytic Narratives," is named after the title of the book written by five political economists (Robert Bates, Avner Greif, Margaret Levi, Jean-Laurent Rosenthal, and Barry Weingast). Just as they maintain, this book takes advantage of "the rich, qualitative, and descriptive materials that narratives offer," and seeks "an explicit and logically rigorous account of the events," which game-theoretic formal models offer (Bates et al. 1998, 12).

of available alternative strategies and then choose the course of action most consistent with their preferences among the set of strategies. Based on this assumption, this book develops two game-theoretic models: one about local finance, rural taxation, and the provision of public goods; and the other about village elections. In the chapters that use game-theoretic formal models, I first discuss assumptions of the model by introducing anecdotes and observations drawn from my field research and previous studies, and set out the stylized facts that pose puzzles. Then I examine theoretical explanations that may account for the puzzles in logically consistent ways. The theoretical explanations are supported by a game-theoretic analysis shown in an appendix to each chapter.

Another benefit of using formal modeling is to help us "make inferences about other sometimes difficult to observe phenomena" (Kydd 2005, 24). One cannot directly infer the actors' preferences from the observed choices of the actors, especially when the actors make decisions strategically. For example, observed compliance might mean satisfaction with policy but might also mean a lack of ways to protest. However, the difficulty of inferring preferences from observed acts does not necessarily mean that one cannot infer actors' preferences at all. On this issue, formal modeling can help "reason backwards from observed events to unobserved beliefs and motivations" (Kydd 2005, 24). Moreover, by casting the central government as the institution that influences local cadres' and villagers' behavior, I infer the central government's preferences from the observed relationship between local cadres and villagers. In other words, I treat the central government not as a strategic player in the formal models but as a player that "governs" the model.

Thus, I assume that central leaders chose particular policies using the available information when they made decisions about what their options were and what the likely consequences would be. This assumption does not necessarily contradict conventional wisdom about policy making in post-Mao China: that it has often been a reaction to local initiatives and experiments (e.g., Kelliher 1992; Tsai 2002; Zhou 1996); that it has constantly shifted and adjusted in the manner of "crossing the river by feeling the stones" (e.g., Oi 1999; K. Tsai 2007; Whiting 2001); and that it has typically been based on incomplete and inaccurate information (e.g., Landry 2008; Manion 2004; Wang and Hu 2001). In this book, I argue that the central government myopically responded to the current, urgent problems in rural China. First, this argument implies that the central government perceived reacting to local initiatives and experiments as a possible option of its policy making. Second, it does not contradict the conventional view that the Chinese central government operates in the manner of "crossing the river by feeling the stones." Equilibrium of the games would show potential scenarios if the central government had a long-term perspective. If the central government's observed behavior contradicted the model's predicted outcome, then the model would provide a good reason to suspect that the government behaved myopically. Third, the assumption that central leaders would use the *available* information to choose particular policies is consistent with the observation that they often have to face the problem of incomplete (and inaccurate) information when making decisions. In other words, the conventional view that policy making in post-Mao China has typically been based on incomplete and inaccurate information is incorporated into my game-theoretic formal models.

PLAN OF THE BOOK

After the theoretical framework of taxation and participation in authoritarian rule is laid out in Chapter 1, this book is divided into two main parts. Part I, consisting of Chapters 2, 3, and 4, sets out the historical and analytical contexts of rural taxation and political participation. Chapter 2 presents how the theoretical argument developed in Chapter 1 compares to the historical context of rural taxation and political participation in China. This chapter also highlights major changes that occurred in rural governance during the post-Mao period. Chapter 3 focuses on how the theoretical argument on taxation and participation fares with rural taxation and resistance in the period of 1980–2005, especially in the 1990s. It documents the growing crisis of legitimacy surrounding the tax and revenue issue, discussing why the agricultural tax was abolished in 2006. Chapter 4 explores the series of rural tax reforms beginning in 2000 and discusses their effects, focusing on the survival strategies of township governments. It reviews how and why the tax reforms brought undesired consequences in the form of local fiscal crises in agricultural areas. It then considers why the central government implemented rural tax reforms despite the evident negative effects they would have on the provision of public goods.

Part II, consisting of Chapters 5, 6, and 7, presents how the development of political and economic institutions – such as rural-to-urban migration, the petition system, and village elections – influenced the political economy of rural tax reform in contemporary China. Chapters 5 and 6 lay out the underlying framework of rural taxation and political participation in the context of central-local relations and local state-society relations in rural China during the post-Mao period. Chapter 5 discusses how the relaxation of restrictions on migration from rural to urban areas influenced the central government's strategy of rural governance and the relationship between villagers and local governments. It argues that the most recent tax reform was the optimal strategy for the central government to strengthen its state authority, sacrificing the local governments' capability to govern, while remaining committed to market-oriented reform. Chapter 6 discusses how the institutionalization of remonstrative participation during the post-Mao reform influenced central-local intergovernmental relations and local state-society relations. It argues that seemingly democratic (or pseudo-democratic) institutions strengthened the central authority while undermining the local governments' capacity for rural governance, especially after rural tax reforms since 2000. Hence, the strategy of strengthening remonstrative institutions was consistent with the CCP leadership's goal of sustaining one-party authoritarian rule, even if it did not lead to the improvement of rural governance. Chapter 7 presents the nature and consequences of village elections in rural China. It argues that this electoral institution was also part of the central government's optimal strategy to strengthen its state authority and maintain authoritarian rule, even though it did not improve the local governments' capacity for rural governance or hold local leaders accountable to villagers. Simple game-theoretic models are shown at the end of Chapters 5, 6, and 7.

The conclusion of this book summarizes my empirical findings and evaluates the logic developed in the previous chapters. It also examines this book's implications for understanding the political economy of the relationship between the local state and the central government in contemporary China, as well as for illuminating theoretical debates about the relationship between authoritarian rule and regime type on the one hand, and taxation and market-oriented economic reforms on the other.

1

The Theory of Revenue and Resistance under Authoritarian Rule in Rural China

The natural starting point for a discussion about rural taxation in contemporary China is how Chinese rulers collect taxes in the countryside, and more generally how authoritarian rulers maximize revenue. In this book, I explore the issue of rural taxation by distinguishing two different types of China's rural areas: one is poor, nonindustrialized hinterland agricultural villages, the other is rich, industrialized periurban villages. My overall finding in this book is that poorer interior agricultural villages have been plagued by bad governance (i.e., lack of the provision of public goods), whereas richer villages have benefited from comparatively good governance (i.e., the provision of public goods). In short, poorer agricultural villages have been losers under the post-Mao market-oriented reform, whereas richer industrialized villages have been winners.

Many political economists argue that simply relying on the repressive apparatus to collect taxes is inefficient. Margaret Levi (1988) raises the idea that "quasi-voluntary compliance" is preferable to coercion. Under this preferred arrangement, taxing "is voluntary in that constituents pay because they choose to... [but it] is quasi-voluntary because they will be punished if they do not and are caught" (ibid., 32). If such a situation had existed in the Chinese countryside, a major overhaul of rural taxation and the abolition of the agricultural tax would have been unnecessary. Three conditions are required to elicit quasi-voluntary compliance: (1) tax collectors must have bargaining power over taxpayers; (2) transaction costs to collect taxes must be relatively low; and (3) uncertainty (discount rates over the future) must be relatively low (ibid., 17–33).

In agricultural areas, post-Mao rural reforms made it difficult to meet these three conditions. The relaxation of state migration policies that had allowed villagers to work in cities diminished local governments' bargaining power vis-à-vis villagers and increased the transaction costs of collecting taxes. The low potential for industrial development discouraged local governments from investing in infrastructure construction, gave them a short-term incentive to extract all they could from villagers, and raised villagers' uncertainty over the future. Since the 1980s, the relaxation of migration policies enabled more than 100 million villagers, known as the "floating population" (*liudong renkou*), to enter cities to work in factories, construction sites, or service industries in pursuit of higher wages and improved living conditions (Cui 2004; Mallee 1988, 1995; Solinger 1999; L. Zhang 2001a, 2001b).

Three things should be noted about this new migration policy during the post-Mao era. First, it was a necessary outcome of the Chinese Communist Party's (CCP) commitment to market-oriented economic reform. The massive flow of rural migrants to cities was the basis for rapid industrialization and a booming urban economy. Tightening migration policies would have eliminated a crucial source of cheap labor and an important stimulus to the industrial economy, especially for export-oriented industries. In short, even though population flows presented a sizable challenge to Chinese socialist modes of state control, the regime had no choice but to keep the current relaxed migration policies to maintain the nation's rapid pace of economic growth. Second, the migration wave was not precipitated by the heavy tax burden. The tax burden peaked in the 1990s, which led to many rural uprisings spurred by tax resistance in the latter part of the decade. Thus, it was not the heavy tax burden that caused the migration wave from rural to urban areas, but rather the market-oriented post-Mao reform that began in the 1980s. Third, as a result of the increased possibility of outbound migration, villagers (taxpayers) gained greater bargaining power over their local government (tax collectors). Opportunities to work outside the village made it easier for villagers to resist payments of levies (taxes and fees). It was difficult to collect levies from those who were absent from the village. As a result, local governments suffered from a shortfall in fiscal revenue. Moreover, as more villagers refused to pay levies, local governments encountered a tipping-point problem. Villagers would pay taxes as long as other villagers would pay. But outbound migration made it increasingly difficult to collect levies from villagers and led the remaining villagers to argue that it was unfair that only they had to pay taxes when others were earning comparatively higher salaries elsewhere and not paying levies. Moreover, as more villagers refused to pay levies, the cost to collect them from any given villager was higher because the resources (both personnel and financial sources) to police collection were limited. Therefore, each villager found it easier to refuse to pay levies.

What could compensate for the erosion of revenue collection in rural China? In other words, what would be needed to gain quasi-voluntary compliance with rural taxation? Levi (1988, 60) suggests that rulers must "provide reassurance that they will deliver... promised goods and services." In industrialized villages, this mechanism worked. Because the potential for the long-term benefits of local economic development gave the local government an incentive to provide public goods by investing in infrastructure construction, villagers could be reasonably certain that the local government would deliver on its promise. In short, Levi's "reassurance" existed in industrialized villages as a function of their potential for local development. In contrast, for villagers to be willing to comply with revenue collection in agricultural areas, some mechanism involving political institutions would be needed to compensate for the lack of reassurance on the basis of the potential for local development. One such mechanism would be regularly scheduled democratic elections (ibid., 62). By exposing officials to periodic evaluations and staking officials' job security on their results, elections would arguably assure local residents that officials would follow through on their pledges to use tax revenue for the greater good (or suffer the consequences for failing to follow through on these pledges). In this sense, the CCP leadership's professed desire to maintain an authoritarian regime limited the available policy choices in rural taxation and spawned negative consequences such as those that emerged from a series of rural tax reforms after 2000.

As Levi argues, rulers "maximize [revenue] subject to the constraints of their relative bargaining power vis-à-vis agents and constituents, their transaction costs, and their discount rates" (ibid., 10). To pursue this goal,

> rulers walk a tightrope. The pursuit of personal ends – within constraints – is the sine qua non of predatory rulers. However, such pursuit may antagonize allies and constituents and enhance the appeal of rivals. On the other hand, too many concessions to allies and constituents could undermine rulers' political and economic power. (ibid., 38)

In this chapter, I explore the factors that may explain how China's authoritarian rulers walk this tightrope. I focus on central-local relations and political participation in the political economy of rural China. The theoretical discussion in this chapter provides a basis for more empirical discussion in the following chapters. I argue that in the political economy of rural tax reforms in China, the central government expanded popular political participation to increase its relative bargaining power vis-à-vis local governments, and as a result, local governments lost their bargaining power vis-à-vis both the central government and villagers.

CENTRAL-LOCAL RELATIONS AND RURAL TAXATION

Although a significant number of villagers failed to pay taxes in rural China, local governments still had an incentive to fill, or at least to artfully disguise, revenue shortfalls. Their motivations for reaching the revenue targets by any means possible had an institutional basis. China's Budget Law required that each level of the government should make ends meet every year, and higher-level governments often promoted local officials who maintained a balanced budget (Zhou 2004, 181–82). Because local cadres were not elected by villagers but appointed by higher authorities, their promotions came from one level up and were thereby based on, among other things, their ability to keep public coffers full (Edin 2003; Whiting 2004). Thus, local cadres often cheated higher authorities regarding their fiscal conditions, and the central government struggled to check their deceptive behavior.

In comparative political economy, there has been a long running and frequently contested debate concerning why developmental policies designed to promote economic growth do not work as intended (e.g., Bates 1981, 1989, 2001; Bates and Krueger 1993; de Soto 2000; Easterly 2001; Easterly and Levine 1997; Krueger 1992, 1993; Ostrom 1990, 2005). Political scientists have argued that from the perspective of state building, this malfunctioning of developmental policies occurs because the state structure in developing countries is often not sufficiently consolidated for the central government's power to penetrate local (both governmental and societal) institutions and organizations (Herbst 2000; Huntington 1968; Migdal 1988).

China's rural governance is no exception. Well-known Chinese precepts such as "the above has policies while the below has countermeasures" (*shang you zhengce xia you duice*) and "we see heaven high and emperor far" (*tian gao huangdi yuan*) suggest that the tendency for local officials to reinterpret central mandates for their own interests has deep historical roots. Jean Oi (1989) and Vivienne Shue (1988) argue that even during the Maoist period, when the central government controlled the resources of villagers' daily lives to an unprecedented degree, leaders in local communities had significant space to exercise resistance against central authorities.

However, Jonathan Unger (1989) disagrees with this "weak central control" argument made by Oi and Shue. Instead, he argues that the central government during the Maoist period had willing accomplices in the grassroots-level cadres, and hence the central government was a powerful, penetrative state under Mao Zedong. He agrees that "most rural Chinese officials played a double-edged game," trying to balance the central government's demands and local interests when they were contradictory; however, because "promotions were granted from above and... if their disobedience were ever discovered, they faced ruin," local officials during the Maoist period followed the central government's demands even if they would be completely detrimental to their local residents (Unger 1989, 121). Agreeing with Unger's argument, Ralph Thaxton (2008) contends that the Great Leap Forward famine occurred in 1958–60 because local officials imposed the central government's grain procurement demands despite the fact that they were impossible to achieve, unless the officials would starve villagers.

By contrast, the divergence between the central government's demands and local governments' discretion became more apparent in the post-Mao era. For example, Cao Jinqing (2000), a Chinese sociologist and a veteran observer of rural China, on the basis of his field research in Henan Province, documents how local governments did not implement nationally mandated policies as the central government expected. Whether local CCP leaders could implement the central government's policy as desired by the central government depended on the issue area and the amount of pressure the central government brought to bear on local officials. National policies with a gap between the central government's expectation and the local government's implementation extended from the family planning (*jihua shengyu*) regulation to rural taxation, local government finances, land allocation, land expropriation, the sale of collective assets, village elections, and the handling of disputes among villagers.

With more Chinese literature available on local governments' actual implementation of national policies at the county, township, and village levels (e.g., Li C. 2002; Li and Dong 2004; Yu 2001; Zhan 2004; Zhang 2000, 2007; Zhou 2004), we now know that the problem Cao reported was prevalent across the entire Chinese countryside. Local governments complained that the central government did not provide sufficient financial resources to implement national policies and to achieve various goals (i.e., local economic development, tax collection, etc.) but simply pressured them through various channels such as the personnel system. In the 1990s, facing pressure from the central government, local governments imposed heavy levies on villagers to satisfy the goals set by the central government and higher authorities, and thus tensions between local governments and rural society increased. Moreover, as villagers became increasingly savvy and informed about their rights stipulated by the central government, local governments faced pressure from villagers to provide public goods.

A body of English-language literature has supported the argument that the central government was dissatisfied with the local governments' neglect of the central government's intentions on national policies (e.g., O'Brien and Li 1999; Peng 1996; Rozelle 1991, 1994; Wedeman 2001). However, another body of literature has suggested that the central government maintained, if not strengthened, its control over local governments through a personnel management mechanism called the cadre responsibility system (CRS) (e.g., Edin 2000, 2003; Huang 1996, 2002; Landry 2008; Shevchenko 2002; Tsui and Wang 2004; Whiting 2004). For example, Maria Edin (2003, 36) argues that "higher levels of the party-state have strengthened their political control over local leaders not only through appointment but also through promoting successful leaders to hold concurrent positions at higher levels and by rotating them between different positions within the county."

The argument that the central government attempted to maximize revenue subject to the constraints of its relative bargaining power vis-à-vis local governments and villagers, its transaction costs to collect revenue, and the discount rates for the future in the locality helps explain the split views on central-local relations. Although the CRS was implemented throughout the whole nation, its effect differed depending on local economic conditions. In industrialized villages, where local officials and villagers expected high future benefits and hence the local discount rates for the future were low, the CRS gave local cadres an incentive to provide public goods and be committed to investing in infrastructure construction and other developmental projects, because local economic development was one of the major criteria for the promotion of local cadres. Villagers did not have a strong incentive to leave their village, expecting local economic development, and hence the transaction costs for tax collection were low.

Meanwhile, in agricultural villages, where local officials and villagers did not expect high future benefits and hence the local discount rates for the future were high, the CRS gave local governments an incentive to deceive higher authorities to hide local problems in order to avoid demotion or other unfavorable treatment in personnel management. Villagers left their village to work in cities, and hence the transaction costs for revenue collection were high. Moreover, conditions for performance contracts under the CRS signed between local governments and higher authorities often included targets of economic development or revenue collection higher than the level feasible for governments to achieve with the given local economic conditions, because cadres of the lower government were at an inferior position to higher authorities in this personnel management system (Bernstein and Lü 2003; Zhan 2006). Therefore, the contracts gave local officials in agricultural villages further incentives to shirk and cheat higher authorities.

In sum, the central government's dissatisfaction with a local government's neglect of the central government's intentions was more likely to occur in agricultural villages, while the central government kept the deviant behaviors of local governments in check in industrialized villages through the CRS. In other words, the central government had more bargaining power vis-à-vis local governments in industrialized villages through the CRS than it did in agricultural villages. With this condition, the central government's optimal strategy to maximize revenue was to abolish the agricultural tax and other levies in the agricultural areas, so that it could eradicate the cause of rural uprisings. Local officials resisted by shirking and created the incomplete information problem for the central government. However, for the central government, villagers' uprisings were more threatening to the stability and survival of the regime than local officials' shirking was.

If local cadres were elected popularly, central-local relations would be different. Local cadres would have an institutional incentive to represent their local residents' interests, to reveal their local problems to the central government or higher authorities, and to negotiate with them to elicit better conditions for the locality. The central government, having obtained actual information about local conditions, could provide subsidies to the localities that needed them most. For example, when local cadres were popularly elected in Russia in the 1990s, they had an institutional incentive to reveal their local problems to the federal government, and the federal government also had an institutional incentive to respond to the local demands with fiscal transfers (Gimpelson and Treisman 2002; Treisman 1996, 1999a). Elections for local leaders gave these leaders a reason to be honest about impending crises, and central authorities endeavored to avert crises before local leaders found it necessary to conceal their local problems in myriad ways.[1]

In contrast, the Chinese central government blamed local governments for their economic and political problems and was able to make its blame a credible threat by the personnel system, whereby higher authorities appointed local cadres at each level of the government. Thus, local officials hid the information about local conditions and did not trust but deceived higher authorities. As a result, the central leaders failed to obtain accurate information about local conditions. In short, the central government used the local governments as a scapegoat for rural governance problems.[2] Local governments struggled to maintain a balanced budget, but local cadres tried to disguise these struggles at all cost to avoid unfavorable treatment in the personnel management system. When it was impossible to reach the goal legitimately or disguise the revenue shortage, local officials increased financial burdens on villagers. These financial burdens became a source of contention between villagers and local officials.

POLITICAL PARTICIPATION AND RURAL TAXATION

As reform-related discontent increased, the CCP leadership became increasingly concerned with instability in rural areas. In the 1980s, Chen Yun and other conservative advocates drew attention to the increase in collective uprisings in the countryside (Bernstein 1999, 210–11). In 1988, when Wan Li – former party secretary of Anhui Province and one of the major leaders of the post-Mao market-oriented economic reform – became chairman of the National People's Congress (NPC), he raised the issue of rural financial burdens for the first time in that body, reflecting the heavy financial strains of levies placed on villagers and their possible destabilizing effects on rural politics and society (*Zhongguo Xinwenshe* [China News Agency], July 6, 1993). In 1992, both Deng Xiaoping and Jiang Zemin expressed their concerns with rural instability (*Renmin Ribao* [People's Daily], overseas edition, January 27, 1993).

Importantly, the CCP leadership not only took note of these problems but actively sought to reconcile them with the institutionalization of participatory

[1] I do not claim that the Russian regime was problem-free. The Russian political system created an incentive for local officials to inflate local problems in order to get more fiscal transfers from the federal government (Treisman 1999a).

[2] Ralph Thaxton (2008) argues for the historical continuity of the practice of the center's use of locals as a scapegoat between the Maoist and post-Mao periods. He contends that the reason local governments do not trust but deceive the central government is that during the Maoist era, the central government pressured local governments to carry out its draconian policies, which damaged the central government's credibility with local officials and villagers, and sometimes damaged even the local officials that had done the central government's (or Mao Zedong's) bidding. Once the Great Leap Forward turned into a disastrous famine, the central government (and Mao himself) blamed local officials for economic and political disasters.

channels. For example, the NPC Standing Committee adopted the Agricultural Law in 1993, which intended to protect villagers from local governments' illegal exactions, "because a wave of rural disturbances prompted regime action" (Bernstein 1999, 212). This law, along with the Administrative Litigation Law (ALL: *Xingzheng Susong Fa*) promulgated in 1989 and the Organic Law of Villagers' Committees (*Cunmin Weiyuanhui Zizhi Fa*: hereafter the Organic Law) established in 1988 (and revised in 1998), gave a legal basis for the institutionalization of participatory channels and formed the norms of laws for three democratic institutions: village elections, petitions, and local courts. Some of these institutional innovations, such as village elections, had evolved independently at the local level and were tolerated afterward by the central government. Others, such as local courts, were introduced intentionally by the central government to reduce the likelihood that rural tension would create political and social instability. In the following section, I examine these three political institutions – village elections, petitions, and local courts – that were established or revamped in order to give villagers participatory channels to express their dissatisfaction with rural governance.

Village Elections

Since the landmark event of China's first village election in Guangxi Province in 1980, such elections have spread throughout China and become one of the most widely researched institutional areas of study in Chinese politics.[3] Through the establishment of the Organic Law in 1988 and its revision in 1998, China's authoritarian regime allowed, encouraged, and required elections to be held at the village level. The Chinese village elections had certain democratic functions, and some scholars and Western nongovernmental organizations expected the village elections to lead to the democratization of the whole nation (Chan 1998; Pei 1995). In the meantime, the CCP hoped that village elections would improve local governance in its vast countryside – where the majority of the Chinese population resided even after large-scale migration from rural to urban areas over the past three decades – by disciplining local officials and preventing massive rural unrest (L. Li 2003; Li and O'Brien 1999; O'Brien 1994b; Shi 1999). Some empirical findings suggest the positive effects for which the regime hoped: villages with elected cadres were more likely to have leaders receptive

[3] The literature on village elections is too large to cite in a single footnote. Major books published in Chinese include the books by Hu Rong (2001) and Tong Zhihui (2004) and the edited volumes by Xiao Tangbiao and his collaborators (i.e., Xiao 2002b; Xiao, Qiu, and Tang 2001). Citations of additional empirical work can be found throughout the text in this book, especially in Chapter 7. One of the best anthologies of case studies on village elections is the volume edited by Li Lianjiang, Guo Zhenglin, and Xiao Tangbiao (2001). For the most comprehensive empirical analyses of village elections, see the works by Baogang He (2007) and John James Kennedy (2002a). For reviews of the English-language literature on village elections, see the articles by Kevin O'Brien and Rongbin Han (2009) and Gunter Schubert (2002).

to popular preferences (Alpermann 2001; Kennedy, Rozelle, and Shi 2004; Manion 1996, 2006; Wang 1997), and the implementation of village elections arguably reduced the likelihood of mass uprisings (Howell 1998; L. Li 2001; O'Brien and Li 2001; Pastor and Tan 2001; Schubert and Chen 2007).

However, there were limitations on these democratic functions. For example: "Village elections are said to be controlled by the Communist Party... [and] technically flawed by township and city governments" (Schubert 2002, 1). Lianjiang Li and Kevin O'Brien also suggest that the implementation of village elections "often involves a struggle between villagers who demand improved accountability and township leaders who, initially at least, refuse to cede their authority to appoint village cadres" (Li and O'Brien 1999, 143). Moreover, township and county officials, especially their party committees (*dang wei*), had many opportunities to employ a strategy of "feigned compliance" to resist the nationally implemented policy of holding village elections (Kelliher 1997, 84). Furthermore, elected village cadres did not necessarily represent all villagers' interests, and the interests of the majority of the villagers were often ignored (He 1997; Liu 2000).

The argument that the central government expanded popular political participation to increase its relative bargaining power vis-à-vis local governments may explain both the optimistic and pessimistic views, although it is closer to the pessimistic one. While village elections spread across the nation, their effects differed depending on local economic conditions. The optimistic scenarios were more likely to be observed in industrialized villages, where elected and nonelected cadres had a common goal of local economic development. Meanwhile, the pessimistic cases were more likely to be found in agricultural villages, where cadres often gave up pursuing local development because of a scarcity of economic resources. Village elections supported elected cadres' legitimacy and strengthened the state's authority in the former case. However, they were not useful for villagers attempting to vote incompetent, often corrupt candidates out of office in the latter case. Thus, the functions of village elections were consistent with the CCP's goal of maintaining authoritarian rule in industrialized villages because they strengthened the regime's legitimacy, while they were also consistent with the goal of regime survival in agricultural villages because they did not enable villagers to replace CCP cadres with candidates whom the CCP did not support but villagers did.

The explanation of why village elections function in this way lies in the institutional setting of village elections and the unique characteristics of the village community. Competitive elections easily led to vote buying with the current institutional setting and community characteristics of the Chinese villages. Competitive elections would hold elected cadres accountable to the electorate only if elections were held at higher levels of local government, such as township or county, in which voters and candidates would not know each other personally. However, this is arguably why the CCP has hesitated to introduce elections for the higher levels of local authorities. If local leaders were actually held accountable to the local electorate, they would be less accountable to higher authorities or the CCP organizations. If local leaders effectively represented local residents' interests, it would be more difficult for the central government to enforce unpopular policies such as the family planning regulation or control over unregistered religious activities.

Petitions

Since the post-Mao reform started, the central government has revamped and supported the petition system (*xinfang zhidu*) as a channel for ordinary people to challenge their local government's decisions and for the central government to monitor local governments.[4] The petition system has existed since the 1950s when both the central government and each level of local government established their formal complaint bureaus and specialized offices (Luehrmann 2000, 37–43). As a result of the social chaos of the Cultural Revolution, the petition system was in a state of flux at the outset of the post-Mao reforms (ibid., 43–51). Nevertheless, petitions began to increase in the 1980s, when the organizations needed for the petition system to function properly were rebuilt and reconstituted (Li and O'Brien 1996). As a result, "long lines form[ed] outside of petition-receiving offices, and hundreds, sometimes thousands, sign[ed] on to daring collective complaints against officials" (Luehrmann 2003, 846).

However, findings from a recent survey suggest that only 0.2 percent of complaints were resolved via the petition process in 2003.[5] While this survey casts doubt on the effectiveness of the petition system, it also raises an interesting puzzle: why did so many people still use the system to attempt to solve their problems when the rate of resolution was so low? In fact, the number of petitions and petitioners increased in the same year that the petition system solved only 0.2 percent of the complaints filed. According to a report of the Chinese Academy of Social Sciences in 2003, the number of collective petitions issued by groups of people to the State Council Petition Bureau increased by 41 percent while the number of people involved increased by 45 percent from the previous year.[6] Moreover, the same report says that in the first quarter of 2004, the number of petition cases and petitioners to the State Council Petition Bureau increased by 99 percent and 95 percent respectively, as compared to the same period in 2003.

I answer this puzzle by focusing on the remonstrative character of the petition system. The number of petitions *actually* submitted is not a good indicator of the effectiveness of the petition system. If local officials are afraid of *potential*

[4] The literature on petitions is too large to cite in a single footnote. Major books published in Chinese include the books by Ying Xing (2001) and Zheng Xin (2005). Citations of additional empirical work can be found throughout the text in this book, especially in Chapter 6. For the most comprehensive analyses of the petition system, see the works by Martin Dimitrov (2010), Laura Luehrmann (2000), and Woo Yeal Paik (2009).

[5] See http://www7.chinesenewsnet.com, accessed November 5, 2004.

[6] See http://chinastudygroup.org, accessed November 19, 2004.

petitions and are committed to good governance such as providing public goods or enforcing policies that reflect residents' demands, then the local residents will *not* petition because they are satisfied with the officials' behavior. So, was China's petition system working effectively to pressure local officials to listen to villagers' preferences? I would answer negatively. It is certainly true that since the recent rural tax reforms, petitions from rural areas have rarely concerned taxation, which is a very different situation from the late 1990s when the majority of petitions involved taxation (*Nanfang Zhoumo* [Southern Weekend], September 3, 2004). There have been few *actual* petitions on taxation recently, which suggests that local officials are afraid of *potential* petitions and refrain from levying illegal fees, given that the most recent reforms made it easier for villagers to prove whether or not levied fees are appropriate and legal.

Then, why has the number of petitions increased sharply since 2000? Although petitions concerning taxation decreased drastically since the implementation of rural tax reforms, petitions concerning land disputes increased markedly. The expected deterrent effect of the petition system against local officials' predatory behavior did not work to solve land issues, because it was difficult for villagers to prove the inappropriateness of local cadres' behavior in these disputes. Many contentious issues concerning land, such as the compensatory sums for confiscation, were difficult for ordinary people to figure out. This observation suggests that for a remonstrative institution to work, the central government would have to establish policies in a simplified manner, so that ordinary people could use those institutions to prove whether the local officials' behavior was appropriate or not.

Why did villagers use the petition system even if it did not solve the filed complaints? Interestingly, petitioners often started direct negotiation with the targeted local officials once they found that their petitioning did not solve their problem, which Kevin O'Brien and Lianjiang Li call "tactical escalation" (O'Brien and Li 2006, chapter 4). When protesters faced the targeted local officials, their position would be strengthened in terms of legitimacy and reasoning of their demands if they had petitioned first (Cai 2010; Chen 2012; O'Brien and Li 2006). Therefore, more villagers used petitions even if they knew that petitioning itself would not resolve their complaints. Most importantly, petitioning followed by tactical escalation against local officials did not directly threaten the stability of authoritarian rule, unless the petitioners went to Beijing.

If the petition system could deter local officials from behaving against villagers' interests, it would strengthen the CCP's capacity for rural governance. This was arguably what Hu Jintao and Wen Jiabao aimed for when they took office in 2002 and adopted a more populist leadership style. Lianjiang Li, Mixing Liu, and Kevin O'Brien find that many of the petitioners went to Beijing because they expected that the regime would be more responsive to their petitions, suggesting: "Heightened popular confidence in the Center, and expectations about its commitment to the well-being of those who had been left behind by reform, activated potential petitioners, reinvigorated dormant ones and hardened the resolve of those who were already active" (Li, Liu, and O'Brien 2012, 332). However, "the new leadership shifted to control and then suppression, as the presence of thousands of petitioners and their increasingly disruptive activities came to be regarded as a threat to stability" (ibid., 333). In short, this change in the attitude of the central leadership suggested that the CCP would encourage people to use the political institution if it was consistent with the regime's goal of maintaining and strengthening authoritarian rule; however, if it threatened the regime's stability, it would suppress the protesters that were raising demands by using the institutionalized channels for political participation.

Local Courts

As a by-product of the post-Mao economic reform, villagers and local cadres often clashed over prices of agricultural products. To prevent this conflict from becoming a source of political and social instability, the central government introduced the Economic Contract Law in 1982 and for the first time allowed ordinary villagers to bring their disputes with local officials to courts for mediation or resolution (Zweig 1997, chapter 6). In 1989, the central government promulgated the ALL and courts could be used to resolve conflicts on a wider array of issues between villagers and local officials (Lubman 1999, 204–16; Peerenboom 2002, chapter 9).[7]

The ideal function of the court system is similar to that of the petition system. If local governments fear villagers' lawsuits, they may become more compliant with laws and regulations and more responsive to popular preferences. Hence, local governments may provide public goods or be committed to better governance. There have been some positive empirical findings. For example, a 1992 survey "found that 74 per cent of the government officials surveyed said that they had begun to exercise greater caution in their work because of the ALL" (Pei 1997). Moreover, in a survey in Jiangsu Province, "73% [of local officials] claimed that the law [ALL] caused them to be more attentive to their duties and . . . 48% agreed that the ALL was helpful in improving the work of administrative agencies" (Peerenboom 2002, 404).

However, institutionally it was very difficult, if not impossible, for villagers to expect a fair trial as long as the same local government that was the defendant in the case also paid the judges. This was a major obstacle for local courts to solve the problems between citizens and local governments.[8] To illustrate, a

[7] For empirical analyses of the people's use of local courts, see the works by Neil Diamant (2000), Benjamin Liebman (1998), Kevin O'Brien and Lianjiang Li (2005), Minxin Pei (1997), Yuen Yuen Tang (2005), and David Zweig (2003).

[8] On November 28, 2008, the CCP Central Committee issued a report that proposed a new regulation under which the central government would be in charge of paying the local court judges. Although it is too early to examine the impact of this change, the new institution may make local courts more independent of local governments. On this report, see http://news.sina.com.cn/c/2008-12-05/015716784999.shtml, accessed May 17, 2010.

county party secretary in Hunan Province claimed that a county judge would not receive his salary from the local government the following month if he were to convict the local government (Yu 2000). Moreover, Kevin O'Brien and Lianjiang Li (2005, 37) suggest: "Judges often find it difficult to resist a Party committee or government department that decides to intervene... in the form of an 'inquiry' about a case or an 'exchange of views' on a legal interpretation."

Interestingly, despite these limitations, villagers increasingly used the law together with petitioning. A recent survey suggests that 63 percent of petitioners first attempted to solve their problems via the legal system.[9] The reason petitioners brought their grievances to the courts was similar to why protesters petitioned before directly negotiating with the targeted local officials. The protesters were able to strengthen their positions against local officials if they brought their issue to court. Because the villagers were only allowed to engage in disputes with local governments, and not with the central government, the political institution of local courts was consistent with the regime's goal of maintaining authoritarian rule.

CENTRAL-LOCAL RELATIONS, POLITICAL PARTICIPATION, AND RURAL TAXATION

Did these political institutions play any role in the decisions regarding the implementation of the rural tax reforms beginning in 2000? More generally, how, if at all, did the political institutions work as channels of political communication between villagers and the CCP? In March 2005, Premier Wen Jiabao, in his report to the National People's Congress, referenced 2006 as the deadline for eliminating the entire agricultural tax, which moved up the planned deadline of 2008 by two years. Although statements from official government reports should be viewed with caution, my field interviews nevertheless confirmed that the agricultural tax was indeed to be abolished and villagers' financial burdens were being significantly reduced. The Chinese government's attempts to reduce the levies imposed on villagers were not surprising. Over the past two decades, the Chinese government had been concerned that the signs of discontent among villagers against a variety of taxes and fees would become a source of political instability. In contrast, the regime's success in reducing the financial burdens of villagers since 2000 particularly struck me because such attempts in the 1990s had failed to have a significant effect. Villagers' financial burdens actually *increased* throughout the 1990s despite the regime's efforts to *decrease* them.

Joel Migdal (1988) points out that in many developing countries local governments operate on policies introduced by the central government in a manner radically different from what is envisioned. China is no exception. While the deviation of the local implementation from central government policies is a historical phenomenon, the divergence between the demands of the central

[9] See http://www7.chinesenewsnet.com, accessed November 5, 2004.

government and the discretion of the local governments became further apparent during the post-Mao reform. With several books and many articles in the Chinese language available on the actual implementation of the central government's policies at various local levels, we now know how the central government struggled with getting local governments to behave as it wanted on rural taxation during the post-Mao period. The central government was dissatisfied with the local governments' disregard for the central government's intentions on national policies. Meanwhile, local governments complained that the central government urged them to target certain achievements, such as rapid economic development, without providing sufficient financial resources or considering local economic and geographic preconditions. Therefore, the local governments' complicity in not reducing villagers' financial burdens in the 1990s is not surprising given their financial difficulties. However, the compliance of local governments with the central government's policy to reduce rural levies and abolish the agricultural tax is puzzling. During my fieldwork, one of the village cadres explained: "The reason we gave up levies was that villagers would otherwise accuse us using petitions. Villagers are cognizant of national policies and are willing to use petitions to higher governments (*shangfang*) if we violate the rules" (Interviewee 75).

Although this village cadre's response appears to reflect an optimistic scenario that the political institutions would enable the central government to monitor local governments and would enable the local governments to be more responsive to popular preferences, in the later chapters of this book I suggest a more mixed and, unfortunately, more pessimistic conclusion. From an optimistic perspective, the recent success of the central government in abolishing the agricultural tax appears to support the position that the CCP became more responsive to popular preferences. For example, Dali Yang (2004) argues that a series of administrative reforms since the 1990s significantly and sufficiently improved the institutional environment for the CCP to adapt to and to navigate future challenges in the twenty-first century. Moreover, the administrative reforms changed the landscape of the central government's struggle for the local governments' compliance with policy implementation. For the optimists, the strong record of economic growth for the past two decades was based on growing governing capacity attributable to the improvement of institution building. Thus, the optimists see resilience and rejuvenation in the current state of the Chinese political order.

In contrast, from a pessimistic perspective, the apparent immediate success of recent administrative reforms did not make the CCP more responsive to popular preferences. For example, Minxin Pei (2006) argues that the lack of political reform and democratization caused rampant corruption and a breakdown of state capacity, which would lead to imbalanced growth, if not economic stagnation or regime collapse, in the near future. For the pessimists, although successful in strengthening the central government's apparent capacity to control local governments in the short run, it would be very difficult, if not impossible, for the CCP to sustain its economic modernization drive without the accountability of local governments to their constituencies. The pessimists point to massive social costs seen in social discontent, popular unrest, and uncontrolled corruption, arguing that the issues were the result of pursuing market-oriented reforms while maintaining one-party rule. Thus, they see decay and fragility in the current state of the Chinese political order.

In this book, I argue that the commitment to maintaining authoritarian rule made it difficult for the CCP leadership to choose optimal policies for taxation and long-term economic development in rural China. In this sense, my argument builds on the debates between these two views but is close to the pessimistic view. It resonates with Pei's argument that the lack of political reform undermined the state's capacity to govern rural areas. At the same time, it is also consistent with the optimistic view in the sense that the CCP has so far succeeded in defusing the dissatisfaction of villagers by abolishing the agricultural tax and giving them limited opportunities for political participation to remonstrate against local governments.

Democratic Institutions in Authoritarian Regimes

Why did the CCP introduce or reform the political institutions that gave villagers some channels for political participation? My argument to answer this question builds on the recent literature of comparative politics that focuses on democratic (or pseudo-democratic) institutions in authoritarian regimes. This literature starts with the interesting observation that most, if not all, authoritarian regimes have some (at least apparently) democratic institutions. But the role of democratic institutions in authoritarian regimes and the motivation for an authoritarian regime to introduce democratic institutions often appears puzzling. How do democratic institutions function in the decision making of an authoritarian regime? How do democratic institutions under authoritarian rule function differently from those under democratic rule? How do democratic institutions influence the survival and demise of an authoritarian regime?

Contrary to the traditional view of dictatorships, which focuses on the means by which a totalitarian leadership exercises absolute control over society (e.g., Arendt [1948] 1973; Friedrich and Brzezinski 1965; Linz 2000),[10] many authoritarian regimes actually have some democratic institutions, especially electoral and legislative systems. While scholars have often considered these democratic institutions in authoritarian regimes a harbinger of democratization (e.g., Mozaffar 2002; Schatz 2006; Schedler 2002), Steven Levitsky and Lucan Way argue that they are rarely "incomplete or transitional forms

[10] The work by Juan Linz (2000) is an important exception in that he distinguishes between totalitarian systems and authoritarian regimes. However, his work does not directly analyze how democratic institutions matter for political participation under authoritarian regimes, but rather focuses on typology to distinguish between totalitarian and authoritarian regimes.

of democracy" (Levitsky and Way 2002, 51). Following Levitsky and Way's argument, a growing body of literature, mostly focusing on elections and parties, has found that democratic institutions help an authoritarian regime survive. For instance, elections helped alleviate intraparty tension over personnel management of party officials in authoritarian regimes in Latin America (Geddes 2006). In Mexico, the authoritarian party discouraged potential opposition powers from cooperating with each other by winning the overwhelming majority in elections (Magaloni 2006). The authoritarian regime constrained, split, and co-opted the opposition powers through elections in the Middle East (Lust-Okar 2005). And in Hosni Mubarak's Egypt, authoritarian elections helped the regime distribute rents and even public goods (Blaydes 2010). Moreover, Jason Brownlee (2007) argues, on the basis of his empirical research on the success and failure of democratization in Egypt, Iran, Malaysia, and the Philippines, that effective authoritarian parties alleviated the intraregime competition over the distribution of rents and official positions. Furthermore, Jennifer Gandhi's (2008) comprehensive comparative analysis shows that authoritarian leaders often use legislatures and parties to co-opt opposition and maintain power. What is common in these examples is that democratic institutions often solve intraregime conflict that would otherwise undermine the regime's stability and jeopardize its survival. The key for the regime's survival strategy is to use elections and other democratic institutions to strengthen the ruling party while also deterring the formation and growth of opposition parties.

Then how are the roles and functions of these democratic institutions in authoritarian regimes different, if at all, from those in democratic regimes? The consensus of recent comparative politics literature is that authoritarian leaders are concerned with popular support for the regime's survival and that democratic institutions are associated not with the regime's demise but with its survival. Samuel Huntington (1968) once argued that institutionalized autocracy was as effective at orderly governance as institutionalized democracy. Since then, however, studies on political institutions have focused overwhelmingly on democratic politics – even though most human beings throughout much of history have lived under authoritarian rule of one kind or another. As a result, we have few theories of authoritarian politics. Combining theoretical insights with empirical research of day-to-day politics in rural China, I provide an assessment of China's experience in introducing market-oriented reform while maintaining authoritarian rule. I endorse the previous literature's argument that democratic institutions in authoritarian regimes primarily function as a survival strategy of the regime. Recent discussions of Chinese politics also show how China's authoritarian regime has pursued its survival strategy by constructing and designing incentive mechanisms to co-opt and manage key players such as entrepreneurs, local officials, and various groups of citizens (e.g., Chen and Dickson 2010; Dickson 2003, 2008; Landry 2008; Schubert 2008; K. Tsai 2007; Wright 2008, 2010).

While the comparative politics literature argues that authoritarian regimes cannot remain in power without popular support, it is dubious whether one can apply this idea to the case of China's authoritarian regime. However, even though the CCP has been in power for more than sixty years, and most of the time without popular support, it has established or revamped the apparently democratic (or pseudo-democratic) institutions that give villagers channels for political participation in rural areas.[11] Many of the authoritarian regimes in countries other than China have used democratic institutions to co-opt various groups of potential rebels into the regime by making them share common interests with the regime.[12] In other words, they bribe potential rebels to prevent them from actually rebelling. China's authoritarian regime has also co-opted various groups in society, especially those who have been empowered in the market economy, to make them support (or at least accept) authoritarian rule (e.g., Chen and Dickson 2010; Huang 2008; Pei 2006; K. Tsai 2007; Whyte 2010; Wright 2010). However, it has also used democratic institutions to strengthen the central government's authority, which sacrificed the local governments' capacity for rural governance. In the following chapters, I show how the democratic institutions in rural China – including village elections, petitions, and local courts – helped the central government smoothly enforce a series of rural tax reforms since 2000. I argue that the democratic institutions in rural China were part of the political economy of reform designed and constructed by the central leadership of the CCP to maintain authoritarian rule.

When authoritarian regimes establish democratic institutions to gain popular support for the regime's survival, they have to face the dilemma that democratic institutions may also strengthen political opponents, which will threaten the regime's survival. Thus, one can imagine that an authoritarian regime should be responsive to popular preferences through democratic institutions only when the regime's survival strategy coincides with the functions of the democratic institutions. In other words, democratic institutions in authoritarian regimes primarily function not to enhance the accountability of the regime but to strengthen the state's capacity to maintain political stability and to consolidate the regime's legitimacy and survival.

Democratic Institutions and Remonstration

The democratic institutions in rural China have remonstrative characteristics. Kevin O'Brien conceptualizes one of the significant new roles of the delegates of the People's Congress as "remonstrators," defining remonstration as an act to "seek attention and transmit information that may help rectify administration... [and] assert a right to recognize injustices and mistakes, and to

[11] Thaxton (2008) argues that the CCP lost popular support in the countryside because of the Great Leap Forward famine and the Cultural Revolution.

[12] For the most theoretically sophisticated discussion of this argument, see the works by Bruce Bueno de Mesquita and his colleagues (e.g., Bueno de Mesquita and Smith 2011; Bueno de Mesquita et al. 2003).

confront leaders" (O'Brien 1994a, 368). With this role as remonstrators, he argues, delegates of the People's Congress serve as "a bridge (*qiaoliang*) from the leadership to the citizenry" (ibid., 360). I concur with O'Brien's definition of remonstration, and note that a crucial characteristic of democratic institutions in rural China is that ordinary people are allowed to *remonstrate* for certain interests against *local* governments, but are never allowed to *represent* certain interests against the *central* government. With the remonstrative characteristics of its democratic institutions, China's authoritarian regime succeeded in strengthening its survival at the cost of local institutions' governance capacity in rural areas. In other words, I argue that remonstrative institutions would not undermine the regime's authority but strengthen it, and that arguably this was why China's authoritarian regime introduced democratic institutions.

The ideal function of remonstration is as follows. A higher-level government should be informed of popular dissatisfaction with a local government through remonstration. The higher-level government would punish the local government if it found that the local government's action was inappropriate. To avoid being punished, local governments should become more compliant with laws and regulations. Moreover, being afraid of *potential* remonstration, local governments should be more responsive to popular demands. Thus, the key for remonstration to work to induce the responsiveness of local governments is whether local cadres will be afraid of *potential* remonstration. Thus, the frequency of *actual* remonstration is not a good indicator of the effectiveness of remonstrative institutions. In other words, actual remonstration is an off-the-equilibrium path, a strategy that is not taken in reality but influences the actual outcome; however, potential remonstration makes responsive governance an equilibrium outcome.[13]

Among the three democratic institutions – that is, village elections, petitions, and local courts – petitions and local courts would have obvious remonstrative characteristics if they function in an ideal way. Writing a petition to a superior government and suing local officials in local courts could both be considered as acts to "seek attention and transmit information that may help rectify administration." The key for these democratic institutions to work effectively to deter local officials from behaving inappropriately or to make them responsive to popular preferences would be whether these officials were afraid of potential petitions or potential lawsuits. Local officials would feel this fear if higher authorities and the central government were committed to seriously responding to petitions and lawsuits with investigations and making their commitment credible. In that way, these remonstrative institutions would strengthen regime legitimacy. However, the Chinese central leaders did not offer the necessary

[13] Melanie Manion (2008) explains the impact of the 1995 political reforms on the outcomes of elections to the local people's congresses from the perspective of an off-the-equilibrium path. She argues that the possibility of CCP candidate losses does not lead to actual losses by CCP candidates, but rather to an improvement in winning candidates' quality.

institutional support for the remonstrative institutions and failed to make their commitment credible. For example, for the petitioning system, after the high tide of petitions in 2003–06, the central government found the demands that petitioners raised to have gone beyond their capacity, took petitions as a threat to political stability and regime survival, and decided to control and then suppress petitions (Li, Liu, and O'Brien 2012). Ordinary people, who had expected the administration of Hu Jintao and Wen Jiabao to be more responsive to popular preferences, were disappointed with the central leaders, and the suppression of petitions since 2006 has significantly weakened people's faith in the central government (especially as compared with their faith in local governments), if such faith ever existed.

Unlike petitions or local courts, characterizing village elections as a remonstrative institution would likely create an immediate objection. Nevertheless, I view this seemingly representative institution as a remonstrative one. In China's rural politics, cadres elected in village elections were not the only ones involved in the decision-making processes – nonelected CCP cadres also exerted influence over village politics. For this institutional reason, the role elected cadres played in the postelection administration was a "bridge" between nonelected local cadres and villagers (Alpermann 2001, 49). As seen in O'Brien's conceptualization of remonstration, "bridging" the local leadership and the constituencies is the central role of remonstrators. Moreover, villagers often found that village elections did not solve their grievances but rather generated them (He 1997; Liu 2000; Xu F. 2004). Instead of seeking resolution by electing their representatives, they preferred solving their grievances by directly negotiating with local officials or other targeted actors (Chen 2009; O'Brien and Li 2006, chapter 4). When they tried to resolve their grievances in direct negotiations with local officials, elected village cadres might help mediate between local officials and villagers (Alpermann 2001).

The requirement for remonstrative institutions to work as an effective means for political participation is different from that for representative institutions, especially in terms of the flow of information on contentious issues. In remonstrative institutions, remonstrators would have to possess sufficient information about existing laws and regulations to justify the legitimacy and validity of their demands. As a result, the laws and regulations that the regime stipulated and the policies that it demonstrated should be unambiguous, so that remonstrators could understand and use them in their remonstrative protests. In contrast, in representative institutions political elites would have an incentive to account for their policy positions to appeal to their constituencies. As a result, constituencies would not have to possess a lot of information about each law and regulation to evaluate who might best represent their interests. Note that I do not argue that the laws on petitioning or other remonstrative institutions should be written in an unambiguous way for the remonstrative institutions to pressure local officials. For example, the laws on petitioning were indeed written in an ambiguous way. However, I argue here that laws on taxation and other economic issues should be written in an unambiguous way for the petitioning system to work in the way that would ideally make local officials more responsive to popular preferences. Laws on tax-for-fee reform and on the abolition of the agricultural tax were written in an unambiguous way. As a result, local officials were afraid of potential petitions and implemented the rural tax reforms, even though they knew that the reforms would lead to fiscal starvation of the local governments.

The logic of remonstrative institutions corresponds with "statutory constraints" control, which Kathleen Bawn (1997) defines as a means for a principal to monitor agents. In this conceptualization, the principal has an incentive to design statutes in advance (ex ante control) in such a way that the principal could monitor agents easily afterward (ex post monitoring). Thus, I hypothesize that the Chinese central leaders introduced remonstrative institutions in a way that would not threaten the regime's survival. In other words, they did not necessarily choose policies consistent with optimizing the responsiveness to popular preferences but rather chose policies consistent with optimizing the likelihood of regime survival. However, I argue that this strategy had unintended consequences on rural taxation and local fiscal health. In order to make potential remonstration a credible threat to local officials, the central government had to make policies sufficiently unambiguous for remonstrators to be able to assert them in their remonstrative acts.

This logic of remonstrative institutions also corresponds with the idea of "fire alarms" oversight as defined by Mathew McCubbins and Thomas Schwartz (1984). Fire alarms oversight is a mechanism where the principal would be notified of agents' actions if some problem occurs – as fire alarms ring when they detect fire. If this oversight mechanism works, such problems should rarely occur, because agents should know that their actions would be revealed to their principal and hence they would try not to cause problems. Thus, the key to whether remonstrative institutions would work to monitor local governments should be whether ordinary people could use existing laws and regulations for their remonstrative acts. If local cadres perceived that ordinary people would use remonstrative institutions if they were dissatisfied, they would have an incentive to be responsive to popular preferences.

The basis for remonstrative institutions to work in the context of rural Chinese politics is what Kevin O'Brien (1996, 33) defines as "rightful resistance," which "entails the innovative use of laws, policies, and other officially promoted values to defy 'disloyal' political and economic elites." Claims of popular rightful resistance should use "authoritarian pronouncements" by the *central* government (ibid., 36). Consequently, remonstrators would not target the central government or the authoritarian regime, but would "need a plausible argument that remonstrating serves state interests" (O'Brien 1994a, 373). In this way, neither remonstrative institutions nor rightful resistance would threaten the regime's survival but both would strengthen the capacity for the authoritarian regime to monitor local governments. However, once an increasing number of petitioners decided to go to Beijing to seek redress, having found that their grievances would not be solved in their locality, the central government took the petition wave to Beijing as a threat to authoritarian rule (Li, Liu, and O'Brien 2012). Thus, since 2006 the central government has collaborated with local officials to prevent petitioning, and this has weakened the ability of ordinary people to express grievances and claims through remonstrative protests. In other words, now the central government has stripped the petitioning system of its democratic content and process.

CONCLUSION

This chapter laid the theoretical background for the discussion about rural taxation in contemporary China in the following chapters. Authoritarian rulers have a primary interest in maintaining their regime and the CCP leaders are not an exception. At the same time, they are also interested in gaining popular support because merely relying on repression is a costly way to rule. The CCP leaders faced this dilemma when they pursued market-oriented economic reform and maintenance of one-party rule. To maximize revenue under the conditions of the market economy and authoritarian rule, they had to seek popular support to an extent that would not threaten the regime's survival. Introducing remonstrative democratic (or pseudo-democratic) political institutions to the authoritarian regime, while pursuing market-oriented economic reform under authoritarian rule, was consistent with the CCP's strategy. However, this strategy brought unintended consequences to its policy making. For remonstrative institutions to function for the central government in monitoring local governments, the CCP had to make policies unambiguous enough so that villagers could use rules and laws for their remonstrative, rightful resistance. Rules and laws implemented during a series of rural tax reforms since 2000 were unambiguously written, and local officials implemented them even though they knew that the reforms would lead to local fiscal crises. As a result, local governments have lost the capacity for rural governance and its functions, such as collecting taxes and providing public goods and services.

There are at least two reasons the central government would prefer having local governments collect taxes and provide public goods – unless it leads to a threat to the regime's survival. First, local governments would be better informed about popular preferences for the state's policies. Second, local governments could more easily enforce the central government's preferred policies if local governments were functioning effectively to collect taxes and provide public goods. However, the central government's interest in having the local governments accomplish these objectives was not as strong as the interest in committing to market-oriented economic reform and maintaining sociopolitical stability for the regime's survival. These two interests conflicted with each other when the increase in local levies sparked rural unrest in the 1990s. The CCP's response was to place its own political survival before any other problems such as local fiscal health. A series of rural tax reforms beginning in 2000 reflected the regime's willingness to sacrifice local fiscal health for the survival of the authoritarian regime.

PART I

HISTORICAL AND ANALYTICAL CONTEXTS

2

Revenue and Resistance in Rural China in History

In this chapter, I review rural taxation and political participation in China in historical context. A full discussion of revenue and resistance in rural China during the past several hundred years is well beyond the scope of this book.[1] The aim here is to lay out some of the core issues that have emerged since the nineteenth century. In particular, I emphasize migration and central-local relations and their impacts on the interaction between rural taxation and political participation. I first consider rural taxation during the imperial period (before 1911), and then I discuss the impact of the 1911 Revolution and of the republican period between 1911 and 1949 on rural governance. In the second half of this chapter, I consider rural governance during the Maoist period (1949–76) with an emphasis on the question of why the Maoist state relied on the agricultural procurement system, rather than agricultural taxes, to transfer resources from the rural to the urban sector. I conclude this chapter by discussing how rural governance in the post-Mao period was different from that in the previous periods, although each regime had the same goal of maintaining its nondemocratic regime.

Douglass North (1981, 21) defines the state as "an organization with a comparative advantage in violence, extending over a geographic area whose boundaries are determined by its power to tax constituents." Although the state (as tax collector) "claims the *monopoly of the legitimate use of physical force* within a given territory" (Weber [1919] 1946, 78: italics in original), the territory and the constituents where the state can monopolize the legitimate use of violence are restricted by the state's ability to collect taxes. Thus, rulers have

[1] For discussions about taxation during the imperial period, see the works by Philip Huang (1990), R. Bin Wong (1997), and Madeleine Zelin (1984). For reviews of political participation during the imperial period, see the works by Qiang Fang (2009), Jonathan Ocko (1988), and Guangyuan Zhou (1993).

a strong incentive to establish efficient taxation to maximize the state's capacity for ruling. Authoritarian rulers also need revenue to co-opt or bribe potential opponents and rebels (Bueno de Mesquita and Smith 2011; Bueno de Mesquita et al. 2003). Political economists and economic historians have found that when rulers pursue the goal of maximizing revenue, relying solely on the suppressive apparatus is a costly way to collect taxes. Thus, rulers have a strong incentive to establish some mechanisms that make taxpayers willing to cooperate with tax collection. One such mechanism is giving taxpayers channels to participate in decision-making processes, so that taxpayers will recognize that they influence how taxes are used.

Do rulers in a single-party authoritarian system, such as China's, create mechanisms that make taxation a mutually beneficial process? I argue that authoritarian rulers have a strong incentive to create such mechanisms, but they must do so while not allowing taxpayers to participate fully in decision-making processes. In other words, they have to pursue the goal of revenue maximization within the constraint of pursuing the even more important goal: maintaining the authoritarian regime. At the same time, as long as the state adopts a market system in its economy – regardless of the regime type – the regime has an incentive to establish efficient taxation to increase its revenue and achieve economic development. How do authoritarian rulers pursue this goal while maintaining authoritarian rule? Historically, how did Chinese rulers achieve this goal under a nondemocratic regime?

In this book, I argue that authoritarian rulers have designed and constructed a political economy of rural taxation while giving the highest priority to the maintenance of the authoritarian regime. Under this regime, higher authorities appoint local officials and set economic goals for local development. While authoritarian rulers pursue the goal of maintaining the regime, they are also interested in gaining popular support, because merely relying on repression to collect taxes is costly and inefficient. This argument suggests that efficient taxation can be established if the state succeeds in providing constituents with the assurance that popular preferences are reflected in the state's decision making and policy implementation. The question then becomes: under what conditions will the state succeed in providing this assurance, and under what conditions will the state fail to do so? Because China has never been a democracy, this question does not have an obvious answer. Lacking regularly scheduled democratic elections, Chinese villagers have never expected their preferences to be reflected in policy making through electoral mechanisms. However, I argue that under some conditions villagers are assured that policies implemented in their locality reflect their popular preferences, and that whether such conditions exist depends on local state-society relations and central-local intragovernmental relations.

To examine how state-society relations and central-local relations created (or failed to create) the expectation for the state to provide public goods in rural China, I should make it clear that I do *not* assume necessarily *conflicting* relations between the state and society. Moreover, I should also make it clear that I focus on *local* state-society relations. In other words, I highlight relations between villagers and local governments in the context of central-local relations. As Pan Wei (2003, 374–75), a Chinese political scientist, notes: "China's 'state' (*guojia*) and 'society' (*shehui*) are mixed with each other . . . [and] grassroots authorities (*jiceng zhengquan*) represent both the state and society." My question is about *how* the state and society are *mixed*, instead of how they are in conflict with each other. My goal is to articulate a new interpretation that is not necessarily inconsistent with the interpretations found in previous studies on China's state-society relations but that may explore other avenues and possibilities. However, while previous works emphasize the importance of not treating the relationship between society and the state's agents as conflicting ones (e.g., Oi 1989; Perry 2002; Shue 1988; Wong 1997), I argue that under each regime (i.e., imperial, republican, or communist) the conflicts between them were significant, and taxation was always one such axis of conflict. The information presented here is well-known to scholars of rural China, but I propose a new interpretation highlighting the theoretical argument of this book.

RURAL GOVERNANCE IN IMPERIAL CHINA

As Bin Wong (1997, 123) notes, "[W]here politics in Europe always had a strong urban component with classical roots, Chinese politics had long been agrarian and imperial." Because imperial China was an agrarian economy, the agriculture-related taxes (e.g., the land tax) became the major source of revenue for the imperial court (Bernstein and Lü 2003, 20–22). For example, in 1766 (the Qianlong Reign) the land tax accounted for 62 percent of total revenue (Caizhengbu [Ministry of Finance] 1994, 23). Thus, Wong (1997, 135) concludes: "The Chinese state maintained an active interest in the agrarian economy, promoting its expansion over larger stretches of territory and its stability through uneven harvest seasons." In other words, the Chinese imperial court had a strong incentive to establish efficient rural taxation in the large territory it ruled. It often struggled to collect taxes in areas remote from the imperial capital. To avoid local military rebellion against the imperial court and to secure the revenue from agriculture-related taxes, emperors often kept rural taxes low. For example, in 1713 the Kangxi emperor called for tax remissions during times of poor harvests (Wang 1971).

However, local leaders, colluding with landlords, often resisted rural taxation policy because they found it difficult to finance the basic administrative functions of local governments with the revenue they were allowed to keep. Hence, it was not unusual for local governments to siphon off the funds earmarked for remittance to the imperial court (Zelin 1984, 37). Therefore, taxation was a primary source of conflict between the central authority and local leaders, and the Chinese imperial court often struggled with tax collection by local governments. However, local discretion in central taxation did not necessarily have a negative impact on the provision of public goods and on local prosperity. Local governments, which understood local conditions better than the central government, often taxed more efficiently, though lightly, and spent the tax revenue on the provision of public goods that reflected the preferences of local residents. Wong (1997, 134) notes: "A burdensome government that levied heavy taxes was more likely to provoke rebellion, possibly raising a serious challenge to social order. The threat of social disorder then required additional resources for military preparations, thereby exacerbating popular dissatisfaction and unrest. Thus Chinese officials reasoned that they should keep taxes light." In this way, in rural China during the imperial period, "elites were . . . oriented toward local society and could fend off the state either to defend the common people or more often to protect their own claims on resources and to control over local society" (ibid., 122). Thus, "elite efforts were seen not as substitutions for but as complements to official efforts to maintain local social order" (ibid., 111–12).

What conditions would make local officials committed to this kind of benevolent governance? Michael Adas argues that in many rural areas in Southeast Asia, "benevolence was encouraged and limits established not on the basis of abstract ethical principles or idealized standards for the behavior of a just king" (Adas 1980, 534). It is true that "officials at all levels depended on local and village leaders, who were not part of the regular bureaucracy extending from the court, in their efforts to collect taxes or conscript peasants for corvee labor or military service" (ibid., 531). Thus, local officials, especially at the grassroots level, might have an incentive to be committed to benevolent governance and the provision of public goods. However, Adas argues: "Moral precepts . . . were far less important determinants of the peasants' welfare than the administrative and technological deficiencies of pre-colonial states and the defense mechanisms which these weaknesses allowed the peasantry to develop to buffer elite demands" (ibid., 530). In other words, whether local officials had an incentive to be committed to benevolent governance would depend on the institutional structure of the state's central-local relationship and what modes of political participation were available for villagers to present their preferences to the government. Adas argues in another article (1986) that the modes of political participation available for peasants in South and Southeast Asia were what he called "avoidance protests," consisting of foot dragging ("everyday resistance") and flight ("exit"), while collective protests were costly. The avoidance protests were effective for tax revolts in small rural communities because "the villagers in many areas of South and South-east Asia were assessed and paid their taxes on a communal basis" (ibid., 70).

In rural China under imperial rule, this benevolent type of local government was sustainable as long as agricultural productivity increased. The equilibrium was maintained as long as local leaders had the capacity to respond to popular preferences and were afraid of the potential revenue loss posed by an avoidance protest. Thus, in rural China, as in rural Southeast Asia, political participation by avoidance protests was effective for villagers to make local officials remain committed to benevolent governance "only in situations where political institutions and social structures remain[ed] viable" (ibid., 72). Under this condition, villagers were assured that policies would reflect their popular preferences, local state agents would respond to popular preferences, and villagers and local officials would share common interests.

However, once the population increased and productivity stagnated, local governments lost the ability to reduce taxes and started levying heavy taxes. This was the case in the late nineteenth century. Philip Huang (1990) argues that although labor input per unit of land kept increasing and total output was expanded, marginal returns per workday diminished. Moreover, the Qing Dynasty had faced foreign invasion since the First Opium War in 1839, and not only had to pay indemnities to foreign powers but also had to build up strong militaries. Thus, the imperial court by then was unable to invest in the infrastructure for economic development, and local officials lost the capacity to be committed to benevolent governance, imposing more financial burdens on villagers. Once rural taxation reached an unacceptable level for villagers, tax resistance became rampant "as a common form of collective action, growing more common in the nineteenth century and continuing into postimperial times" (Wong 1997, 231). This shift of villagers' strategies into collective protests corresponds with Adas's finding of villagers' behavior in Southeast Asia: "Conditions of social and political deterioration and severe economic scarcity force[d] peasants to turn to more radical, and risky, measures to protect their interests, and often, merely to survive" (Adas 1986, 72).

This pattern of tax resistance in China was different from that in Europe. In Europe, tax resistance emerged after 1500, but it "stopped being a collective form of protest in the nineteenth century, when connections among representation, citizenship, and taxation were affirmed" (Wong 1997, 231). This was when tax regime variants – high-tax democracies versus low-tax autocracies – emerged in Europe. The democratic governments of Britain and Holland succeeded in collecting taxes with relative ease, maintaining high tax rates and investing in the infrastructure for economic development. Meanwhile, the autocratic governments of France and Spain struggled to collect taxes and endured low tax rates. Moreover, they had to expend more revenue on bureaucracies for tax collection, as they relied on repressive means to monitor taxpayer compliance. In sum, tax resistance in Europe and the state's reaction to it led to the emergence of more efficient tax systems through the creation of more representative political regimes. In contrast, tax resistance in rural China further reduced the power of the imperial court, which had been weakened already by indemnity payments imposed by foreign powers. The imperial court was bankrupt by the beginning of the twentieth century. Moreover, the tax resistance created opportunities for the rise of local informal powers, some of whom had overlapped with local leaders during the imperial period but others who had not (Perry 1980). Eventually, the fiscal crisis led to the collapse of the Qing Dynasty in 1911.

Why did Chinese and European states, which faced the same challenge of mobilizing fiscal resources, take different paths? One reason is that the Chinese imperial court had an institutional capacity to collect taxes far beyond the abilities of European states until the nineteenth century (ibid., 132). In European states, which relied on commercial taxes, the central government struggled to collect taxes from merchants through local officials because merchants were geographically mobile (Beik 1985). In contrast, because the fiscal revenue of the Chinese imperial court relied on agriculture-related taxes, such as the land tax, local officials could collect taxes more easily because Chinese taxpayers were not mobile (Will 1990). Another reason is the difference in the state's need to mobilize fiscal resources. In medieval European states, this came from wars. Thus, the European states, each of which was a small political unit in terms of the population, needed to collect taxes efficiently to combat the external pressure of wars. In this sense, it is suggestive that the less populated smaller states such as Holland and Britain introduced a representative regime earlier than the larger states such as France and Spain (Hoffman and Norberg 1994a). For the goal of financing wars, establishing a representative regime to induce taxpayers' cooperation was a viable choice for the preindustrial European states. In contrast, the main goal of the Chinese imperial court had been to maintain political stability in its large territory until the Chinese empire faced foreign invasion in the nineteenth century. In other words, the Chinese imperial court did not face the external pressure of wars as much as the European states, but faced the internal pressure of rebellions.

This favorable fiscal condition in China changed once the imperial court faced the external pressure of wars in the nineteenth century. From the Opium Wars on into the twentieth century, such wars escalated and the indemnity payments increased. As long as the Chinese empire maintained the political stability of its large territory, it could collect taxes easily on the basis of land because taxpayers were not geographically mobile. However, whenever the Chinese court faced the need to increase taxes, it could and did impose heavy financial burdens on villagers – immobile taxpayers. As a result, unlike European countries, the Chinese state did not have a strong incentive to introduce a representative political regime to induce taxpayers' cooperation, and collective tax resistance became rampant beginning in the nineteenth century.

RURAL GOVERNANCE IN REPUBLICAN CHINA

The Republic of China (ROC), which ended imperial rule and assumed the state's authority from the Qing Dynasty in 1912, did not create efficient taxation or a representative political regime.[2] After the Republican Revolution ousted the Qing Dynasty, the weak central power of the Nationalist

[2] A national election was held from late 1912 to early 1913 under the ROC regime, and "the election was generally considered to be fair, free and a surprising success... [and is still considered] the first and only popular election of a national government" (Gilley 2004, 3). Twenty million voters participated, although the franchise covered only one-eighth of the adult population because it was restricted to educated taxpayers and property owners.

(*Kuomingtang*: KMT) government allowed each rural community's informal groups to "become an uncontrollable power in local society, replacing a host of traditional arrangements of local governance" (Duara 1987, 133). With the KMT's initial failure to create an effective national government, rapacious warlords and local bandits ran rampant after 1915, leading many local communities to form their own village militias to combat growing lawlessness (Perry 1980, 87–88). Overall, during ROC rule, "both the central authorities and the peasants lost out, while local officials, often in collusion with local social and economic elites, gained" (Bernstein and Lü 2003, 25). The central government faced major resistance from local leaders in its attempt to collect taxes. The fiscal decentralization reform during this period not only failed to lessen the financial burden on villagers, but even increased it. Local officials, supported and protected by community-sponsored militia, emerged as a local power because they were able to collect taxes and other exactions more easily than the central government from local people. At the same time, they gained legitimacy to levy originally illegitimate or quasi-legitimate surtaxes and enjoyed the financial benefits (ibid., 29).

The War of Resistance against Japan (1931–45) exacerbated the problem of rural governance. Because the KMT had trouble in collecting local taxes in the face of warlord and bandit competition, its leadership turned to national sources of revenue generation. Even before the War of Resistance, as Ralph Thaxton points out, the Chiang Kai-shek–led Ministry of Finance intensified the quest for money; it transformed the enforcement arm of the *gabelle* – the salt tax administration – into "a national paramilitary tax police force, which proved far more responsive to the center's demand for more salt revenue and far less tolerant of the controls of county magistrates, who usually were preoccupied with local political stability" (Thaxton 1997, 58). The Japanese invasion and war, which destabilized the KMT's salt tax force, worsened the situation, and made it more difficult for the central government to collect resources. Cut off from rich coastal cities, the KMT government had to raise revenue from poor rural areas, where the Japanese and the Chinese Communist Party (CCP) were competing for such revenue. Lloyd Eastman (1984) also finds that in the KMT-controlled territory, the KMT government had to rely on levies from rural areas to finance the war, especially after it was cut off from rich coastal cities. In some cases, the Japanese Army raised provisions from local levies, worsening the plight of the villagers. For example, in one northern village, located in what is now Hebei Province, the Japanese-controlled government levied a tax rate of 50 percent on villagers – one-fourth of which was as grain procurement and the other three-fourths as cash and material contributions (Friedman, Pickowicz, and Selden 1991, 47).

The economic conditions of rural residents did not improve after the Japanese were defeated. There were many protests and uprisings against taxation in the KMT-controlled areas. During the civil war (1945–49), the KMT government not only struggled to collect taxes but also had to send a large number of soldiers to quell tax resistance in its own territory. Eastman (1984) argues that the KMT was not able to devote enough soldiers to the civil war because it had to spare a number of them to respond to outbreaks of tax resistance. In contrast, Steven Levine (1987) argues that the levies in the CCP-controlled areas in the northeast were lower than in the KMT-controlled areas, which apparently minimized popular resistance in the CCP-controlled areas and contributed to the CCP's victory in the civil war.[3] Moreover, Thaxton (1997, 44) argues that in North China "the Kuomintang state effort to reestablish the salt monopoly, driven by the pressures of international debt, endangered the market performance of village people, whose protest against state intrusion into the space of habitual market routines became closely associated with their participation in the Communist-led revolution."

Republican China displayed apparent similarities to the current China. The weak central government struggled to establish efficient taxation while local governments relied heavily on informally surcharged levies for financing themselves, and taxation and levies were a major source of villagers' grievances and protests. Needless to say, as with imperial China, the regime's reaction to tax resistance never resulted in the creation of a representative political regime. At the same time, the republican period was when the traditional functions and roles of the rural community and leadership declined. Village community leaders under warlords often sought to further their own personal interests and feathered their nests by colluding with militarized gangster groups. In this sense, as Liu Ya (2004, 32), an expert in Chinese rural politics, argues, the republican period was the beginning of the search for a modernized form of rural governance after the traditional form had collapsed. Both the KMT and the CCP aimed to establish an institutionalized form of rural governance. However, as Lucien Bianco (1971, chaps. 5–6) contends, neither side had any intention of establishing a representative political regime.

RURAL GOVERNANCE IN MAOIST CHINA

After the People's Republic of China was established and Mao Zedong was put in power by the Communist Revolution in 1949, major changes occurred in rural governance. First, land reform confiscated land from landlords and distributed it to villagers. Following the land reform, agricultural production was collectivized. After agricultural collectivization, the central government's primary concern shifted from creating efficient taxation to creating an effective compulsory grain procurement system (*tonggou tongxiao*).

Along with these changes, village leaders were officially treated as "state cadres" (*guojia ganbu*), and their roles changed from leaders of the rural community to agents of the state. Did this change in the status of village leaders

[3] However, Jun Chang and Jon Halliday (2005) contend that the CCP's rural taxation was quite predatory.

simply transform rural cadres into Mao's willing accomplices? One body of the literature has answered this question negatively. Jean Oi argues that although village leaders officially represented the state as its agents, they were "a distinct entity whose interests cannot be assumed to be the same as or even compatible with those of the central government" (Oi 1989, 3). Village leaders acted as a cushion between the CCP and villagers (or the state and society more generally) in the way that "peasants . . . pursue clientelist politics as a means of getting ahead and receiving special consideration in the distribution of the rewards available in a system that theoretically prohibits unequal access to goods and resources" (ibid., 153). Moreover, Vivienne Shue suggests that grassroots leaders played active roles in villagers' interests, as "for the great majority of rural-dwelling Chinese throughout the Mao period, all the meaningful social relationships of a lifetime would still be with other men and women *inside* these highly localized social units – the village and the commune" (Shue 1988, 49: italics in original). Local leaders during the Maoist period skillfully balanced their obligation to higher authorities (the state) and their responses to villagers' interests (society), and were overall able to serve their local villagers; Shue notes that "local leaders had to pursue a combined strategy of administrative activism *and* local political and economic entrepreneurship to serve their localities well" (ibid., 58–59: italics in original). Furthermore, Elizabeth Perry emphasizes the importance of considering interactive relations between the state and society, arguing that state-society relations are "not always conflictual, and sometimes even quite complementary" (Perry 1985, 414).

By contrast, another body of the literature argues that the shift of the village leaders' official status to state cadres made them agents of the state and Mao's willing accomplices. For example, Ralph Thaxton (2008) contends that the CCP leaders of Da Fo Village in Henan Province – where he conducted oral history field research – used occasions to communicate with villagers to carry out the state's (the central government) policy that contradicted local interests and villagers' preferences. In Da Fo Village, villagers preferred individual production and market-based distribution of products for their agriculture. Thus, collectivization and the creation of the people's commune during the Great Leap Forward contradicted villagers' interests. However, the CCP leaders in the village turned the institutionalized occasions to meet with villagers, such as public criticism sessions, into opportunities to carry out the unpopular state policies.

In this book, I argue that the CCP's primary goal of regime survival determines central-local relations in rural China. Under a regime where local officials are appointed by higher authorities, local leaders are institutionally constrained from responding to residents' demands and preferences. This argument is closer to the "Mao's willing accomplices" argument than to the argument that local leaders responded to villagers during the Maoist period. As Jonathan Unger (1989, 121) argues, "rather than simply 'glove the hand of the state,' most rural Chinese officials played a double-edged game, mindful that promotions were granted from above and that, if their disobedience were ever discovered, they faced ruin." It is true that the implementation of state policies was not always in line with the central leaders' or Mao's preferences in rural China during the Maoist period (Shue 1988, 68). However, it was not always in line with local villagers' preferences, either. Perry claims that "the production teams and brigades, which often replicate traditional communal groupings" were "salient vehicles of contemporary rural action" and concludes: "It would be incorrect... to interpret the continuity in local society as a *circumvention* of state policy. Rather, in important ways, the communal structure of contemporary China is a direct product of government initiatives" (Perry 1985, 439: italics in original). Oi (1989) argues for local leaders' positive roles in bridging the state and society, focusing on the leaders of production teams, which is at the level of traditional natural villages. Unger's argument and Oi's argument are not contradictory. In the following sections, I show that when local leaders and villagers interacted through clientelistic personal networks to pursue their own interests, local leaders faced the constraints of and pressure from the personnel system. As a result, the central policies that did not always benefit villagers – such as collectivization (most typically the establishment of people's communes) and rural taxation – were still implemented even though the central government was not satisfied with the implementation of the policies in rural areas. Collectivization of agricultural production (especially the establishment of people's communes during the Great Leap Forward) and rural taxation were the central policies that villagers did not always welcome, but local leaders enforced them regardless of villagers' preferences. In other words, the willing accomplices had little choice but to go along with the central government's dictates and yet tried to mitigate some of the worst effects of the Maoist central government's outrageous and ruinous extractions.

Collectivization of Agricultural Production

In the 1950s, following land reform, the CCP introduced an institutional transformation with the collectivization of agricultural production (Teiwes 1997, 56–67). Moves toward a socialist transformation in rural areas had begun with the development of mutual aid teams (MATs: *huzhuzu*) in the CCP-controlled areas even before the establishment of the People's Republic of China (PRC). Each MAT consisted of six to ten households. Under this organization, villagers shared productive resources and worked together while land was still owned privately. By 1952, about 40 percent of rural households were in the MATs (ibid., 57). While the First Five-Year Plan (1953–57) advanced socialist transformation rapidly in urban areas, the collectivizing moves were accelerated in rural areas. The agricultural producers' cooperatives (APCs: *nongye shengchan hezuoshe*) were introduced and spread across the whole nation. The APCs were institutionalized in two stages. In the first stage, called the Lower APCs (*chujishe*), each APC consisted of thirty to forty households. Under this organization, land was pooled and productive resources were controlled by the Lower APCs, although each villager received a dividend according to their relative contribution of land *and* labor. In the second stage, called the Higher APCs (*gaojishe*), each APC consisted of 100–150 households. Land was owned by the Higher APCs and each villager was paid exclusively by their labor contribution. By 1955, 63 percent of rural households were in the Lower APCs and only 4 percent were in the Higher APCs; however, by December 1956, 8 percent were in the Lower APCs and 88 percent were in the Higher APCs (ibid., 58). After these collectivizing moves, the problem in agriculture in the late 1950s was how to increase agricultural output while state investment was devoted to the heavy industrial sector under the Leninist economic regime (Lieberthal 1997, 93). Mao answered this question by relying on the same strategy he used in the Communist Revolution: mobilize the underemployed labor power in rural areas (ibid., 98). Mao called this strategy the "Great Leap Forward" (GLF: *Da Yuejin*).[4]

New political institutions and organizations emerged in rural China along with the GLF. In 1958, rural local cadres of Henan and Shandong Provinces started to organize groups of villagers even larger than the Higher APCs, primarily to combat massive flooding of the Yellow River, calling these organizations the "people's communes" (*renmin gongshe*). The people's communes started as voluntary organizations. However, after the *People's Daily*, the CCP's official newspaper, reported what is now known as Mao's famous remark, "the people's communes are good" (*renmin gongshe hao*), as the headline on August 18, 1958, most of the nation's rural households were in people's communes by the end of the month regardless of their local economic and geographic conditions.[5] Mao's leadership and charisma were not the only reason that people's communes spread so rapidly; local cadres also took Mao's statement as a signal that every local government had to follow the policy of organizing people's communes regardless of local conditions (Bachman 1991; Bernstein 2006; MacFarquhar 1983, chapter 5; Yang 1996, chapter 2). Under a political regime where local officials were appointed by higher authorities, and under an economic regime where the agricultural production target was given by higher authorities, the GLF imposed intense political pressure on local cadres to compete and to exaggerate agricultural production in their localities. During the GLF, local cadres gave higher authorities false reports of miraculously rising grain yields. Consequently, in 1958 the official estimate of the grain harvest was 375 million tons, an increase of more than 90 percent from the 1957 output (Lardy 1983, 42). Responding to these exaggerated reports, central planners raised the amount of the central government's demand for state

[4] For detailed discussions about the GLF, see the work by David Bachman (1991) for an institutional perspective of the famine, the work by Thaxton (2008) from the perspective of villagers' responses, and the work by Dali Yang (1996) from the perspective of how the GLF influenced people's attitudes toward the post-Mao reform.

[5] Roderick MacFarquhar (1983, 81) says: "The paper [*People's Daily*] did not attribute the assertion to Mao, but by now most alert cadres must have been aware of the Chairman's [Mao's] attitude. The die was cast."

grain procurement and shifted land from grain to economic crops, diverting many agricultural laborers into industrial sectors (Yang 1996, 65). The state's increased demand for grain procurement led local cadres to coerce villagers ruthlessly to collect the required grain quotas, which resulted in widespread starvation.[6]

Through the collectivizing moves of the GLF, each people's commune became an extremely large unit, which on average consisted of approximately 6,000 households. Mao wanted each people's commune to be large enough to be economically self-sufficient. However, the scale of each people's commune was too large for villagers to maintain their motivation for working in agriculture (Lieberthal 1997, 95–96). The GLF ended with disastrous results: a steep decrease in agricultural production and a massive famine. As a result, the size of each people's commune was scaled down to approximately 1,000 households in 1962. For the administration of rural governance, production brigades (*shengchan dadui*), which were essentially the same size as the former Higher APCs of 100–150 households, were established under each people's commune. Production teams (*shengchan dui*), each of which consisted of fifteen to twenty-five households, were established under each production brigade. One of the unique characteristics of the people's communes, production brigades, and production teams was that they were not only the primary economic units of agricultural production but were also the primary political units of governmental administration and of people's social lives (*zhengshe heyi*) (Oi 1989; Shue 1980; Siu 1989; Zhang 1998). With these organizations, the Chinese state could control not only people's economic and political activities but also their daily lives to an unprecedented degree.

In sum, the experiment of the people's communes system ended in failure.[7] Labor productivity plunged, agricultural revenue decreased, and living conditions worsened during the Maoist period (Lin 1992, 45–69). Although the system's failure was recognized during the GLF, it continued until the late 1970s. At the local level, the attempts to introduce a more market-oriented economic system for agricultural production and distribution started in the early 1960s, after the disaster of the GLF. For example, in 1962 in Anhui Province approximately 90 percent of the farm land was distributed to villagers, who

[6] Thaxton (2008) examines petitions written by farmers in Henan Province to the CCP's central leadership in 1958. One of the petitions, addressed to Tan Zhenlin, agricultural chief during the GLF, on August 11, "complained that party cadres were falsely overreporting the harvest output so they could justify appropriating more of the food crop for the party-state and thereby achieve greater glory in the eyes of their superiors" (Ibid., 1). Another petition, sent to Mao on October 20, said that "cadres were consistently breaking the law by severely beating farmers who did not obey their orders, targeting especially those who accurately reported the harvest output" (ibid., 2).

[7] For reviews of why the people's communes system failed to function, see the works by Lin Yifu (1992, 45–69) and Zhang Letian (1998, chapter 12) for the Chinese-language literature, and the works by Jean Oi (1990) and Vivienne Shue (1984) for the English-language literature.

were allowed to farm the land themselves instead of farming collectively under the guidance of people's communes (Liu 2004, 70–72). However, Mao criticized these attempts as "capitalism" and "revisionism," and the Socialist Education Movement (1963–65) and later the Cultural Revolution stopped the attempts to adopt the market system in agricultural production (Baum 1975; Lieberthal 1997; Yang 1996, 93–96). It was as late as 1977 that the central government once again recognized Anhui and Sichuan Provinces as advanced places for market-oriented rural reforms.

Rural Taxation

Along with the changes in administrative institutions in rural areas during the Maoist period, the people's perception of village leadership had also changed since the Communist Revolution. Although villagers perceived village leaders as the "rural community elite" (*xiangshen*) during the imperial period, leaders of production brigades were given the status of state cadres. The rural community elite before the Communist Revolution was mainly made up of landlords or other wealthy people who did not necessarily represent the villagers' preferences or the whole village's interests; however, they were at least *rooted* in the village community and championed villagers' interests to a certain extent (Shen and Zhang 2003, 11). After the Communist Revolution, however, the CCP leadership established the party branch (*dang zhibu*) in each production brigade and "penetrated to the grass roots, gaining unprecedented organizational access to the villagers of the whole country" (Bernstein and Lü 2003, 36). In other words, the CCP organizations were not rooted in the village community but *implanted* from outside the community.

In addition to these administrative organizations for rural governance, another important political institution that the Maoist regime established in the 1950s was the household registration (*hukou*) system, which differentiated urban households from rural households and restricted those with rural household registration (*nongcun hukou*) from migrating into urban areas. During the Maoist era, the migration from rural to urban areas was virtually prohibited. This policy produced a large gap in economic wealth and social welfare between urban and rural areas, and as a result, productivity in rural areas was far lower than productivity in urban areas when the post-Mao reform started. In 1978, although 74 percent of the labor force was in rural areas, it represented only 32 percent of the nation's GDP (Cui 2004, 7–8).

Even with the new administrative system for rural governance, the Maoist regime still failed to create efficient taxation in rural areas. The state's fiscal revenue (at the county level and higher) from the agricultural tax was surprisingly small and continued to decline throughout the Maoist period. Moreover, during the Maoist period "the proportion of foodgrain procured by the state . . . declined, and the share allocated for redistribution within rural areas [fell] even faster" (Lardy 1983, 174). To make these problems worse, the county governments often failed to update their information about land and agricultural production, even though production had increased in most rural areas since the 1960s. For example, Oi (1989, 18–20) shows that in Minhou County of Fujian Province, the county government imposed the agriculture tax on 87 percent of the harvest in 1962 but on only 38 percent in 1983; and the agricultural tax accounted for 32 percent of the county's fiscal revenue in 1957 but dropped to 9 percent in 1983. One of the reasons this inefficient tax collection occurred in rural China was that leaders in local communities, especially leaders of the production teams, did not impose policies in the way that the central government intended. Despite the unprecedented degree of state control over economic resources and over people's daily lives, the space for local leaders to exercise their power against central authorities still existed. For example, Vivienne Shue (1988, 76) argues that "lower-level politicians pursue[d] evasive, defensive, and sometimes aggressive strategies that frequently confound[ed] central intentions." Oi (1989, 6) also suggests that leaders of production teams routinely interpreted state laws and national policies in a way that would protect villagers' interests. This tendency was accelerated after the failure of the GLF became evident in the 1960s. Underreporting of grain production by production team leaders increasingly became a more common phenomenon beginning in the 1960s.

However, it is important to note that inefficient tax collection in rural areas did not necessarily mean light financial burdens for villagers during the Maoist period. Although villagers were residual claimants to the harvest, the share that villagers could claim after the central government and people's communes had taken their share was very small. The central government controlled not only the amount and the price of public grain (*gongliang*) – the de facto tax – but also the amount and the price of surplus grain (*yuliang*). Originally, procurement prices were "set with the objective of stimulating the relatively voluntary delivery of the products" (Lardy 1983, 19). Thus, in 1953–54, the central government offered so high a price for the procured grain that villagers supported the new socialist procurement system (Shue 1980, chapter 5). However, the procurement system quickly lost popular support when the government-set price started to drop immediately after its initial short success in the early 1950s (Oi 1989, chapter 3). Although the price for procurement was high when the system started in the 1950s, it remained unchanged for more than a decade after that even though prices of other products rose, and it significantly increased villagers' financial burden. Disappointed villagers started to complain. Oi suggests: "The voluntary nature of grain sales soon took on an oppressive character that has led to calling these sales 'forced procurements' and 'hidden forms of taxation'" (ibid., 43).

In addition to the financial burden created by the procurement system, there was another hidden burden: the scissors effect (Bernstein and Lü 2003, 36). Mao was "antagonistic to the concept of specialized production based on comparative advantage," aiming for self-sufficiency, rather than setting prices for economic efficiency of agricultural production and distribution (Lardy 1983, 49). When the CCP devoted state investment to the heavy industrial sector to pursue the national goal of industrialization under a command economic system, it procured grain and raw materials cheaply and set high prices for the sale of industrial goods in the countryside. One estimate suggests that this policy transferred 600–800 billion yuan from the rural sector to the urban sector in the three decades from the 1950s to the 1970s (*Renmin Ribao* [People's Daily], June 29, 1988). This transfer amount means that the average annual per capita financial burden of each rural household attributable to the scissors effect was approximately 30 yuan, while the annual per capita rural household income between the 1950s and the 1970s peaked at 134 yuan (Bernstein and Lü 2003, 36–37). By contrast, in the brief period of the early 1960s when Deng Xiaoping's post-GLF reform took place and the market-oriented economic system for agricultural distribution was introduced, the scissors effect was alleviated. Nicholas Lardy finds that in the early 1960s, producer inputs to agriculture increased and "the industrial sector produced tractors, pumps, chemical fertilizers, insecticides, electricity, and other products that were purchased by the agricultural sector in growing quantities" (Lardy 1983, 110). Unfortunately, the post-GLF reform was soon replaced with the Socialist Education Movement and the Cultural Revolution, the price system of agricultural products was again based on the state's plan instead of the market system, and the scissors effect resumed, imposing financial burdens on villagers.

In sum, the rural financial burden was very heavy during the Maoist period.[8] This does not mean that the villagers' tax burden was heavy but means that their financial burden from the procurement system was heavy. The rural financial burden based on compulsory grain procurement became very heavy because the state-set amounts of procurement were designed to meet the needs of resource transfers for urban industrialization instead of considering villagers' needs for their own lives. To make things worse, in order to prevent villagers from selling their grain outside the artificially low price structure imposed by compulsory purchase, the government closed down markets for agricultural production in the late 1950s (Oi 1989, chapter 3).

Then why did the Maoist state rely on the procurement system instead of agricultural taxes to transfer resources from the rural sector to the urban sector? In other words, why did the Maoist regime create an effective procurement system, but not an efficient tax system? One reason is that the way for the Maoist regime to obtain accurate information about local conditions of agricultural

[8] However, this does not necessarily mean that a villager's burden was heavier than before the Communist Revolution. A villager's burden depended on the amount of the land rental fee paid to the landlord rather than the tax rate before the land reform, and it was the landlord who paid the land tax to the state. For example, in a village of Hunan Province, an old villager told me that his financial burden lightened after the Communist Revolution, compared with the rent he had to pay to his landlord before the land reform (Interviewee 77).

production was gone. This, combined with Mao's relentless push for village grain resources, drove the countryside into famine during the GLF and, in turn, made villages and village leaders do anything they could to avoid the reach of grain-grabbing cadres – including eating unripe grain in the fields before the cadres could seize the harvest (Thaxton 2008, chapter 6). Having learned a lesson from the famine during the GLF, local village leaders, especially those in charge of the production teams, conspired with villagers to hide grain from higher authorities, sabotaging grain procurements (Oi 1989). Dali Yang (1996) finds that this tendency for local discretion in central commands and policies was more likely to occur in the localities where the GLF's damage was largest. The central government's failure to grasp accurate information about grain yields in each locality paralyzed collection of the agricultural tax and made it very difficult, if not impossible, to establish efficient taxation in rural areas. Instead, the Maoist state had to rely on the compulsory procurement system of public grain and keep the price of both public grain and surplus grain low, so that it could transfer a large amount of money from rural areas to urban areas for investment in industrialization.

Then why did the procurement system work during the Maoist period? This occurred because the migration from rural areas to urban areas was virtually prohibited. Under the household registration system, those who had a rural household registration could not migrate to live in urban areas. They could not find a place to live nor could they have access to grain rations in cities. In this way, rural residents had to stay in the countryside and be engaged in agriculture. Because villagers were not able to move out of their village, they had no choice but to comply with the procurement system, even though the government-set price of grain was very low. As long as villagers complied with the procurement system, the Maoist state did not have to establish efficient rural taxation, and, needless to say, it had no incentive to establish a representative political regime.

CONCLUSION

In this chapter, I laid the historical background for an analysis of revenue and resistance in authoritarian rule in China, which will focus on rural taxation and political participation in the period of 1980–2006. China's imperial courts were unable to levy high tax rates without provoking rebellion under their authoritarian rule. Unlike Europe's historical experience after the sixteenth century, the end of imperial rule did not create a representative political regime or efficient taxation; rather, tax resistance lingered in rural China. Similar to previous regimes, the Maoist regime was also unable to establish efficient rural taxation, and hence, it had to rely on the compulsory grain procurement system. The financial burden imposed on villagers was very heavy because the procurement system was designed to sacrifice rural financial interests for urban industrialization. Moreover, under the Maoist regime the central government did not have access to accurate information about local conditions, especially accurate information about grain yields in each locality, which paralyzed rural taxation.

Liu Ya (2004), a Chinese political scientist who has studied historical changes in rural China, argues that state-society relations in that area have been in continuous flux and in search of modernized rural governance since the political and social system based on the traditional community collapsed in the late imperial period. During the republican period, the rampancy of warlordism and the reliance on the militia for rural governance weakened the authority of the traditional community. As a result, the KMT regime failed to gain popular support in rural areas. The Maoist socialist experiment uprooted traditional grassroots elites, and collectivization and the people's communes system ended in failure. During the post-Mao reform period, the CCP leadership has aimed to restructure rural governance while committing itself to the twin goals of market-oriented reform and authoritarian rule. These two goals – and the conflicting logics thereof – have been significantly shaped by and constrained the political economy of post-Mao rural China. Under the authoritarian regime where local officials are appointed by higher authorities, central-local intergovernmental relations define the constraints and characterize rural governance. I now turn to the issues of rural taxation and political participation during the post-Mao period, focusing on rural-to-urban migration and central-local relations.

3

Revenue and Resistance under Authoritarian Rule in Post-Mao Rural China, 1980–2005

The discussion of the historical background of rural taxation and political participation in the previous chapter suggests a fundamental problem in China's rural governance: the central government – whether the imperial court, the republican system, or the Maoist regime – struggled to establish efficient rural taxation in the countryside. Because the central government gave the highest priority to maintaining the authoritarian regime – and local cadres were appointed by higher authorities – local officials were under pressure to implement policies whether or not they would benefit villagers. Thus, the question is whether the post-Mao reform has continued the Mao-era pattern of poverty and rule in rural China. My finding suggests that rich industrialized villages benefited from the local governments' relationship with the central government through economic and political rewards, whereas poor interior agricultural villages were plundered and left out of the vertical flow of patronage from the central government.

In this chapter, I provide an assessment of rural taxation and political participation during the post-Mao period, 1980–2005. Similar to the government of the Maoist period, the post-Mao regime failed to raise sufficient fiscal revenues through taxation in rural China in the 1980s and the 1990s. The increase in outbound migration, a new phenomenon in the post-Mao period, made tax collection more costly. Local cadres, suffering from revenue shortfalls as a result of villagers' outbound migration and the 1994 tax-sharing system (*fenshuizhi*), when they could not collect sufficient revenue from the villagers, colluded with gangsters to collect levies in an oppressive and violent manner so that they could meet revenue requirements imposed by higher authorities. After the post-Mao reform started, fiscal decentralization that began in the 1980s and was modified in the 1990s sharpened local fiscal tensions and increased villagers' financial burdens in rural areas. Concerned that the villagers' dissatisfaction with these burdens would become a source of political instability that would threaten the regime's survival, the Chinese Communist Party (CCP) leadership initiated a series of rural tax reforms in 2000 (Chen 2003; Li C. 2006; L. Li 2006, 2007; Li and Wu 2005; X. Li 2003; Lin, Tao, and Liu 2007; Lin et al. 2002a, 2002b; Oi 2004; Yep 2004). These rural tax reforms started with the tax-for-fee (*feigaishui*) reform and culminated in the outright abolition of the agricultural tax and other fees. Although the reforms alleviated villagers' financial strains, they also created a new set of problems: local fiscal crises (Chen 2007; Chen and Chen 2004; Huang 2005; Kennedy 2006; Li and Dong 2004; Oi and Zhao 2007; Xiang 2004; Zhao 2010). In areas that had relied heavily on the agricultural tax, local government officials, especially at the county and township levels, found themselves with inadequate revenues and limited incentive to improve the provision of public goods.

The purpose of this chapter is to highlight some of the basic observations of the Chinese countryside that are crucial for my argument. In this book, I argue that by implementing rural tax reforms in contemporary China, the central government put local governments in poor areas in impossible situations vis-à-vis its own claims and the rights of villagers, and that this central government strategy optimally functioned to maintain the authoritarian regime. In short, the central government used its advantageous position in central-local relations for the survival of its regime. To make this argument, in this chapter I identify three main elements of the fiscal situation in the 1990s, which conditioned the rural tax reforms beginning in 2000:

1. The villagers' financial burden was very heavy in the primarily agricultural areas that did not develop rural industry such as township-and-village enterprises (TVEs: *xiangzhen qiye*). Moreover, among villagers, the financial burden was even heavier if their income relied exclusively on agricultural revenue.
2. The fiscal reform in 1994, which introduced the tax-sharing system, gave the central government a larger share of tax revenues and did not change the central-local share of expenditures. Moreover, higher authorities took a larger share of formal exactions in intragovernmental contracts than lower-level authorities at every level. Therefore, grassroots authorities, especially at the township and village levels, increasingly relied on extrabudgetary funds (EBFs: *yusuanwai zijin*) and other ad hoc exactions imposed on villagers.
3. Fiscal transfers in the 1990s rewarded economic development by transferring more financial aid to richer local governments, which put poor localities at a disadvantage. As a result, fiscal transfers did not alleviate intrarural disparities, but rather exacerbated them.

Rural governance deteriorated in agricultural areas in the 1990s and its improvement was an urgent goal when the central government started a series of rural tax reforms in 2000. Overall, however, the rural tax reforms of the past decade instead had negative effects on the provision of public goods in agricultural areas. In fact, the reforms led to a host of governance problems in many localities whose income levels were average or below average as compared with the rest of the country (Liu et al. 2009; Tao et al. 2011; Wong 2009; Zhan 2009b). This result gives rise to the question that motivates this chapter: why did the reforms fail to enhance the provision of public goods in the areas that needed it most? Why were local governments, especially at the county and township levels, unable to provide public goods? I argue that in agricultural areas, the central government urged local governments to institute the reforms without providing sufficient financial resources or considering initial economic conditions. To make matters worse, the central government then blamed inadequate governance on local governments, further undermining the popular legitimacy and administrative capacity of local governments.[1]

DECOLLECTIVIZATION OF AGRICULTURAL PRODUCTION

The CCP leadership realized that the problem of stagnating agricultural production during the Maoist period was rooted in collectivized production under the people's commune system and state-controlled grain distribution under the compulsory procurement system. Thus, one of the first post-Mao reform policies implemented by the leadership headed by Deng Xiaoping was decollectivization of agricultural production, called the household responsibility system (*jiating lianchan chengbao zerenzhi*), which made each rural household a unit of agricultural production. Under this system, each household would lease a specific plot of land from a production team under a contract. Initially, contracts were to be no longer than one year, but this quickly became three years, fifteen years, thirty years, and then fifty years (Naughton 2007, 241). Each household was to present a certain amount of grain to the production team but could keep the remaining amount to sell in the market as household income. Under the post-Mao agricultural reform, per capita grain production increased rapidly from approximately 300 kilograms in 1978 to more than 400 kilograms in 1983 (ibid., 253), and by the end of 1983 almost all rural households were converted to household farming (ibid., 88–90).

Once agricultural production was decollectivized and people's communes were dismantled, the post-Mao CCP regime realized the need to establish efficient taxation in rural China, which would replace the compulsory procurement system. The post-Mao reform policies produced winners and losers in rural areas by the end of the 1990s. A virtuous circle between economic development and tax collection emerged in the areas that originally had better conditions for local development, while a vicious circle between poverty and taxation emerged in the areas without favorable conditions for rural industrialization. On the one hand, local governments in the areas that succeeded in

[1] Of course, there is economic disparity within rural areas, for which various factors may account. For a discussion explaining rural disparity in post-Mao China, see the article by Jiang Xu (2004).

developing rural industry were able to establish more efficient taxation based on the taxes levied on rural industry, to secure sufficient fiscal revenue for providing public goods, and to promote further industrialization. On the other hand, local governments in the areas that relied on agriculture struggled to collect taxes levied on agriculture, suffered from the lack of fiscal revenue to provide public goods, and failed to promote rural industrialization.

THE RELAXATION OF MIGRATION POLICIES

Two of the most significant changes that appeared in rural areas during the post-Mao period were that villagers had the ability to earn nonagricultural revenue in the 1980s and to migrate to urban areas in the 1990s.[2] With these changes, the proportion of the agricultural labor force to the total labor force dropped from 74 percent in 1978 to 60 percent in 1988, and to 50 percent in 1998 (Cui 2004, 9). The changes occurred in two stages. First, in the 1980s, along with growth of TVEs, many villagers started working in local TVE factories while continuing to reside in their village (*li tu bu li xiang*). Then, in the 1990s, with rapid commercialization, a booming urban economy, and the relaxation of state migration policies, over 100 million villagers, known as China's "floating population" (*liudong renkou*), left their local villages and streamed into large cities.

In the 1980s, as TVEs prospered in rural China, many villagers started working in local factories. Yasheng Huang argues that the TVEs developed more in poor inland provinces than in rich coastal provinces and were the driving force "to transition out of low value-added agriculture and to move beyond... abject poverty" (Huang 2008, 83). Because of the improved efficiency of agricultural production and the prosperity of rural industry, rural areas achieved 15 percent annual income growth from 1978 to 1984 (Aubert and Li 2002). Moreover, the ratio of per capita urban to rural income decreased from 2.5 in 1978 to 1.8 in 1983 (Li and Han 2004, 3). At this time, a majority of the labor force did not leave the local province and interprovincial migration was on a small scale. For example, in Dongguan Prefecture of Guangdong Province, where rural industry prospered at the fastest pace in China in the 1980s, 72 percent of the labor force was still from inside Guangdong Province in 1988 (Cui 2004, 10).

This trend changed in the early 1990s. Per capita grain production stagnated after the mid-1980s and stayed around 350 kilograms throughout the 1990s (Naughton 2007, 253). The gap between rural incomes and urban incomes consistently expanded after the mid-1980s. The speed of its increase was slow until 1997 when the ratio of per capita urban to rural income once again

[2] For the most comprehensive research on rural migration, see the book by Cui Chuanyi (2004). For studies on migrant workers' lives in cities, see the works by Hein Mallee (1995), Dorothy Solinger (1999), and Li Zhang (2001a, 2001b).

reached 2.5 – the same level as that of 1978. However, the ratio rose sharply after 1997 to reach 3.2 in 2005 (Li and Han 2004, 3; Lin, Tao, and Liu 2007, 2). The small-scale production that characterized Chinese household-based agriculture created a bottleneck for any further boost in productivity. Moreover, many TVEs failed to survive because of surging competition in the 1990s (Naughton 2007, 285–86).

In the meantime, especially after Deng Xiaoping's Southern Tour (*Nanxun*) in 1992, enterprises in coastal regions demanded an enlarged work force, and many migrant workers (*mingong*) from inland rural areas started crossing provincial borders. For example, in Dongguan Prefecture in 1993, 70 percent of the labor force was from outside Guangdong Province (Cui 2004, 11). Once a significant number of migrants flowed into urban areas from rural areas, their network enabled even more to migrate to cities (Solinger 1999, chapter 5). With these economic and social mechanisms, the number of migrant workers skyrocketed in the early 1990s. The number of urban workers with rural household registrations was less than two million in 1983, nine million in 1987, and forty to fifty million in 1994 (Cui 2004, 9–11). In 1994, approximately half of the urban workers with rural household registration worked in a province different from their local province. In the late 1990s, however, the increase in the rate of migrant workers slowed, though the number stayed high. According to the Ministry of Agriculture's estimate, the number of urban workers with rural household registrations increased by 12 percent in 1994 and 5–8 percent in 1995, but did not increase significantly between 1996 and 1998 (ibid., 11).

Industrialization of rural areas in coastal regions and outbound migration of villagers from inland regions brought two important changes to agricultural areas. First, villagers earned a large share of their income – compared with their agricultural income – from working in factories, construction sites, or service industries. For those who had both agricultural and nonagricultural incomes, the nonagricultural income became much higher than the agricultural income because of the low productivity of China's small-scale agriculture. For example, a villager in Hubei Province said that his nonagricultural income was twenty times higher than his agricultural income in 2003 (Interviewee 47). Thus, income differences appeared not only between rich villages and poor villages but also within villages, between those with access to nonagricultural income and those without. Second, the mobility of villagers made it difficult for local cadres to collect agricultural levies (taxes and fees). Under the household responsibility system, each household was allocated (leased) land on the basis of the number of household members, regardless of whether they were farming in the village or working outside the village; the agricultural levies were exacted on the basis of the land allocated to the household. Thus, local cadres had to collect levies from each household regardless of whether they were living in the village.

The ability to "exit" from the local village did not necessarily give villagers power to resist local cadres; it might, instead, have *hurt* villagers in the regions without high potential for industrialization and economic development because the increasing probability of outbound migration eroded the basis for local officials to collect levies in agricultural areas.[3] As the ease of migration led to a significant drop in fiscal revenue and the local government failed to meet the revenue target given by its superior government, local cadres would take any available suppressive means to collect taxes and fees from those who remained in the village, and might hire local gangsters to collect levies.

To implement this predatory way of tax collection, collusion among local cadres, the local police, and local gangsters emerged in agricultural areas.[4] Uninhibited by a remote central government, local cadres could levy and collect outrageously high financial burdens by force, colluding with underground powers. Four cases from Anhui Province reported in *An Investigation of Chinese Farmers* (Chen and Wu 2004, chaps 1–4) are the results of this collusion. One case takes place in 1993, when Mr. Ding Zuoming, an ordinary farmer in Luying Village, petitioned to the township government about the collection of excessive amounts of the village fees. The village party secretary, who had been accused of this offense by a township cadre, ordered the local gangsters – who were officially police officers – to beat Mr. Ding to death in the village police office, and Mr. Ding was killed. In 1998, villagers in Zhangqiao Village petitioned the township government to inspect the village office's account. One of the village cadres, who was himself part of the local gangsters, called his company to attack the villagers making up this inspection team. This attack killed four villagers and severely injured another. In still another case, in 1997, villagers in Dagao Village repeatedly refused village cadres' ad hoc fee collection and petitioned to higher authorities about the collection of excessive amounts of the village fees. The village chief mobilized the local police, including the armed police (*wuzhuang jingcha*), and local gangsters, and arrested fifty-two villagers. The final example dates from 1994 when a group of villagers in Wangying Village had petitioned to the county government about the collection of excessive amounts of ad hoc village fees. The village cadres, colluding with local gangsters and the county party secretary, attacked the villagers and beat them up.

In sum, the relaxation of migration policies brought different outcomes for different areas. In successful areas, local rural industry developed in the 1980s and kept developing in the 1990s. Many villagers found employment

[3] The term "exit" is borrowed from the book by Albert Hirshman (1970). I will discuss this argument in greater depth in Chapter 5.

[4] Minxin Pei (2006, chapter 4) conceptualizes this collusion as "local mafia states." A famous Chinese documentary film, *Taishi Cun* [Taishi Village], reports an interesting case that occurred in Taishi Village of Guangdong Province in 2005. Local cadres hired gangsters to suppress villagers' protests against the village cadres' handling of land expropriation. The villagers also made legal demands for the dismissal of the village cadres, who harassed, attacked, and arrested the lawyers working on these issues. For an article about this case, see http://www7.chinesenewsnet.com/gb/MainNews/SinoNews/Mainland/2005_9_14_20_6_54_969.html, accessed October 4, 2005.

opportunities in factories, where incomes were generally much higher than those they could earn from agriculture. Local governments earned fiscal revenue from corporate taxes and profits from rural industry as long as it remained profitable. By contrast, in unsuccessful areas, local rural industry did not develop at all, or developed in the 1980s and then failed in the 1990s. Many villagers left their village for work in cities in the 1990s. Once local governments were no longer able to expect profit from rural industry, they had to depend primarily on revenue from agricultural production and had to levy heavy exactions on villagers for their financing. While the villagers who migrated to cities earned a higher income than friends and neighbors who stayed on the farm, local governments struggled to collect agricultural levies, and a shrinking tax base was forced to pay for a revenue target given by superior governments. This became a primary source of increased tax-based tensions between villagers and their local cadres in the 1990s.

RURAL ADMINISTRATION AND TAXATION

In the early 1980s, people's communes were dismantled as part of the post-Mao reform and a new administrative structure was established.[5] Because people's communes had been the unit of *both* agricultural production and political administration during the Maoist period, one of the first measures adopted in the post-Mao reform was to separate the two functions. While households became the primary units of agricultural production, township governments took on the administrative functions of people's communes. Township governments replaced people's communes, and two governmental organizations at the village level – villagers' committees (VCs: *cunmin weiyuanhui*) and village party branches (VPBs: *cun dang zhibu*) – replaced production brigades.

The Township Level

Township governments were established in a unique position in the administrative structure of rural China. They had not existed before the Maoist period or before people's communes were established. When they replaced people's communes, they became the lowest unit of official local governments. As official governments, they were supposed to play a crucial role in enforcing

[5] For a review of the decision-making process by the central government to establish a new administrative structure, see the book by Joseph Fewsmith (1994, chapter 1). Anita Chan, Richard Madsen, and Jonathan Unger (1992, chapter 10) vividly describe how the administrative reforms influenced villagers' lives in Chen Village of Guangdong Province. The changes in rural society occurring along with the post-Mao rural reforms are described in both the English-language and Chinese-language literature. For the English-language literature, see the books by Daniel Kelliher (1992), Jonathan Unger (2002, chapter 5), and Kate Zhou (1996). For the Chinese-language literature see the books by Yu Jianrong (2001, 309–24) and Zhang Letian (1998, chapter 13).

national policies such as the family planning (*jihua shengyu*) regulation (i.e., the one-child policy) and compulsory education financing, as well as in providing public goods such as constructing and repairing roads, building and maintaining water facilities, and supplying social welfare services. Were these services in reality ever provided to villagers by township governments? The central government intended to supply them, but what happened to the central government's effort to provide public services to villagers in rural China? Here I focus on compulsory education (i.e., six-year elementary school and three-year middle school) as an example of a public good.

As the lowest level of the official state structure in rural areas, township governments had to play a central role in the collection of taxes and fees. Although village governmental offices (such as VCs and VPBs) shouldered a heavy responsibility, township governments were the lowest level of government with a tax bureau. While responsible for enforcing national policies and providing public goods, they had to finance themselves by collecting the township fees (*tongchou fei*) from villagers.[6] In the example of compulsory education, they had paid for 78 percent of the expenditure for compulsory education in rural areas before education reform started in 2001 (Su 2002). This burden on township governments was then typically transferred down to villagers through education fees and other quasi-legal exactions. Only 9 percent was paid out of the county treasury; the central government took care of a minuscule 2 percent (ibid.).

In the 1990s, when the central government tried to implement the policy to "spread nine-year compulsory education" (in Chinese it is called "*yiwu jiaoyu 'pu jiu' gongzuo*": hereafter the *pu jiu* policy), township governments took it as the "goal" that they had to achieve at whatever cost they had to pay (this kind of goal is called "*da biao*" in Chinese). Zhao Shukai (2010, 202–03), one of the leading scholars on rural governance, explains, on the basis of his interviews with township cadres:

> Township cadres complain heavily about the *pu jiu* policy. They think that the central government did not spend sufficient money to implement this policy. However, the central government used the form of a strong "administrative order" (*xingzheng mingling*) to implement the goal of *pu jiu* (*gao pu jiu da biao*), which led to skewed results. It is true that the hard infrastructure was improved, such as fewer dangerous school buildings and wider roads approaching schools. However, it brought a serious hangover, because grassroots governments (*jiceng zhengfu*) and farmers (*nongmin*) had to pay for it. Grassroots government increased debts to build schools under the pressure from higher authorities, schools increased fees, and many farmers had to withdraw their children from school. As a result, in many villages the ratio of school-age children going to school only increased to 30–40 percent. However, as an evaluation of the government's performance, the goal of *pu jiu* was reached. Since then the number of children

[6] Institutionally the township fees, also called "five unified fees" (*wutong*), covered the following five items: compulsory education (*jiaoyu fujia fei*), family planning regulation (*jihua shengyu fei*), welfare for veterans (*youfu fei*), training for the militia (*minbing xunlian*), and construction of the roads (*xiangcun daolu jianshe*).

has decreased [because of the one-child policy], schools have been merged, and many school buildings built by debts have become empty. Some of the schools have become a place to raise pigs and chickens. When talking about this, township cadres sighed.

Zhao's analysis shows how the central government's intention and implementation to provide public goods in fact created debt for local governments and more financial burdens for villagers while achieving little in actually providing public goods. This unintended consequence took place because of the personnel system where local officials were appointed by higher authorities. In other words, the personnel system under the authoritarian regime undermined the state's capacity to provide public goods in rural China.

Township governments had financed compulsory education by collecting fees from villagers in rural China until the "State Council's Decision Concerning Fundamental Education Reform and Development" (*Guowuyuan Guanyu Jichu Jiaoyu Gaige he Fazhan de Jueding*: hereafter the FERD) was introduced in 2001: a directive that sought to alleviate the financing burden placed on villagers. The FERD ordered that teachers' salaries, which constituted a significant portion of the budget for compulsory education, be paid chiefly out of the county treasury. While well-intentioned, the central government implemented this reform by basing teachers' salary levels on conditions in the cities, ignoring living standards that varied greatly between China's urban and rural areas (Xiao 2004). Not surprisingly, this decision put county governments in agricultural areas with average incomes far below the urban baseline in an untenable position. Reflecting the failure to tailor the FERD to local conditions, expenditures for education currently account for a heavy 30–35 percent of the budget in rich counties, a heavier 50–60 percent in poor counties, and an unbearable 80 percent in impoverished counties (ibid., 41).

Another major change stipulated in the FERD was that 40 percent of the expenditures for compulsory education would be paid out of the central treasury (Interviewee 50).[7] Following this provision, a significant proportion of funds transferred from the central government to the county governments were earmarked for compulsory education in 2002. Moreover, the central government decided to "bring rural education into the formal budgetary system nationwide by 2010, which would necessitate a major increase in central government transfers" (Naughton 2007, 440). However, there is good reason to suspect that the funds transferred for compulsory education from the central government to county governments became a target for misappropriation. Zhou Qingzhi (2004, 195), one of the leading Chinese sociologists on rural governance, reports that on the basis of his fieldwork in W County of Inner Mongolia Province, it was a "practice" (*guanli*) in the late 1990s that the county government arbitrarily included the subsidies earmarked for

[7] According to this informant, "Premier Zhu Rongji originally expressed that the nine-year compulsory education should be completely paid out of the central treasury. But then the central government found it impossible to do so" (Interviewee 50).

education (such as a new school building, school heating expenses, school repair, and so on) in the account to pay officials' salaries that were in arrears or to use the funds to cover administrative costs. As a result, the Education Office (*Jiaoyu Ju*) was one of the richest offices in the county government, because "earmarked transfers for local education from the central government . . . paid officials' salaries (*yang ren*), paid the costs for officials' sedans (*yang che*), and maintained the administrative costs (*weichi yunzhuan*)" (ibid., 195).[8]

The situation was different in urban areas, where the municipal governments were responsible for implementing compulsory education; more importantly, compulsory education was financed by taxes in urban areas. In contrast, villagers had to pay fees *in addition to* rural taxes in order to finance compulsory education in the countryside.[9] In rural areas, the villagers' financial burden from combining taxes and fees was very heavy if their incomes relied exclusively on farming. My interviewees told me that in the 1990s, it was not unusual for their financial burden to exceed their agricultural income (Interviewees 5–11, 28–29, 31–41, 43, 47, 51, 57, 77, 86, 88–89, 93–94, 96–102). Li Changping (2002, 21), in a letter he wrote to Premier Zhu Rongji in 2000, said that in his town each household on average had to pay 2,500–3,000 yuan every year, while the annual average income from farming was approximately 3,200 yuan. Many villagers barely earned their livings with wages they obtained from working in factories or construction sites in their off-season. In terms of the composition of their financial burdens, villagers had to pay much more in fees than in taxes, and fees were a major source of their complaints. For example, in Chenliu Town of Henan Province, while villagers paid 15 yuan per mu for agricultural taxes, they paid 50 yuan per mu for fees in 1995 (Cao 2000, 526).[10] Concerned that the villagers' grievances would become a source of political and social instability, when the central government initiated a series of rural tax reforms at the beginning of this century, it started with the tax-for-fee reform, which integrated all the fees into a single agricultural tax.

[8] The Education Office had access to not only earmarked fiscal transfers for education but also "education fees" (*jiaoyu fei*). It was also a common practice for the Education Office to appropriate education fees for other purposes such as building (or repairing) government offices or for entertainment allowances. One of the informants in Hunan Province also told me that funds for education were a major source to finance the new county government office building (Interviewee 63). Other offices perceived as rich offices in a county government were the Financial Office (*Caizheng Ju*), the Judiciary Office (*Sifa Ju*), the Public Safety Office (*Gong'an Ju*) (in charge of the police organization), and the Water Supply Office (*Shuili Ju*). The Financial Office was rich for an obvious reason: it was in charge of the budget (Zhou 2004, 195). The Judiciary Office and the Public Safety Office were rich because they both had access to various fines (ibid., 199). The Water Supply Office was rich because it handled subsidies for construction and the repair of water facilities for agriculture such as reservoirs and irrigation canals (Interviewees 52, 62, 77). The Water Supply Office was rich and powerful only in the counties with good access to water – mostly provinces such as Hunan, Hubei, and Jiangxi located along the Yangtze River.

[9] A similar case was the implementation and financing of the family planning regulation.

[10] One mu is 1/15 hectare or 1/6 acre.

The Village Level

During the Maoist period, production brigades were supposed to take the initiative to provide public goods in each rural village. Institutionally, they had both economic control over agricultural production and political control over people's daily lives. However, in reality they did not provide public goods in many villages. As a result of the failure of tax collection and later the chaotic social conditions during the Cultural Revolution, CCP cadres in each production brigade often lost the authority and capacity to provide public goods (Liu 2004, 76–80). For example, in 63 percent of production brigades in Guizhou Province one or more party cadres were replaced at the beginning of the post-Mao reform because they had been neglectful of their duties during the Maoist period (ibid., 78).

Thus, in the 1980s Chinese villages faced the serious problem of paralyzed community leadership. Before the Communist Revolution, the village elites still filled the role of community leaders, although their power and authority had declined since the late Qing period and throughout the warlord period during the republican era (Duara 1988, chapter 6; Shen and Zhang 2003, 11–15). They played an important role in turning the imperial court's official policies into villagers' interests. Then, along with the rampancy of warlords during the republican period, the community's informal groups gained power as they were militarized. Although there was a difference in the source of power – wealth during the imperial period and arms during the republican period – local leadership existed at the village level before the Communist Revolution.

However, traditional grassroots elites were uprooted through the land reform early in the Maoist period (Hinton 1966; Shue 1980). The socialist transformation in the 1950s replaced the grassroots leaders with CCP cadres and established a party branch in each production brigade. The new village cadres did not necessarily function as the community's true leaders to champion villagers' interests; rather, they functioned as the state's agents to implement the regime's policies (Friedman, Pickowicz, and Selden 1991; Siu 1989). Although they still functioned as the state's agents during the 1950s, the Maoist system was paralyzed after the Great Leap Forward (GLF: *Da Yuejin*). During the GLF, local cadres were caught between the higher level's demands for greater grain deliveries and the villagers' inability to deliver more grain (Chan, Madsen, and Unger 1992, 24–41). After that, the state cadres in reality functioned neither as the state's agents nor as the villagers' champions in many villages (Siu 1989).[11] Therefore, there was a power vacuum in many Chinese villages when the post-Mao rural reform started.

[11] However, in quite a few villages, the new village elite emerged as advocates for villagers' economic interests and experimented with market-oriented reforms in the 1970s. These villages became the front-runners of Deng Xiaoping's nationwide economic reforms once the post-Mao reform started. For example, Chan, Madsen, and Unger (1992, chaps. 6–9) describe the case of Chen Village.

Before the Communist Revolution, community leaders played a role in bridging the state and society in traditional villages. However, even then community leaders such as estate managers and gentry leaders "used their power to distribute tax burdens unevenly, to collect high interests from delinquent members, and to pocket the difference" (ibid., 6). Thus, "tax collection by ancestral trusts had its well-known problems. Though the managers sheltered lineage members from grasping tax officials, they could also turn against weaker ones" (ibid., 74). However, local cadres had a strong interest in maintaining "the cultural traditions that provided a sense of unity to the entire region" (ibid., 54). By contrast, during the Maoist period, when the CCP aimed to implement socialist transformation in rural areas, it "attacked culture and ritual that signified meaningful moments in life's cycle, including birth, marriage, and death as well as those communal experiences associated with temples, lineages, and festivals, thus desecrating much that gave meaning to Chinese lives" (Friedman, Pickowicz, and Selden 1991, 269). In addition, "the collective, by squeezing out cash, was making it difficult for families to live in morally proper ways that required many cash expenditures" (ibid., 205). Thus, "as the socialist state consolidated its networks of power, it made nepotism, personal ties, and unquestioned loyalty decisive in determining who moved ahead" (ibid., 285). Therefore, "foreign economic dogmas [i.e., communism] that treated household farming... and commerce as evil and exploitative, while treating increasingly statist and collectivist control as liberating, hurt the economy, alienated villagers, and undermined peasant household rationality" (ibid., 269).

During the Maoist period, village cadres increasingly became the state's agents instead of society's champions. Whenever receiving financial pressure from higher authorities, they turned the pressure into financial burdens on villagers. While villagers had maintained social networks outside of the village by trade and travel before the Communist Revolution, they faced pressure from village cadres within the cellularized village community after the revolution, as villagers were confined to the production brigade "by a system of household registration enforced by the state and backed by a rationing system" (Siu 1989, 143). Moreover, "when the economic autonomy of local society shrank after collectivization, the [local] cadres' ability and willingness to draw on traditional resources decreased correspondingly" (ibid., 193).

Although villagers lost their sources of power to confront the state's agents, village cadres also lost their legitimacy during the GLF by imposing impossible procurement targets on the farmers' shoulders (Friedman, Pickowicz, and Selden 1991; Thaxton 2008). The GLF "demonstrated the cadres' willingness to follow the party at tremendous cost" (Siu 1989, 195), and "during the famine, [while] victims primarily blamed particular corrupt and careerist local officials, [r]ulers at the center... strove to focus outrage on foreigners and traitors" (Friedman, Pickowicz, and Selden 1991, 272). Thus, at the dawn of the post-Mao reform, local cadres had lost the capacity and legitimacy for rural governance and there was a power vacuum in rural China.

To fill this power vacuum in villages, VCs were established all over the nation. Unlike production brigades or people's communes, VCs were villagers' innovations and were later confirmed and institutionalized by the central government. In contrast, production brigades and people's communes had evolved at the Maoist regime's initiative. More importantly, in some villages, villagers held popular elections to determine the members of their VC. The election in Hezhai Village of Guangxi Province in 1980 was the first village election in China.[12] Then, when the central government institutionalized village elections through the establishment of the Organic Law of Villagers' Committee (hereafter the Organic Law) in 1988, village elections spread throughout the nation. Since the revision of the Organic Law in 1998, every village has been *required* to have a contested election to elect members of a VC. In addition to a VC, each village has another organization vested with the authority to make policy decisions: a VPB, a CCP organ at the village level. Although the Organic Law stipulates that the VC is the village's highest decision-making organization, previous studies (e.g., Guo and Bernstein 2004; Jing 2004; Liu 2004; Xu F. 2004) have shown that in reality a VPB is more powerful than a VC. While VC members are elected by villagers, VPB members are not exposed to periodic evaluations by villagers. Thus, although elections are held at the village level, village cadres are not necessarily accountable to the villagers.

Similar to township governments, village bodies had to finance themselves by collecting fees (*cun tiliu* or *jiti tiliu*) from villagers. These fees, called "three retained funds" (*santi*), covered administrative costs (*guanlifei*), village cadres' wages (*gongjijin*), and the provision of public goods (*gongyijin*). These fees accounted for a much larger part of the villagers' financial burdens than the agricultural tax and hence became a source of their grievances. To help alleviate this burden, the central government decided to abolish fees before abolishing the agricultural tax in the tax reforms that were implemented starting in 2000.

FISCAL REFORMS AND RURAL TAXATION

During the post-Mao reform, many state-owned enterprises (SOEs), which had been key players in Chinese industrial development during the Maoist period, lost their competitiveness against the enterprises that entered the market in the 1980s.[13] In the meantime, TVEs became the primary unit of industrial production in rural areas and one of the key engines of the nation's economic growth in the 1980s (Huang 2008; Lin 2001; Oi 1999; Pan 2003; Whiting 2001; Zhang 2009). Reduced revenue from the inefficient SOE sector, meanwhile, placed new strains on both central and local governments to maintain fiscal solvency (Steinfeld 1998, chapter 3). The steep declines in revenue transfers

[12] Xu Yong (2003, 3–14), one of the leading Chinese scholars on rural politics, documents China's first village elections in detail.

[13] For a review of the process of post-Mao SOE reforms, see the book by Barry Naughton (2007, chapter 13).

from SOEs meant that these governments had to rely more on taxes collected from the people to provide public goods, to pay salary to officials, and in general to maintain the functions of government. Therefore, taxation became a key source of tension between the state and villagers (Lü 1997), and the division of tax revenue became a point of contention between the central and local governments (Zhan 2009a). There were two major fiscal reforms: the 1980 fiscal contract system and the 1994 tax-sharing system.

The 1980 Fiscal Contract System

At the beginning of the post-Mao reform, the biggest fiscal problem for the Ministry of Finance was that the central government was responsible for all provincial government expenditures, even though it struggled to collect sufficient revenue to finance them (Zhan 2006, 61). To solve this problem, a new fiscal system, popularly referred to as "cooking and eating in separate kitchens" (*fenzao chifan*), was introduced in 1980 (ibid., 63). Under this system, the central government and provincial governments delimit *both* revenues and expenditures through a contract. Moreover, each local government similarly signed a fiscal contract with its superior government. The central government originally welcomed this new fiscal contract system because it released the central government from the burden of unlimited responsibility for expenditures by local governments. However, the central government soon noticed that it also lost many revenue sources while local governments, especially at the provincial level, gained these sources with the new fiscal system. This occurred because local governments were able to retain the extra revenue that exceeded the target set in the fiscal contract. As a result, the revenue of local governments increased more rapidly than the revenue of the central government during the economic growth of the 1980s (ibid., 66).

One of the most serious negative consequences of the decline in the central government's share of fiscal revenue was the increase in regional inequality (Fan 1995, 1997). While in some areas rural industry developed in the 1980s and kept progressing throughout the 1990s, in other areas economic growth started dragging in the mid-1980s. Although the expansion of the regional income gap motivated the central government to adopt redistributive policies, the central government was unable to adjust the gap through income redistribution with its declining share of total revenue (Zhan 2006, 67). More importantly, the situation was made worse for local governments from poorer regions, which were at a disadvantage in negotiating fiscal contracts with superior governments because they often lacked economic leverage in the negotiations. This gave the CCP regime an incentive for the 1994 tax reform, called the tax-sharing system.

The 1994 Tax-Sharing System

The tax-sharing system redefined fiscal responsibilities for revenue and expenditure between the central government and each level of local government. As

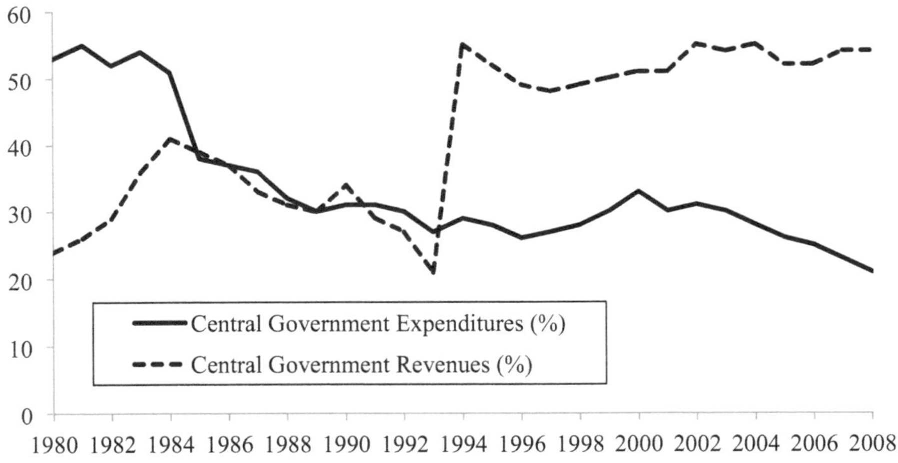

FIGURE 3.1. Central Government's Share of Total Revenue and Expenditure, 1980–2008. *Source:* Guo (2009, 625). Copyright © 2009, John Wiley and Sons.

Figure 3.1 shows, the biggest effect of the tax-sharing system on the central-local fiscal relationship was that the central government sharply improved its share of budgetary revenue. Jing Vivian Zhan (2009a, 454) summarizes: "the most obvious effect is that the new tax-sharing system increased the central share of budgetary revenue. It shared a majority of the voluminous taxes that are easy to collect, such as value added tax (VAT) and consumption tax, but left to the localities the taxes that are small in volume and hard to collect." Moreover, when the tax-sharing system was implemented, the central government opened its own tax bureaus (the national tax bureaus) at each local level. The national tax bureaus had authority to collect not only the taxes whose whole revenue the central government was able to claim (central taxes) but also the taxes whose revenue had to be divided by the central government and local governments (central-local shared taxes). In this way, the central government also had authority to decide when to refund the local share of the central-local shared taxes to local governments (ibid., 454–56).

From the perspective of the local governments, the biggest problem with the tax-sharing system was that the local governments' share of budgetary expenditure was largely unchanged even though local governments lost major revenue sources when the central government took over the tax duties. Local governments were the major provider of public goods in rural areas. Because the tax-sharing system cut many revenue sources from local governments, the central government had to set up a fiscal transfer system to provide sufficient funding for the operation of local governments (Zhan 2006, 74–78). However, the fiscal transfer rule along with the tax-sharing system enabled richer local governments to claim a larger amount of the transfer from their superior government. The transfer that local governments were able to claim was *positively*

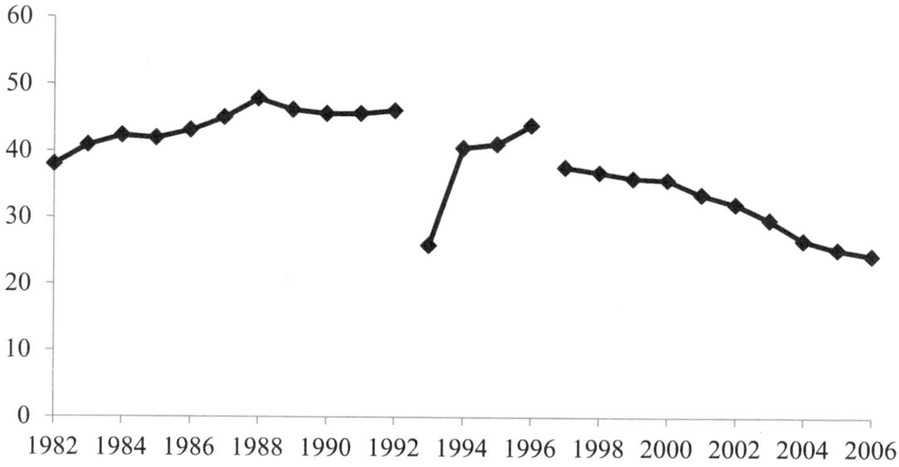

FIGURE 3.2. EBFs' Share of Local Governments' Revenue, 1982–2006 (%). *Source:* Caizhengbu [Ministry of Finance] (1993–2008).

associated with local economic development. The central government intended this rule to encourage local governments to develop their local economies by treating economic development as the achievement and fiscal transfer as the reward. However, this rule put local governments in poor areas at a disadvantage to claim fiscal transfers even though it was the poor local governments that needed these transfers the most.

Local governments that had lost a major part of their revenue sources with the tax-sharing system further relied on EBFs. Since the founding of the People's Republic of China, a local government's revenue consisted of two parts: within-budget funds (WBFs: *yusuannei zijin*) and EBFs. While EBFs had not played a significant role during the Maoist era, it became an important funding source for local governments during the early 1980s (Bernstein and Lü 2003, chapter 3; Lü 1997; Oi 1999, chapter 2; Wong 1992, 2009; Wong and Bird 2008; Zhan 2009a, 2009b). WBFs were based on within-budget taxes, which local governments had to share with superior governments, while EBFs were based on local taxes and nontax levies, which local governments were able to keep. After the tax-sharing system had been implemented, national tax bureaus were established to collect central taxes and central-local taxes, but local tax bureaus kept the right to collect and retain the revenues from local taxes and nontax levies. Therefore, local governments had a strong incentive to maximize EBFs, especially given that the tax-sharing system forced local governments to share a larger portion of WBFs.

Figure 3.2 shows the EBFs' share of local governments' revenues.[14] The Chinese government changed the definition of EBFs twice, in 1993 and in 1996

[14] My thanks to Jing Vivian Zhan, who shared with me the data she compiled.

(the latter implemented in 1997). Coinciding with these changes in the definition, the line is fragmented at 1992–93 and at 1996–97. In 1993, local governments were not allowed to collect after-tax revenue of SOEs and include it in their EBFs (Zhan 2009b, 401). In 1996, the central government reclassified thirteen major items of funds (accounting for approximately 150 billion yuan) from EBFs to WBFs (ibid., 401–02). The portion of EBFs in local governments' total revenue consistently increased once the post-Mao reform started. It increased from 38 percent in 1982 to 46 percent in 1992. Then, although it decreased to 26 percent in 1993 as a result of the redefinition of EBFs, it increased steeply to 41 percent when the tax-sharing system was implemented in 1994. After the redefinition of EBFs in 1996, it stayed high at 36–38 percent throughout the late 1990s until it began decreasing in 2000 alongside a series of rural tax reforms.

The tax-sharing system worsened the tension between villagers and local officials. Local governments that had lost a significant portion of revenue sources further depended on exactions from villagers using EBFs, and these exactions caused villagers to resent local officials. Villagers viewed EBFs as unfair and illegitimate fundraising, especially as its level had grown (Bernstein and Lü 2003, chapter 3; Lü 1997; O'Brien and Li 1995). Although not always informal or illegal, EBFs were often ambiguous and could easily be manipulated by local governments when they collected them.[15]

Many incidents of rural protest were reported in the 1990s.[16] With rural areas becoming more unstable, China's central leaders institutionalized apparently democratic (or pseudo-democratic) channels for political participation to alleviate the tension between villagers and local cadres. Optimally, it expected the institutionalization of the means of expressing grievances to help defuse popular discontent, to reduce mass protests, to stabilize rural society, and to get local cadres to listen to popular preferences. However, the attempt by authoritarian rulers to institutionalize communication channels for political participation could theoretically cut two ways. While it might alleviate tension between villagers and officials, it might also stimulate popular dissatisfaction by giving legitimacy to popular protests, and hence the rulers might face a rising tide of expressed grievances.

[15] Naughton (2007, 439) summarizes: "Given the fact that EBFs are irregular and imposed at local discretion, there is little to prevent a corrupt local official from arbitrarily imposing a new fee to fund his own administrative expenses."

[16] No public quantitative data exist on the frequency, intensity, or types of rural protests in China, but from sporadic media reports and scholars' field interviews and observations, there were thousands of contentious episodes in the Chinese countryside every year in the 1990s. For example, "3,200 collective protests occurred in the first half of 1998 alone, of which more than 420 involved confrontations in which rural government buildings were surrounded, with casualties topping 7,400, including more than 1,200 officials of police wounded" (O'Brien 2002, 141).

Although China's authoritarian rulers hoped that rural political reforms would alleviate the tension between villagers and local governments, the actual consequences in the 1990s were disappointing. The rise of rural protests suggests that the political institutions that were established (or revamped) during the reforms did not function as the rulers had intended. One might expect that local cadres would be willing to listen to villagers' preferences, afraid of the possibility that villagers might vote them out of office, petition to higher authorities, or sue them in court; in turn, villagers would comply with the local government's policies, seeing that the local government compromised with their preferences. Hence, both social stability and good local governance would be achieved. However, in reality rising incidents of protests using non-institutionalized means such as riots were reported (Bernstein and Lü 2003; Chen 2012; O'Brien and Li 2006; Pei 2006; Unger 2002; Yang 1996). During the post-Mao period, especially after the introduction of the tax-sharing system, villagers suffered from heavy financial burdens. Local cadres not only disregarded their demands but also retaliated violently against those villagers who made their demands using institutionalized means.

FINANCIAL BURDENS IN RURAL CHINA

What were the financial burdens shouldered by villagers – often referred to as "peasant burdens" (*nongmin de fudan*) – that caused the tension between local governments and villagers during the post-Mao period? Table 3.1 shows a list of the major financial burdens levied on villagers in rural China between 1994 and 2000. Thomas Bernstein and Xiaobo Lü (2003, 50–68) classify the financial burdens into five categories: (1) state taxes; (2) township and village fees; (3) compulsory labor; (4) miscellaneous fees; and (5) fines. Among these categories, only state taxes were included in WBFs and the other four categories were in EBFs. The agriculture tax and other agriculture-related taxes listed here were the local taxes that local governments were able to claim under the 1994 tax-sharing system. Moreover, none of the financial burdens classified as EBFs were illegal. It is important to note that EBFs were not "illicit nontax levies by governments and their agencies outside both the budgetary and extra-budgetary management systems," but "various sorts of nontax revenues outside budgetary management... collected by government agencies, institutions, and social organizations when performing government-delegated duties or acting on behalf of the government in accordance with laws, rules, and regulations" (Zhan 2009b, 392).

The township and village fees were legal exactions set by laws and regulations, especially by the Law on Agriculture passed in 1993, which had integrated relevant laws and regulations issued since the late 1980s (Bernstein and Lü 2003, 51–53). In fact, problems of the township and village fees were not rooted in their legitimacy but in their burden. Although the Law on Agriculture

TABLE 3.1. *Financial Burdens, WBFs, and EBFs in Rural China, 1994–2000*

Within-Budget Funds (WBFs)	Extrabudgetary Funds (EBFs)
State taxes	Township and village fees
Agricultural tax	Township fees for:
Other agriculture-related taxes	Compulsory education
Special products tax	Family planning regulation
Slaughter tax	Welfare for veterans
Farmland utilization tax	Training for the militia
Contract tax	Construction of the roads
Animal husbandry tax	Village fees for:
Education surcharge	Administrative costs
Other	Village cadres' wages
	Provision of public goods
	Labor services (if monetized)
	Compulsory labor on:
	Flood prevention
	Local afforestation projects
	Other local projects
	Accumulation labor on:
	Water conservancy
	State afforestation projects
	Other state projects
	Miscellaneous fees
	Road or school construction
	Purchase of insurance
	Marriage certificates
	Other ad hoc charges
	Fines
	Birth control violations
	Other infractions

Sources: Bernstein and Lü (2003, 50); Oi (1999, 39, 217).

stipulated that the township and village fees should not exceed 5 percent of the previous year's per capita income of the township inhabitants, this limit was often exceeded in many localities (ibid., 51–52). For example, in 1991 the rate of the township and village fees across the nation reached 8 percent (Bernstein and Lü 2000, 743). As a result, financial burdens consisting of the agriculture-related state taxes, the township and village fees, and other miscellaneous fees imposed on villagers were very heavy if their incomes relied exclusively on agricultural revenue. In the 1990s, it was not unusual for this total to exceed agricultural income, and villagers barely made a living by working in cities in their off-season. Moreover, fees (including both the formal township and village fees and informal miscellaneous fees) were a source of complaints and protests from villagers, as they had to pay more in fees than in taxes.

Labor service was required of all villagers. Each villager had to contribute fifteen to thirty days of work per year for small-scale projects at the township or village level, such as flood prevention, road repair, school construction, and water management.[17] However, many of my interviewees told me that during the 1990s, when their family members had worked in the cities, they had often paid a cash equivalent instead of contributing their labor services (Interviewees 5–6, 28–29, 31–34, 38–39, 47, 88–89). Bernstein and Lü (2003, 52) suggest that as more people went to the cities to work and earned nonagricultural incomes, more paid cash instead of providing labor services. It is interesting that local officials often preferred the cash payment to labor services and pushed villagers to pay cash even though a regulation issued in 1993 prohibited the practice of replacing labor services with cash payments (*Fazhi Ribao* [Legal Daily], March 21, 1996). Local officials had this preference because they were able to combine these payments with miscellaneous fees and fines for EBFs and use the cash to fund their administrative expenses for officially specified purposes.[18]

Fines were another important revenue source for local governments. For example, many local governments in Henan Province collected fines for an excess child under the family planning regulation as a major revenue source at the county, township, and village levels in agricultural areas (Cao 2000, 16). Local governments preferred having a certain number of villagers violate the family planning regulation. Corresponding to the local cadres' preference, some of my interviewees perceived the fine for an excess child as an "application fee" (*shenqingfei*) for having another child (Interviewees 7–11, 28–29).

In sum, local governments had a strong incentive to collect the cash substitutes for compulsory labor, the miscellaneous fees, and the fines as the funds they would not have to share with the central government. This practice especially helped local governments cover the inadequacy of regular budgetary allocations after the tax-sharing system was introduced in 1994 (Wong 2009; Zhan 2009b). The tax-sharing system gave the central government a larger share of state taxes than local governments, and gave higher authorities a larger share of the revenues for WBFs than lower-level governments in every intergovernmental fiscal contract (A. Chen 2008; Zhan 2009a). As a result, one of the biggest problems that the tax-sharing system generated was that the

[17] Bernstein and Lü (2003, 50–53) distinguish the "compulsory labor" (*yiwu gong*), which required five to ten days of work per year on local projects, from the "accumulation labor" (*jilei gong*), which required ten to twenty days of work per year on state projects. However, many of my interviewees did not distinguish these two categories and called both the "compulsory labor" (Interviewees 5–6, 28, 29, 31–34, 38–39, 47, 88–89). Thus, I use the term "compulsory labor" to denote what Bernstein and Lü classify as the compulsory labor and the accumulation labor.

[18] Strictly speaking, the monetized compulsory labor was not included in EBFs starting in 1993 when it became illegal. However, local officials were able to disguise the cash as some ad hoc fee charge to be included in EBFs.

new system cut many revenue sources from local governments, even though the central-local share of expenditures remained largely unchanged. The central government set up a fiscal transfer system to fill the gap for funding local government expenditures. However, fiscal transfer rules enabled richer local governments to claim more from higher authorities, because the central government treated fiscal transfer as the reward for local economic development. In short, local governments in agricultural areas, especially at the township level, were put at a disadvantage and had a strong incentive to maximize various ad hoc charges after the 1994 tax-sharing system. They even collected fines to cover administrative budget shortfalls and replaced compulsory labor with cash payments to maximize the resource basis of EBFs. These financial demands for EBFs – and illicit charges – were the exactions that villagers resented.

RURAL TAX REFORMS STARTING IN 2000

Concerned with the rise of resentment over exactions in rural areas, the CCP leadership took a direct measure in its fiscal policy: an attempt to eliminate the sources of people's resentment – that is, financial burdens imposed on villagers – through a series of rural tax reforms that were implemented starting in 2000. The central government first ordered local governments to integrate all *legitimate* fees (nontax exactions) that had been assessed for various reasons into a revamped single agricultural tax. The central government also directed local governments to consolidate all the agriculture-related state taxes into the integrated agricultural tax. As part of these reforms, the central government placed a ceiling on the maximum agricultural tax rate that each local government was able to collect at 8.4 percent (Li and Han 2004). The central government then required that each local government reduce the integrated agricultural tax by three percentage points every year, so that by 2008 the agricultural tax would be phased out completely.[19] But how effective were these reforms in alleviating the financial burdens placed on villagers?

The reforms had a surprisingly significant impact in this regard. In March 2005, Chinese Premier Wen Jiabao, in his report to the National People's Congress, referenced 2006 as a deadline for eliminating the agricultural tax, moving up the planned deadline of 2008 by two years (Huang 2005; Yu 2005). Although a statement by a CCP leader should be viewed with caution, reports by other Chinese officials also suggest the full implementation of the reforms and reduced burdens.[20] Among China's thirty-one provinces (including five

[19] Although the central government ordered the reduction of the integrated agricultural tax rate by one percentage point per year, in reality a number of provinces, mostly in central China, reduced their tax rate by three percentage points. Thus, the agricultural tax was phased out completely in many places by 2006.

[20] Because comprehensive data at the national level of actual implementation of the rural tax reforms and reduced burdens is unavailable, I rely on official reports to examine Wen Jiabao's statement.

autonomous regions and four provincial-level cities), twenty-eight had already abolished the agricultural tax completely by July 2005, and the other three (Hebei, Shandong, and Yunnan) stated their intention to do the same by 2006 (Li and Lei 2005; Yu 2005). Local officials like those in Shaanxi Province, who gradually pared their per capita agricultural tax of 109 yuan to zero by 2005, made similar claims (Li and Lei 2005).

Moreover, my field interviews with villagers confirmed that the agricultural tax was indeed to be abolished and financial burdens were significantly reduced. In the five inland provinces (Guizhou, Hebei, Hubei, Hunan, and Jiangxi) where I conducted interviews, thirty-three of thirty-seven interviewees (89 percent) said that the agricultural tax had become easier to tolerate since 2002 (Interviewees 5–11, 28–29, 31–41, 43, 47, 51, 57, 77, 86, 88–89, 93–94, 96–102). It is true that the amount villagers claimed they had been paying was usually higher than the amount that the local government officially announced. For example, Mr. Wu, an ordinary villager in Hubei Province, still paid 100 yuan per mu in 2004 and would be likely to pay some smaller amount of the agricultural tax in 2005, while the provincial government declared that it had completed the abolition of the agricultural tax in that year (Interviewee 47). However, he paid a much smaller amount of the agricultural tax in 2004 than in 2002 when he had paid 230 yuan per mu, and he expected that the agricultural tax would further decrease in 2005.[21] In short, even though there was a disparity between rural residents' and local governments' accounts of the overall reduced amount, there was always agreement over the general trend. The financial burdens imposed on villagers fell in many areas and disappeared altogether in some others.

My interviews also indicated that because of the reduction of the financial burdens for the first time in recent memory, villagers had little to say about their dissatisfaction with local cadres who had taxed heavily (although cadres became the object of the villagers' ire for numerous other reasons). This was a very different situation from that of the late 1990s, when the majority of the petitions had involved taxes and fees. Supporting these on-the-ground observations, a study of the Institute of Rural Development at the Chinese Academy of Social Sciences (CASS) found that only 1.9 percent of the news stories on the rural issues between August 2003 and June 2004 concerned taxation (*Nanfang Zhoumo* [Southern Weekend], September 3, 2004).

[21] The agricultural tax was levied on land, not on income. Land was distributed to individual households depending on the number of household members (including women and children). For example, in Mr. Wu's household, he, his wife, and his child were counted for land allocation and his household was allocated three mu – one mu per capita was standard in most of China's interior rural areas. Therefore, his household had paid 690 yuan before the recent rural tax reforms while it paid 300 yuan in 2004. Because the agricultural tax was de facto a capitation, villagers suffered most from the levy when the crops failed or the prices of agricultural products were low.

Both my interviews and the CASS survey suggest that the overwhelming majority of rural protests have been over land since the turn of the century. For example, in J Prefecture of Hubei Province there was a steep drop in the number of complaints related to taxation sent to the prefectural government from the countryside, but there was a significant increase in the number of complaints regarding land disputes. In 2003, 88 percent of the complaints were related to local cadres' handling of land, rather than taxes (Interviewee 45). Villagers complained about low compensation when local governments expropriated their land for building an industrial zone or a freeway. They also complained that local governments then sold the confiscated land to developers at a much higher price, so that local cadres could cover the funding shortage arising from reduced tax revenues.

In sum, although villagers complained and protested that local officials were abusing their power over land issues, the recent tax reforms had reduced the financial burdens on villagers, and the disputes about these burdens decreased drastically. The reason this result was so striking is that previous attempts at tax reform in the 1990s had failed to have such a remarkable effect. For example, as noted earlier, in 1991 the ratio of township and village fees to the previous year's per capita income reached 8 percent although its level set by national laws and regulations was 5 percent. And while there is no reliable comprehensive data measuring the villagers' financial burden over time, anecdotal evidence from the likes of then Premier Zhu Rongji in March 2001 and the Ministry of Agriculture all suggest that the burden grew during the 1990s (Bernstein and Lü 2003, 52). In short, the villagers' financial burden *increased* throughout the 1990s, but *decreased* after the 2000 tax reform.

Even though it was indeed good news that rural tax reform reduced financial burdens imposed on villagers, all was not well in rural China. As is common in the post-Mao era, solving one dilemma created others. In this case, the newly emergent problems are: (1) fiscal crises confronting local governments; and (2) the substitution of land sale revenue for agricultural taxes and fees by local governments. After 2000, county and township governments in agricultural areas saw their revenues shrink and watched as the central government did too little to address their funding shortages. Because the tax-for-fee reform made local governments unable to levy fees – whether legitimate or not – on villagers, local governments were not able to depend on EBFs for their fiscal revenues. Figure 3.3 shows the change in the EBFs' share in local governments' revenue from 1997 to 2006. Until the tax-for-fee reform started in 2000, the portion of EBFs in the local governments' total revenue had stayed at 36–38 percent throughout the late 1990s. Then, after 2000 it consistently decreased, down to 25 percent in 2006. In order to cope with the aggravated funding shortage, local governments sold village land to developers for huge sums, for which villagers themselves got very little. This became the biggest source of rural protest. Land sale revenue was apparently not included in any budgetary

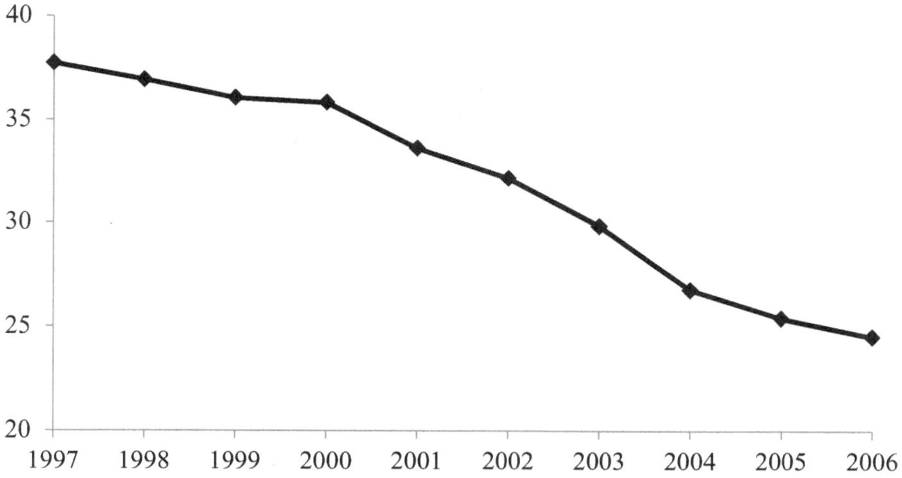

FIGURE 3.3. EBFs' Share of Local Governments' Revenue, 1997–2006 (%). *Source:* Caizhengbu [Ministry of Finance] (1998–2008).

account (neither WBFs nor EBFs).[22] In the next chapter, I discuss central-local relations and local state-society relations in regards to the local fiscal crises and the land sales issue.

CONCLUSION

There were significant similarities as well as differences between the post-Mao regime and previous regimes. Similar to the late imperial and republican periods, financial burdens became a source of contention between villagers and local governments. Similar to the Maoist period, nontax financial levies made the villagers' burdens heavy. Similar to the rampancy of warlords during the republican period, local cadres colluded with local informal forces – especially armed gangsters – to collect levies and maintain their authority. Similar to the imperial and republican periods, the central government struggled to get local governments to implement national policies. Similar to any other period, there was a tug-of-war between the central government and local governments regarding fiscal revenue sharing. However, I do not claim that the issues in post-Mao rural China were merely a playback of the past. In contrast to the Maoist period, villagers were able to move out of their villages to work in cities during the post-Mao period. The relaxation of migration policies and the development of TVEs in industrialized villages brought villagers opportunities

[22] Christine Wong (2009, 945) notes: "Since 1997 the government has required provinces to report land revenues in the 'fund budget,' but compliance with this reporting requirement is spotty."

to earn nonagricultural incomes far higher than agricultural incomes, which created intrarural disparity. At the same time, the tax base of local governments was eroded as opportunities for outbound migration increased in agricultural areas. The tax base was further eroded by the tax-sharing system in the 1990s.

A series of rural tax reforms starting in 2000, which ended with the complete abolition in 2006 of the agricultural taxes and various fees that had been imposed by township and village governments, further eroded the tax base of local governments in rural China. As a result of the reforms, local governments in agricultural areas lost revenue sources and struggled to cover administrative costs. Moreover, they lost the authority to govern as villagers blamed their *local* governments for the quality of governance. Villagers became far more discriminating in how they evaluated the performance of the state. Following the rural tax reforms, villagers drew sharp distinctions between local and central levels of government.[23] On the one hand, during my interviews it was common to hear villagers thanking Premier Wen Jiabao and the *central* government for introducing beneficent tax policies (Interviewees 77, 86, 88–89, 93–94, 99–102).[24] On the other hand, it was also common to hear villagers castigating local leaders, especially township officials, for their failure to provide public goods and govern effectively. According to my interviews, villagers believed that poor rural governance occurred because township officials were inherently corrupt, not because township governments were facing serious fiscal crises that had more complicated institutional origins (Interviewees 28–29, 31–34, 88–89, 93–94, 96).

The reason villagers praised the central government and blamed local governments is because the central government had a way to advertise its policy. While the state media actively reported the central government's implementation of the tax reform policies and its apparent concern with villagers' interests, local governments did not have a channel to appeal to villagers. Moreover, villagers did not have as good of mutual relations with local officials, at and above the township level, as they did with village cadres.[25] Village cadres were usually residents of the village but local officials above the village level were often sent from another locality. Therefore, it was hard for villagers to understand what local officials were doing. Hence, township officials easily became a target of villagers' complaints. In short, township governments in agricultural regions lost both the ability and the authority of rural governance.

[23] Xiaolin Guo (2001) reports that these unique central-local dynamics existed in some cases of land disputes even before the most recent rural tax reforms started in 2000.

[24] For example, one of my interviewees, an old villager in Hunan, compared the current leadership with emperors in history, saying: "No emperor abolished crop procurement but the current regime with President Hu Jintao and Premier Wen Jiabao is the first one that has gotten rid of farmers' obligation of procurement" (Interviewee 77).

[25] However, Lianjiang Li's (2004) survey results find that village cadres are at least as unpopular as township cadres.

In this chapter, I argue that during the post-Mao reform, as in the Maoist period, the central government's policies caused various problems in rural governance. There is indeed continuity between the Maoist era and the post-Mao era in the sense that the central government uses local governments as a scapegoat for the problems that the center has created (e.g., Friedman, Pickowicz, and Selden 2005). The central government put local governments located in poor areas in impossible situations vis-à-vis its own claims and the rights of villagers. The consequences of a series of rural tax reforms beginning in 2000 also followed a similar pattern. Studies on rural China have put an emphasis on local predatory governments to locate the cause of the problems in governing the countryside (e.g., Bernstein and Lü 2003; Chen 2012; O'Brien and Li 2006; Pei 2006; L. Tsai 2007a). My argument in this book is different, although it does not necessarily contradict the findings of the previous studies. I argue that the cause of the problems in rural governance was attributable to the way the central government had structured rural power relations between the central and local governments, between local officials and villagers, and more generally between the state and society. These power relations created tension between local officials and villagers, and this tension was caused by the central policy. In this situation, what were local officials supposed to do? How did local officials respond to the unfavorable situation that they faced once the agricultural tax was abolished? I will turn to this issue in the next chapter, focusing on the response of township governments.

4

Survival Strategies of Local Governments

From Predatory Taxation to Land Trade

The discussion in the previous two chapters shows that rural taxation was regressive from the imperial period to the abolition of the agricultural tax in 2006. The tax rates of richer industrialized villages were lower than those of poorer agricultural villages, exacerbating the regressive tax situation. Intrarural economic disparity expanded in the 1990s when rural industry, such as township-and-village enterprises, developed in some villages and the opportunities for rural-to-urban migration increased. In agricultural villages where rural industry had failed to develop, local governments imposed heavy financial burdens on villagers, which caused protests in rural areas. Concerned with social instability, the central government initiated a series of rural tax reforms, starting with the tax-for-fee (*feigaishui*) reform in 2000 and ending with the complete abolition of the agricultural tax in 2006.

The tax reforms created a new problem: local fiscal crises. As a result of the rural tax reforms beginning in 2000, local governments, especially at the county and township levels, faced fiscal crises in agricultural areas. Also, county and township governments were subsidized by higher authorities in the fiscal system. In 2004, the county and township levels accounted for only 21 percent of national fiscal revenue but represented 71 percent of officials whose salaries were paid out of national fiscal expenditures (Hu 2004).

These developments raise the following two questions: (1) why did local governments implement the rural tax reforms even though they could easily expect the reforms to undermine their fiscal capacity; and (2) how did they respond to the problems that emerged as consequences of the reforms? After briefly discussing the influence of the tax reforms on county governments, my analysis in this chapter focuses on the influence of the tax-for-fee reform and the abolition of the agricultural tax on the local governments that suffered most from the rural tax reform: township governments. I explore the township governments' survival strategies for these reforms, which began in 2000.

I discuss township officials' fears of the county government in the personnel system under China's intergovernmental relationship and central-local relations. Although the tax reforms reduced the financial burdens of villagers, the Chinese Communist Party (CCP) still faced serious problems in establishing taxation that could finance grassroots governments such as townships. As a response to fiscal starvation as a result of the tax reforms, township governments attempted to keep the same number of township personnel and to maintain over-quota staff despite reduced budgets, relying on creative and deceptive ways to provide salaries for its personnel. In this chapter, I discuss how township governments adapted to the new conditions that tax reform had created.

LOCAL FISCAL CRISES AT THE COUNTY LEVEL

The fiscal impact of the rural tax reforms was smaller at the county level than the township level. This is primarily because county governments relied less on revenue from the agricultural tax than township governments did. Even if most townships in a county depended on agriculture, some counties had enterprises from which they were able to collect corporate tax. For example, in S County of Hubei Province, most townships relied on agriculture, but two enterprises paid corporate taxes of 62 million yuan to the county government, a figure that accounted for half of the county's corporate tax revenue. Further, this corporate tax accounted for more than 65 percent of the county government's revenue in 2003 (Interviewee 50). This case notwithstanding, the rural tax reforms still affected county governments, in part through the misappropriation of subsidies.

As the agricultural tax was reduced, county governments increasingly relied on subsidies from higher authorities. Gang Guo (2008, 73–74) shows that the average subsidy per capita for counties and county-level cities increased from 195 yuan in 1999 to 539 yuan in 2003, while the average population of counties did not significantly change over the same period. These subsidies were distributed through China's vertical (*tiaotiao*) administrative system that ran from the central government to provincial governments, from provincial governments to prefectural governments, from prefectural governments to county governments, from county governments to township governments, and from township governments to village governmental organizations. The vertical transfer of funds gave rise to a vicious circle of unintended problems that began with the misuse of subsidies and, as they were filtered through China's unique set of institutions, affected the quality of the provision of public goods.

As a result of strong economic growth throughout the post-Mao period, the agricultural tax only accounted for 2.2 percent of budgetary revenues. Thus the regime had sufficient financial resources to offset the local agricultural tax losses by means of fiscal subsidies when the agricultural tax was to be abolished (Naughton 2007, 440). However, it is not clear to what extent the subsidies were used to allow local governments to function and to provide public goods.

Among the fiscal transfers to the county governments, earmarked subsidies (*zhuanxiang zhuanyi zhifu*) were transferred for specific projects, usually for the provision of public goods. However, statistical analyses in previous studies have found that there is no evidence that an increase in the amount of earmarked subsidies led to an increase in a county government's expenditure for providing public goods (e.g., Duan and Zhan 2009; Guo 2008; Shih and Zhang 2007). Thus, the fiscal transfers earmarked for public goods were not necessarily used for that purpose. I explore how fiscal transfers were actually used and what made subsidies ineffective because of corruption and misappropriation, based on field reports in previous studies and the evidence I acquired through my field research.

In the cases I discuss here, governments misappropriated funds when the subsidy reached the county level. One example of misappropriation is that public funds were used for private purposes – in a word, corruption. In a county in Jilin Province, the provincial government had provided 300,000 yuan in subsidies to the local government to construct a middle school building.[1] The county government then used these earmarked funds to purchase a luxury sedan, which not so coincidentally cost 300,000 yuan.[2] The middle school addition was never constructed, and because the number of students in the area in question had decreased over the past ten years as a result of the one-child policy, it apparently was not needed.

However, at a deeper level, the misappropriation of subsidies was related to China's unique set of institutions and was a process that cannot be summarized in a single word. Although many county governments had a fiscal deficit, the Budget Law (*Yusuan Fa*) required that they make ends meet every year, and higher-level governments promoted local officials who maintained a balanced budget. Zhou Qingzhi (2004, 181) describes how the misappropriation of subsidies occurred in W County, Inner Mongolia Province, in 1994–97:

> Although the fiscal conditions were in deficit, we heard the same concluding phrase every year from the fiscal report to the People's Congress by the Director of the Finance Division: "We have made ends meet and even have a little surplus. We have again achieved our goal of fiscal balance this year." After looking at the "fiscal balance" in the "report," one can easily find that this was a result of accounting manipulation. This occurs because: (1) the Budget Law requires a balanced budget every year and never allows deficit financing; and (2) to encourage a balanced budget, the superior government gives subsidies as a reward for the balanced budget while cancelling or decreasing subsidies as a punishment for deficit financing – as well as pursuing political responsibility in the performance evaluation system of local officials.

According to Zhou's (ibid., 180) observation, appropriating earmarked subsidies helped disguise the accounting manipulation in the balanced budget. Table 4.1 shows how much of the fiscal deficit was covered by appropriating

1 This example is based on my interview with a scholar in Beijing conducted in March 2005.

2 According to the informant, some villagers taunted that cadres were "riding in a middle school" (*zuo zhongxue*) when the officials traveled in the sedan.

TABLE 4.1. *Fiscal Deficits and Earmarked Subsidies in W County, 1994–97 (million yuan)*

	1994	1995	1996	1997
Fiscal Deficit	21.0	20.3	22.0	20.3
Appropriated Earmarked Subsidies	6.6	7.4	12.1	10.5

Source: Zhou (2004, 180–81).

earmarked subsidies. The amount used to cover the fiscal deficit was not used for the original purpose for which the subsidies had been earmarked. This is one of the reasons an increase in earmarked subsidies did not necessarily lead to an increase in the provision of public goods.

It may be surprising that the misappropriation of subsidies occurred despite the prefectural government's audit. The reason the audit did not prevent misappropriation is simple: the audit was formalistic. The formalistic audit did not alleviate corruption but accelerated it. The cost for a county government to have a prefectural government's audit was drawn mainly from expenditures as an entertainment allowance. This cost was often a substantial burden on the county government's budget. For example, in the quote just discussed regarding W County approximately 80,000 yuan was spent on entertainment expenses for auditors in 1999; however, the official total entertainment allowance in the budget was 50,000 yuan (ibid., 157–59). The county government financed the shortage by appropriating other items in the budget – such as the infrastructure construction fee, the office administration fee, the enterprise development fund, and so forth – for the entertainment allowance. Herein, one can see the vicious circle among cheating auditors, excess entertainment allowances, and the budget shortage that causes cheating auditors.[3] In short, auditing of county governments by higher levels was ineffective because the county government paid off auditors using the entertainment allowance to cover the misappropriation of subsidies; and to make things worse, paying off auditors increased the budget shortage.

LOCAL FISCAL CRISES AT THE TOWNSHIP LEVEL

As pernicious as the effects detailed in the previous section seem to be on county governments, it is important to explore the influence of the rural tax reforms implemented since 2000 on governments lower than the county level: township governments. To do so, I focus on another pattern of problems.

[3] The county government's audit of the township's accounting was ineffective in preventing the misappropriation of subsidies for the same reason that the prefectural government's audit of the county's accounting was ineffective. A local official in W County explains: "The county audit is merely going to the township government's office, listening to its official report, and bringing back well-prepared documents to the county government. This is still the case for a serious auditor. Some auditors merely go to the township government's office to drink, gamble, and chat" (Zhou 2004, 161).

However, it merits emphasizing that this vicious circle cut a more destructive path because the township governments are at the bottom of the official Chinese state structure. Therefore, township governments were reliant on the county government for the transfer of funds and were more vulnerable to popular complaints when they collected various fees and/or failed to provide public goods. The irony of the recent rural tax reforms is that the reforms strengthened the central government at the expense of local governments, especially township governments. Township governments suffered through a vicious circle that included the accumulation of debt and the buying of taxes and concluded with the misappropriation of funds. In the following sections, I explore these issues caused by the township fiscal crises focusing on the two towns where I conducted field research: Fire Mountain Town in Hebei Province and Long Port Town in Jiangxi Province.

Fire Mountain Town

In a sense, the fiscal crises of township governments were a consequence of the success of the rural tax reforms, which deprived township governments of revenue sources based on the agriculture-related taxes and the township fees. Many township governments did not have sufficient funds to pay officials' salaries and administrative costs. For example, Jean Oi and Shukai Zhao (2007, 83) find that among the twenty townships they studied, eight did not have sufficient funds to pay officials' salaries and five were able to pay but not on time.

Needless to say, the township governments that had such difficulties did not spend their budget on providing public goods. Consider an example from Fire Mountain Town in Hebei Province. The town's party secretary said that the total revenue for 2003 barely covered the expenditures of officials' salaries and administrative costs (Interviewee 23). In 2003, the town government still had revenue of 900,000 yuan from the agricultural tax, which accounted for 50 percent of the town's revenue (the other 50 percent was from the corporate tax). In 2004, the town had difficulty paying officials' salaries on time because the agricultural tax was reduced significantly. The party secretary said that he would expect more difficulty in paying officials' salaries and covering administrative costs in 2005 when the agricultural tax would be completely abolished across Hebei Province (Interviewee 23). The town's total expenditure was 1.8 million yuan – 1.2 million yuan was spent for officials' wages (*gongzi*) and 600,000 yuan was for other administrative costs (*bangongfei*). Thus, the party secretary said: "Everything is spent for operating costs (*chifang caizheng*) of the government. There is no room to spend on public goods or services (*gonggong jianshe* or *gonggong shiwu*)" (Interviewee 23).

According to the party secretary, the biggest challenge for the town government was reducing the number of officials (Interviewee 23).[4] The town

[4] I refer here to the issue of reducing *kuaikuai* (township) cadres, not *tiaotiao* (county) cadres. I do not have data on the personnel of *tiaotiao* cadres.

government employed 110 regular officials (not including leading cadres), which had been decreased by thirty-two from the previous year. The superior county government required the town government to employ no more than sixty regular officials, which means that the personnel "target" given and financed by the county government to this town was sixty regular officials. Thus, the town government faced strong pressure to reduce the number of regular officials. However, the party secretary said: "The recruitment of township officials is based on connections (*guanxi*), so reducing officials is not a straightforward task" (Interviewee 23). In other words, officials are hired not because of economic rationale but because of personal connections, which makes reducing the number of officials very difficult. The county government subsidies for the township treasury, however, were based on the target number of regular officials. Thus, if the number of regular officials exceeded the target, the financial burden for excess officials would directly impact the township treasury. In other words, regular officials suffered from the pressures of dismissal while leading cadres suffered from the pressures of finance; and, overall, regular officials suffered more than leading cadres, because leading cadres still had jobs, even though the tax reforms had made their jobs more difficult. In this way, the personnel target gave authority to the county government and made township cadres afraid of county cadres.

After losing revenue sources from the rural tax reforms, how did the Fire Mountain Town government finance its budget? It attempted to cover the shortfall in fiscal revenue by collecting fees from villagers. Although the collection of fees had become illegal with the tax-for-fee reform, township governments could still collect some fees if the fees were levied for a *specific* purpose and *solely* on those concerned with the purpose. The education fee (*wenjiaofei*) was a typical example. Two villagers in Fire Mountain Town told me the following interesting story (Interviewees 28–29). In 2003, the town government collected 300 yuan per *student* from the households that had elementary or middle school students in the name of the compulsory education fee. However, it wrote "50 yuan" on the receipts that the town government gave to the villagers when they paid the fee. This phenomenon suggests that of the amount collected, one-sixth went to the county treasury to be redistributed to the compulsory education budget, while the remaining five-sixths was used to cover the shortfall in fiscal revenue and to pay officials' salaries and administrative costs of the town government. This fee itself was legal because it was not levied on all the villagers but *solely* on the households that had elementary or middle school students. However, its operation was illegal because the town government in reality levied the fee to cover its administrative costs, instead of using it for the specified purpose of compulsory education. In the case of Fire Mountain Town, however, this illegal operation did not cause any protest (neither uprisings nor petitions) because, as both villagers said, "the fees levied now are much lower than the fees levied in the late 1990s," even though they both raised this incident when I interviewed them as the most dissatisfying thing about the town government (Interviewees 28–29).

In addition to writing false receipts for collected fees, another means to cover the shortfall in fiscal revenue was turning in false reports about villagers' income to the county government. One of the informant villagers in Fire Mountain Town told me another interesting story: "The town government is submitting a false report about villagers' revenue to raise wages and bonuses of officials" (Interviewee 29). A township with a larger economy often received a larger personnel target for the government's official employment. The county government only subsidized the payment of wages for township officials within the target number. Thus, the township government had a strong incentive to exaggerate villagers' income in the report to the county government. The problem was that this would no longer work once every township turned in an exaggerated report. At the same time, the township government would be punished if it did not exaggerate villagers' income while the other townships did exaggerate it, given that the county government funds for this subsidy were limited. As a result, no township government benefited from the false reporting, although none were able to stop turning in a false report, and the county government failed to have accurate information about each township government's fiscal condition.[5]

Long Port Town

One of the clearest trends to emerge from the rural tax reform was the township governments' growing debt. The township governments' debt problem was not a totally new phenomenon, but the reforms have made it more pressing in recent years. One of the major causes of township debt was a shortfall in tax revenue.[6] In the 1990s, a growing number of villagers went to cities to work in higher-paying factories, construction sites, or service industries. Outbound migration made it increasingly difficult to collect taxes and fees from villagers. This led the remaining villagers to argue, as I heard from two villagers in Fire Mountain Town, that "it is unfair that only I have to pay taxes" when others were earning comparatively higher salaries elsewhere (Interviewees 28–29). Moreover, as township officials in both Hebei and Jiangxi complained during my field research, the tax reforms exacerbated the problem because villagers

[5] The same logic could explain what happened during the GLF. No local governments benefited from a falsely exaggerated report of agricultural production, but they would be harmed if they did not submit one. See the books by David Bachman (1991) and Ralph Thaxton (2008).

[6] Other causes of township debt are: bankruptcy of township-and-village enterprises; investment in infrastructure; educational expenses; investment in projects to attract business; salaries for township officials; and the collapse of rural credit collective associations (Oi and Zhao 2007, 85–88). Major causes related to corruption include: construction of a luxurious building for the township government's office; the purchase of luxury cars for township officials; and the capitalization of officials' private expenses by the government (put more simply: eating and drinking on the government's budget). For the most comprehensive analysis of the township debt issue, see the works by Lynette Ong (2006, 2012).

were able to further justify their refusal to pay on the grounds that the taxes were to be abolished in the near future (Interviewees 14, 81–82).

Although a significant number of villagers failed to pay taxes, township governments still had an incentive to cover, or at least to artfully disguise, revenue shortfalls. While the CCP government decentralized economic decision making by empowering local officials, in each vertical intergovernmental relationship a superior government retained authority and resources to sanction a lower government under the personnel management system for leading cadres called the cadre responsibility system (*gangwei zerenzhi*) (Edin 2003; Whiting 2004). Pierre Landry explains: "A large number of agents are monitored by a multiplicity of principals who each have *some* authority to grant rewards (promotions) or inflict punishments (dismissal or demotion)" (Landry 2008, 117: italics in original). Of course, similar to other political systems in China, the actual operation of the cadre evaluation system may be different from what the formal rules say. However, on the basis of his survey of county officials in Jiangsu Province, Landry finds: "Local officials believe that formal rules matter . . . [and] the cohesion among respondents speaks to the capacity of the Party to instill and maintain formal norms" (ibid., 150). Therefore, township officials had a political incentive to borrow money to compensate for fiscal revenue shortfalls and they did so in creative and quasi-legal ways such as the next topic of discussion: tax buying (*mai shui*).

What is tax buying? It is probably better exemplified than defined.[7] Here is an example from Long Port Town. When I was staying in the town, one of the town officials gave me the town chief's (*Zhenzhang*) report to the Town People's Congress (Interviewee 79). According to the report, the town had revenue from industrial and commercial taxes (*gong shang ge shui*) of 3.3 million yuan in 2004. However, I found that there were no major corporation activities that could substantiate industrial and commercial taxes of 3.3 million yuan. When eating lunch together, one of the officials told me that tax buying financed more than 1.2 million yuan of the reported industrial and commercial tax revenue (Interviewee 82).[8] The officials of Long Port Town used their personal connections to locate corporations in another township that agreed to pay their industrial and commercial taxes in Long Port Town.[9] These corporations enjoyed a 30 percent discount because of their willingness to pay elsewhere. It cost 400,000 yuan up front for the government of Long Port Town to pay

[7] Oi and Zhao (2007, 91–92) call this act poaching or hijacking taxes. Among twenty townships they researched, five townships committed this act to fill the gap between actual tax revenue and targeted tax revenue.

[8] I do not have information about how the remaining 2.1 million yuan was financed. This informant did not talk about tax buying at a formal interview in his office, and I judge that what he said during the conversation over lunch was more reliable than what he said during the formal interview.

[9] Many of the corporations that paid their industrial and commercial taxes in Long Port were located in townships close to Nanchang, the provincial capital of Jiangxi.

this amount as a kickback to the other township. However, the government of Long Port Town eventually earned revenue of more than 1 million yuan through this mutually beneficial exchange. Officials knew that such an act was technically illegal, but the official said that it was worth the risk because losing revenue would be tantamount to losing his job (Interviewee 82).[10]

To use this strategy, the officials of Long Port Town needed personal connections not only with the corporations but also with the officials of the township where the corporations were actually doing business. Obviously, this act caused the township government where the corporations were based to lose revenue. Hence, officials needed a very close relationship with the officials of the township government that lost the revenue. If the relationship was close enough, township officials would put personal relations (*guanxi*) ahead of legal commitments. Moreover, officials in "host" localities might receive rebates personally – which cost 400,000 yuan in the case of Long Port Town in 2004 – and the host township governments might count these rebates as additional revenue in extrabudgetary funds. Thus, the host township's officials were not necessarily losers in tax buying.

In keeping with the theme of a vicious circle, I close my discussion of problems at the township level where I began at the county level: with the misappropriation of funds. In addition to tax buying, Long Port Town government appropriated subsidies to cover fiscal shortages. When the government decided to construct a new office building in 2004, it sent a funding request to the county government for a 900,000-yuan subsidy to level nearby farmland (Interviewees 81–82, 88). In reality, the leveling project cost 300,000 yuan, but the funding request was awarded despite the obviously inflated estimate, which enabled the town to get a new office building as well as some discretionary funds on the side. This case becomes more intriguing when factoring in the county government's complicity in the process. The county regulation on vertical transfers included a loophole that stated that a subsidy for leveling land should be 3,000 yuan per mu, a figure that was about 2,000 yuan per mu more than the actual cost (Interviewee 81). Hence, a tacit understanding existed that the town government could use the overage to cover its officials' salaries and administrative costs when it received a subsidy (Interviewees 78, 81–82).

THE LAND SALES ISSUE

In order to cope with the aggravated funding shortage, local governments increasingly used the practice of selling village land to developers for huge

[10] According to the informant, a new regulation would be applied in 2005 (Interviewee 82). Under the regulation at that time, a business was able to pay its owed taxes anywhere as long as a receipt indicated payment. However, under the new regulation, "the tax receipt must indicate which township's tax bureau has received the tax, so there will be no way to collect taxes located in a different township. Thus, one cannot buy taxes anymore" (Interviewee 82).

sums, for which villagers were able to get very little compensation. As You-tien Hsing (2010, 5–6) describes: "Land has moved to the center of local politics... [and has been] commodified in the cities and the countryside" as the national policy objective has shifted to emphasizing urbanization.[11] In other words, local governments have substituted land sale revenue for agricultural taxes and fees after 2000. Although the conversion of rural land to nonagricultural use was widespread in coastal provinces as early as the mid-1980s, the rural tax reforms implemented since 2000 extended the local governments' land sales issue to interior provinces (Ho and Lin 2004). As a result, according to Keliang Zhu and Roy Prosterman (2007), land-related problems became the number one cause for rural grievances and unrest in China, which reported 17,900 incidents of farmers' protests (in which 385,000 villagers participated) in the first nine months of 2006. Among these land-related problems, approximately 80 percent of these incidents were related to illegal land takings. Moreover, according to a survey of 1,962 villagers conducted in 17 provinces in 2005, "incidents of land takings" increased by more than 15 times since 1995 (ibid., 5).

My field research in J Prefecture of Hubei Province supports this finding. The following is a list of the issues petitioned by villagers to the prefectural government in 2003:[12]

1. Local cadres' legal but inappropriate use of power over land (65 percent).
   - Expropriating land for building an industrial zone or a freeway.
   - Expropriating land for a low price and selling it for a high price.
   - Demolishing villagers' houses, and paying too small an amount of compensation and/or not paying it on time.
2. Local cadres' illegal use of power over land (15 percent).
   - Illegally yielding or selling collectively owned farmland.
   - Illegally expropriating residential areas.
   - Using collectively owned farmland for purposes other than legally allowed.
3. Local cadres' corrupt attitudes (12 percent).
   - Neglecting their duties.
   - Failing to solve petitioned issues.
   - Selling resources for agricultural production (such as chemical fertilizers and agricultural chemicals) at too high a price.[13]

[11] For an analysis of the local politics of corruption over land in urban areas, see the article by Jiangnan Zhu (2012). For an analysis of homeowners' reactions to the corrupt behavior of local governments and developers in urban areas, see the article by Ngai-ming Yip and Yihong Jiang (2012).

[12] The data were given by Interviewee 45, and the issues were categorized by the interviewee.

[13] There are extreme examples where local officials intentionally overcharged for inferior goods, colluding with producers. In one of the reported cases, Mr. Peng in Henan Province killed himself on March 30, 1010, after he had been sold inferior seeds and was beaten when he protested against the village cadres. According to the report, his cousin said: "We know a lot of farmers who've bought fake seeds in this area.... The government does nothing to

- Abusing their official authority for their private benefit, including: lining their own pockets; yielding collective property under the table to the one(s) with whom they have connections; misusing collective money; and manipulating fiscal management.

4. Conflicts among villagers over land (8 percent).
   - Requesting to return the land originally allocated after coming back from working in a city.
   - Demanding that the local government implement the original contract for land allocation.

Overall, 88 percent of the complaints were related to land, most of which accused local cadres of mishandling land issues. Interestingly, unlike the finding of Zhu and Prosterman (2007), most of the petitions over land in this data did not accuse local officials of illegal acts but complained about their legal but inappropriate handling of land disputes between local officials and villagers.

One reason it was difficult for villagers to claim that local cadres' land expropriation was illegal was the ambiguous nature of property rights in rural areas. Article Eight of China's Land Management Law (*Tudi Guanli Fa*) stipulates that land in rural areas is owned by "collectives" (*jiti*), and the Chinese government has deliberately kept the term "collective" ambiguous in articulating land rights (Ho 2001).[14] Thus, land ownership depends on who the collectives are. Local cadres interpreted this stipulation to mean that village cadres were the collectives, whereas villagers interpreted it to mean that they were the collectives themselves. Under the current scheme, compensation was not paid directly to villagers but to a collective, which means that village governmental organizations had the authority to receive compensation and decide the amount to be distributed to villagers. In a survey of 1,962 villagers in 17 provinces, approximately two-thirds of the respondents indicated their dissatisfaction with this process (Zhu and Prosterman 2007, 6). In sum, because of ambiguously legislated property rights, villagers were unable to rely on the laws to justify their demands to protect their land from local cadres' expropriation.

Conflicts among villagers over land became a new type of petitioned complaints, which increased since the tax-for-fee reform started in 2000. Unlike the 1990s, farming became more profitable because villagers' financial burdens were reduced since the rural tax reforms had been implemented. Thus, more villagers were willing to go back to their home village from cities where they had worked for higher wages. When they went back to these villages, they found that the land originally allocated to them had been allocated to other villagers who had stayed in the village. Conflicts might then emerge between

protect them, and some suspect that those responsible for the bad seeds have connections with officials." For this report, see http://www.mcclatchydc.com/2010/05/25/v-print/94804/cheated-on-seeds-deprived-of-justice.html, accessed June 17, 2010.

14 I cite China's Land Management Law from the book by Li Rui (2009, 289–312).

TABLE 4.2. *Illegally Used Land Area in China, 2000–2002 (ha)*

	2000	2001	2002
Province	263 (0.83%)	264 (0.95%)	1,487 (4.71%)
Prefecture	548 (1.73%)	1,504 (5.42%)	858 (2.72%)
County	5,669 (17.89%)	3,914 (14.10%)	2,433 (7.71%)
Township	1,698 (5.36%)	1,824 (6.57%)	1,117 (3.54%)
Village	5,561 (17.55%)	4,735 (17.06%)	4,974 (15.76%)
Government Total	13,742 (43.37%)	12,238 (44.09%)	10,867 (34.43%)
Enterprise	9,623 (30.37%)	9,021 (32.50%)	14,181 (44.93%)
Individual	8,317 (26.25%)	6,495 (23.40%)	6,511 (20.63%)
Total	31,687 (100%)	27,756 (100%)	31,562 (100%)

Sources: Percentages and total land area figures from Paik and Lee (2012, 277), reprinted by permission of Taylor and Francis Ltd., http://www.tandf.co.uk/journals. Other land area figures calculated by the author.

the villager who was originally allocated the land and the villager who was currently cultivating it.

Although it is not easy to obtain reliable comprehensive data on local governments' illegal or quasi-legal land sales, Woo Yeal Paik (2009, 211) compiled statistical data regarding illegally handled land.[15] Table 4.2 shows data on officially recorded illegally used land and on the users of illegally taken land between 2000 and 2002.[16] During this period of time, approximately 30,000 ha of land were illegally used by government organizations, enterprises, or non-enterprise individuals.[17] Although there is a limit on the ability to read a long-term trend from three years of data, one can make a few interesting observations. First, approximately 5,000 ha more land was illegally used by enterprises in 2002 than in 2000, while 3,000 ha less land was illegally used by some governmental organizations (province, prefecture, county, township, or village) and 2,000 ha less land was illegally used by non-enterprise individuals in the same period of time. On the basis of this observation, one can surmise that approximately 5,000 ha of land were illegally sold to enterprises by governmental organizations or individuals between 2000 and 2002. Second, because county, township, and village governments all reduced illegally used land holdings from 2000 to 2002, one can surmise that these lower-level local governments, rather than provincial or prefectural governments, sold the illegally used land to enterprises. Third, among governmental organizations,

[15] For Paik's other analysis on the politics of land development in suburban China, see the article by Wooyeal Paik and Kihyun Lee (2012).

[16] Paik (2009) compiles the data from *Guotu Ziyuan Nianjian 2001–2003* [National Land Resource Yearbook]. In the data, county governments include district (*qu*) governments, and township governments include street (*jiedao*) governments.

[17] Because this is official data, one can easily imagine that the actual land area illegally used could be even larger.

TABLE 4.3. *Illegal Land Expropriation and Occupation in 2002 (ha)*

	Land Occupation	Land Expropriation	Land Trade
Province	1,232.72 (8.49%)	–	0.28 (0.02%)
Prefecture	384.77 (2.65%)	–	12.98 (0.93%)
County	1,032.34 (7.11%)	48.04 (49.55%)	35.87 (2.57%)
Township	484.96 (3.34%)	10.72 (11.06%)	96.57 (6.92%)
Village	2,038.55 (14.04%)	29.99 (30.93%)	316.93 (22.71%)
Government Total	5,173.34 (35.63%)	88.75 (91.54%)	462.62 (33.15%)
Enterprise	5,757.03 (39.65%)	4.44 (4.58%)	611.39 (43.81%)
Individual	3,590.70 (24.73%)	3.76 (3.88%)	321.53 (23.04%)
Total	14,521.07 (100%)	96.95 (100%)	1,395.55 (100%)

Sources: Percentages and total land area figures for land expropriation and land trade from Paik (2009, 233). Other land area figures calculated by the author.

higher-level local governments (province and prefecture) increased illegally used land holdings from 2000 to 2002. Thus, illegally used land was transferred not only from local governments to enterprises but also from lower-level local governments to higher-level local governments.

Table 4.3 shows the official data on the expropriators, occupiers, and traders of illegally taken land in 2002.[18] According to the official record, in this year approximately 14,500 ha of land was illegally occupied, almost 100 ha was illegally expropriated, and almost 1,400 ha was illegally traded.[19] Lower-level local governments (county, township, and village) were engaged in more than 90 percent of the illegal land expropriation, although they occupied only one-fourth of the illegally taken land. By contrast, enterprises occupied approximately 40 percent of the illegally taken land although they were rarely engaged in land expropriation. Moreover, enterprises were involved in almost half of the illegal land trades while lower-level local governments were involved in more than one-third of the illegal land trades.[20] Thus, one can surmise that in a typical process of illegal land trade, a lower-level government would sell the land that it expropriated to an enterprise. Moreover, higher-level governments (province and prefecture) were never involved in illegal expropriation but occupied approximately 10 percent of illegally handled land. Thus, one can surmise that illegally expropriated land would be traded not only to enterprises but also to higher-level local governments. Overall, these observations based

[18] Paik (2009, 212) compiles the data from *Guotu Ziyuan Nianjian 2003* [National Land Resource Yearbook]. Land expropriation includes its evaluation and approval. As in Table 4.2, county governments include district governments, and township governments include street governments.

[19] As with the data in Table 4.2, given that this is official data, one can easily imagine that the actual area illegally occupied, expropriated, or traded could be even larger.

[20] The data might count land trades between local governments, enterprises, and non-enterprise individuals twice.

on Tables 4.2 and 4.3 are consistent with the widespread belief of the practice of local governments, especially at the county, township, and village levels, selling land to developers for huge sums to cover their fiscal deficits.

FROM PREDATION CRISES TO FISCAL CRISES

The shortage of local government funds was not a new issue in the twenty-first century. Deep indebtedness plagued local governments long before the phase-out of the agricultural tax and was especially aggravated by the 1994 tax-sharing system. What was new in this century was that local governments stopped transferring their fiscal shortages to villagers in the forms of various fees. Consequently, rural financial burdens imposed on villagers were significantly reduced while township fiscal shortages were aggravated in agricultural areas as a result of the rural tax reforms beginning in 2000. Therefore, the new situation in the twenty-first century was better for villagers than in the 1990s; and local governments attempted to balance their budgets by stealing from above by appropriating subsidies, rather than stealing from below by levying heavy miscellaneous fees on villagers. In short, the rural tax reforms replaced local predation crises with local fiscal crises. In either case, local governments had no incentive to provide public goods because local cadres needed the money for themselves. They needed the money both to survive and to live an affluent life. The former is an institutional reason created by the central government's fiscal policies and the latter is corruption. The cases introduced in this chapter show both patterns.

To what extent did collective resistance influence the consequences of the rural tax reforms that began a decade ago, which culminated in the outright abolition of the agricultural tax and other fees? Yongshun Cai (2010) argues that collective resistance in an authoritarian regime may help ordinary people to defend their interests and lead to policies more favorable for them under certain conditions. The outcome of the reforms suggests that collective resistance over levies may satisfy the conditions for resistance leading to favorable results for villagers. I argue that the tax-for-fee reform clarified the misconduct of grassroots local officials. Hence, officials were afraid of their misconduct being made public (through petitions, for example) and refrained from levying illegal fees. In other words, the clarification of misconduct by the tax-for-fee reform made the implementation of subsequent policies more favorable for villagers.

As a result of the reforms, fiscal revenues of local governments were reduced and they had to rely increasingly on subsidies from higher authorities. Earmarked subsidies were misappropriated as a result of the institutional incentives of the performance evaluation system of local officials – specifically their promotion and bonuses based on the balanced budget. Although many local governments, especially at the county and township levels, had a fiscal deficit, local officials had a strong incentive to disguise an unbalanced budget. Before recent reforms, when it was impossible to reach the goal of a balanced budget legitimately, county and township governments in agricultural areas had four choices: (1) increase the financial burdens on villagers; (2) juggle amounts and sources of revenue; (3) stop paying officials' or teachers' salaries; and (4) borrow through personal connections from a local government in another county or township, or from a superior government (such as a prefectural or provincial government). In the 1990s, before the tax-for-fee reform was instituted, local governments had used some combination of the four but relied most heavily on the first. Thus, they had exaggerated the amount of revenue from agriculture-related taxes and legally permitted fees and levies, and then increased *illegal* fees to meet the exaggerated figure. To cover any remaining shortfall, they had used creative bookkeeping and trimmed officials' or teachers' salaries.

After the implementation of the tax-for-fee reform, county and township governments were no longer able to rely on taxes and fees to balance the budget, because villagers could easily recognize illegal fees if their local government levied miscellaneous fees, and because they became more cognizant of the central government's reform policies. Under the new regulations in the tax-for-fee reform that stipulated that fees should be integrated into a single agricultural tax, local governments could not increase miscellaneous fees – either legal or illegal – to compensate for revenue shortfalls. In contrast, in the 1990s when many tax reforms attempting to reduce financial burdens imposed on villagers ended in failure, local governments *could* levy *legal* fees. Thus, they collected miscellaneous fees for superficially legal reasons even though many of the fees were in reality not used for those legally designed purposes. Moreover, as a result of the popularization of television sets in rural areas, villagers became increasingly aware that the central government had implemented the rural tax reforms. The state media actively reported the central leadership's intention for reform and its apparent concern with the interests of villagers and rural issues. By appearing to side with the ordinary people against the predatory agents of local governments, the central government managed to rechannel the blame for bad governance to local officials – thereby strengthening its own authority by sacrificing the local government's authority.[21] Because local officials were not popularly elected but appointed by the superior government in China's authoritarian regime, they had few venues through which to articulate their grievances against the central leadership or higher authorities when harmed by national policies.

Have local officials resented the central government for rechanneling the blame for bad governance to them to a point where they intentionally and tacitly support protest against central policies? In other words, has the central government unwittingly driven local officials to align with angry protesters on some issues in rural areas? So far, we have not observed such cases. Apparently

[21] As a result, according to surveys, villagers and local officials had very different views on their village's socioeconomic conditions, and villagers saw local officials as unfairly advantaged (Chen 2005b; Jennings and Chen 2008).

the central government has succeeded in restricting protesters' target to local officials. However, local officials have instead used what I would call "stealing from above" as a strategy to face the challenges posed by the rural tax reforms. In their attempt to keep the number of township personnel and maintain over-quota staff under the condition of fiscal starvation, they have taken creative and deceptive measures to misappropriate the subsidies from higher authorities, which originate in the central government. In addition to the cases discussed in this chapter, field research conducted by Chinese scholars has suggested that misappropriation of subsidies is a response to fiscal starvation. For example, three Chinese researchers from the Ministry of Agriculture report that one of the townships where they conducted research spent the entire amount of the subsidies earmarked for rural public construction (*nongcun gongyi shiye jianshe*) on the unpaid salaries of the township officials (Zhu, Zhang, and Yan 2004, 281). They conclude that in most of the agricultural areas where they conducted field research, earmarked subsidies were spent on unpaid salaries of the township's leading cadres and teachers while regular officials were fired as a result of fiscal starvation (ibid., 290).

Moreover, villagers became more willing to use legal mechanisms such as petitions to superior governments when local governments violated the rules and policies implemented by the central government (O'Brien and Li 1995). As a result of institutional reforms of political participation in the 1990s, villagers had more institutionalized means to communicate with local governments and express their demands to the state (Li and O'Brien 1996). Engaging in mass demonstrations or public protests, villagers became adept at using laws, rules, and institutional mechanisms that the central government had created and/or legitimated to express dissatisfaction with local governments (O'Brien and Li 2006). Thus, villagers might petition to higher authorities if their local government levied a miscellaneous fee. Before the tax-for-fee reform, it was difficult for villagers to prove which fees were illegal, therefore they gave up using the petition system. Now that local governments knew that villagers *could* more easily prove that fees were illegal, they might give up levying miscellaneous fees to fill the revenue gap, afraid of *potential* petitions. Therefore, as a result of the rural tax reforms implemented beginning in 2000, a growing number of county and township governments suspended payment of officials' and teachers' salaries in order to cover their fiscal deficits. And when a local government received a subsidy, it used the subsidy to pay officials' salaries rather than fund projects. In some cases local officials desperately needed subsidies to live, and in some other cases officials used subsidies to live beyond their means (i.e., corrupt behavior). This chapter discussed both cases, though highlighting the cases where local officials needed to keep their jobs.

My argument here implies that the change in behavior of township governments was not because of the new basis for promotion and bonuses under the performance evaluation system of local officials, but rather because of clearer identification of misconduct at the grassroots level. In the past, the amount of revenue collected played a large role in the promotion of leading cadres. Since the tax-for-fee reform was implemented, this criterion was downgraded. More importantly, local governments behaved strategically by not levying miscellaneous fees as a response to the clearer identification of exaction misconduct. In this strategic calculation, local officials were as afraid of *potential* petitions as they were fearful of actual petitions of any kind, because reported petitions to higher authorities would have a negative influence on their promotion. Thus, they complied with the reduction of rural financial burdens through the tax-for-fee reform and the outright abolition of the agricultural tax. Would the same deterrent effect work to solve land disputes? I would answer negatively.

I have argued that in the rural exaction issue, interventions by higher levels demarcated the legal feasibility of levies and charges, and the infringement of villagers' rights or violations of national laws was thus more clear-cut. By contrast, laws and regulations regarding land were so complicated that it was difficult for villagers to prove the inappropriateness of local officials' behavior in land disputes. My position is consistent with Cai's argument that the key for success in collective resistance is "to seek favorable intervention from higher authorities" because "those local officials who are worried about citizens' reporting on their misconduct may be more responsive to the citizens' grievances and even make concessions to silence them" (Cai 2010, 8–10). I do not argue that the land right issue was exceptionally complicated, but I do argue that the rural tax reforms significantly simplified laws and regulations regarding rural exaction. In general, individual rights and entitlements in any single policy area are complicated, as they are legislated and implemented in the bureaucratic maze of laws, regulations, arrangements, and practices at both central and local levels (O'Brien and Li 1999). Despite the complication of rights and entitlements stipulated in laws and regulations, land-related disputes were rising throughout the past few years while local governments adopted predatory strategies on rural land. Many of the land disputes were clear-cut violations of national laws, as compensation was much lower than legal stipulation, eviction and confiscation occurred without compensation, and excessive violence was deployed by local officials or thugs employed by them. However, unlike the rural exaction issue, clear identification of misconduct over land disputes did not help local officials become more responsive to the people's grievances or make concessions.

Hsing (2010, chaps. 5–7) argues that township officials are more willing to work with villagers in richer areas, while they are more predatory in poorer areas. Villagers benefit from land deals when farmland is converted to urban uses in industrialized villages and "former peasants continue to live in the residential parts of the village" (ibid., 123). Villagers even take initiatives to advance land deals and "carve out a space of autonomy in the increasingly urban-centered metropolitan governance" (ibid., 124). Township officials know that they are able to earn large profits from expropriating land and leasing it to outside developers, and they do not want to lose such benefits by inducing collective resistance from villagers. As long as compensation and compromise are possible without hurting their material and monetary interests, township officials have a strong incentive to consider villagers' interests and allow them to "maximize land use by building up on their own reserved housing land" (ibid., 141).

By contrast, villagers in poor areas often lose their land when township officials are interested in selling land to outside developers. Hsing says that "between 1980 and 2003, somewhere between 50 and 66 million Chinese peasants lost all or part of their farmland and houses" and hence "land grabs and forced evictions have become the primary cause of peasants' protests since 2000" (ibid., 182). In contrast to land deals in industrialized villages, residents in agricultural villages tend to lose their houses when township officials confiscate their land. These villagers are relocated and lose their local ties with the community. Thus, relocation "triggers physical, social, and discursive processes," which cause villagers to "lose land, livelihood, networks of social support, and collective identities" (ibid., 184–85). This is different from the cases in industrialized villages where villagers or village leaders take the initiative to trade land by pooling "land parcels into larger industrial estates" or by creatively pooling funds for further development to increase the commercial value of their land (ibid., 133). In sum, in land disputes, it is not laws or regulations but financial interests shared by villagers and local officials that may give local officials an incentive to support or compromise with villagers' interests and to defend villagers' legitimate rights.

CONCLUSION

In this chapter, I have explored the survival strategies of local governments to adapt to the new conditions posed by the rural tax reforms, focusing on township governments. Since 2000, local governments in agricultural areas saw their revenues shrink and watched as the central government did too little to address their funding shortages. The tax reforms pressed local governments in agricultural areas to reduce their personnel, but these governments resisted the pressure by various creative means. In order to maintain over-quota staff despite the aggravated funding shortage, local governments misappropriated earmarked funds and sold village land to developers for huge sums, for which villagers themselves got very little. This became the biggest source of rural protest.

My analysis in this chapter suggests that collective resistance might have a significant but limited impact on the responsiveness of local governments in rural China. In the authoritarian regime, the lack of government's responsiveness is a default setting, as Cai (2010, 21) suggests that "citizens' legitimate or legal rights have been ignored by state agencies or businesses in the fast changing socioeconomic context."[22] However, officials may be responsive to popular preferences under some conditions. For example, at the village level – a small rural community where people know each other in person and interact with each other on a daily basis – cadres could be held accountable if the village has what Lily Tsai (2007a) calls the "encompassing and embedding solidary groups" in whose activities cadres participate. At the township level (or higher), where ordinary people do not interact with local officials on a daily basis, the key for successful collective resistance is to seek support from state actors such as local officials, because "those local officials who are worried about citizens' reporting on their misconduct may be more responsive to the citizens' grievances and even make concessions to silence them" (Cai 2010, 10).

In the case of the rural tax reforms, clearer identification of misconduct brought on by the tax-for-fee reform made local officials afraid of potential petitions. This gave them an incentive to implement the subsequent pro-villager reforms that ended with the abolition of the agricultural tax. A similar deterrent mechanism worked on land disputes in industrialized villages. Local leading cadres were keenly aware that they could benefit immensely from expropriating land and leasing it to developers (Hsing 2010, chapter 6). At the same time, they did not want to have this benefit tarnished by collective resistance. With this cost-benefit calculation, officials were willing to compromise with popular preferences, and villagers could earn a significant amount of compensation while selling farmland but keeping their houses. This deterrent mechanism did not work on land disputes in agricultural villages. Local officials benefited from expropriating and selling land to cover the fiscal shortage. However, unlike in industrialized villages, villagers had a strong incentive to keep farmland in agricultural villages because they did not have any industry other than agriculture. Local officials were not willing to compromise with villagers because a large amount of compensation might cancel out the low value of land in nonindustrialized areas. Moreover, higher authorities were not sympathetic to land-losing villagers because confiscation of land was legitimatized under the national policy of urbanization. In sum, clear identification of misconduct was not enough to make (potential) collective resistance lead to favorable policy for ordinary people. Popular demands must be consistent with a national policy for the state to respond. Otherwise, people will be unable to find support from state actors, which is essential to pursue legitimate rights and interests, especially in the authoritarian regime.

In sum, a series of rural tax reforms beginning in 2000 did not resolve local governance issues in poorly endowed agricultural areas. Fiscally starved local governments relied on land sale revenue, as well as misappropriating fiscal transfers, as the last resort for financing their administrative costs. Remonstrative political participation, such as the petition system, alongside the

[22] For discussion of how the CCP has maintained legitimacy by limited but effective political reforms, see the article by Gunter Schubert (2008).

tax-for-fee reform that had clarified identification of misconduct deterred local officials from levying illegal exactions. However, rural participatory institutions did not succeed in checking local officials' proclivity for misappropriating fiscal transfers, nor did it succeed in protecting villagers' interests in land disputes against local governments. I now turn to the question of what conditions, if any, might make political participation work effectively to improve local governance. In Part II, I put together the building blocks laid out here and develop an account of bargaining between local officials and villagers with democratic institutions under China's authoritarian regime.

PART II

ANALYTIC NARRATIVES

5

Exit Strategies of Villagers

Migration and Taxation in Rural China

In this chapter and the two following chapters, I merge the arguments from the four previous chapters by showing how rural-to-urban migration and remonstrative political participation affected local state-society relations in rural China. In this chapter, I explore how the relaxation of migration policies affected the bargaining between villagers and local governments. I focus on the relationship among rural-to-urban migration (exit from the village), rural discontent over the heavy tax burden, and the difficulties of the local governments in collecting taxes from missing outbound migrants. Finally, I address the consequences for the central government's appropriation schemes and local governments' fiscal dilemmas.

In China, as in other authoritarian regimes, the state aggregates preferences poorly and people often become frustrated with existing institutionalized opportunities for political participation (e.g., Bernstein and Lü 2003; Cai 2006, 2010; Frazier 2010; Gallagher 2005; Gilley 2001; Hurst 2009; Lee 2007; O'Brien and Li 2006; L. Tsai 2007a; Yang 1996). While popular grievances about the lack of responsiveness from the authoritarian state have received a lot of attention, authoritarian regimes on some occasions respond positively to the demands of their citizenry. How can ordinary people strengthen their position vis-à-vis the authoritarian state?

Scholars studying politics in rural China have examined how the institutionalization of political participation interacts with various local socioeconomic conditions, such as geographic issues (e.g., Bernstein and Lü 2003), legacies of the Maoist period (e.g., Pan 2003; Whiting 2001), the roles of social networks (e.g., L. Tsai 2007a), and the personal competence of the leadership (e.g., Gilley 2001). An institutional change that has so far received little attention is internal migration from rural to urban areas. Although a number of studies have examined the effects of rural-to-urban migration on urban governance (e.g., Solinger 1999; L. Zhang 2001b), few have examined its effects on rural governance. Since the 1980s, the relaxation of migration policies enabled more than 100 million villagers to enter cities to work in factories, construction, or service industries in pursuit of higher wages and improved living conditions. Did the increasing possibility of outbound migration limit the predatory behavior that state officials might otherwise take?

The theoretical discussion in this chapter and the next reformulates and extends Albert Hirschman's (1970) argument of *Exit, Voice, and Loyalty* to explore the effects of allowing outbound migration on the state's response to the local people. Hirschman argues that when people are angered in a society, they may not only voice their dissatisfaction but also exit from their society. Hence both voicing (participation) and exiting (migration) are protest options against the state. To develop a theoretical discussion of this issue, I introduce a simple game-theoretic model to analyze an ordinary form of political participation in rural China. William Clark, Matt Golder, and Sona Golder (2007) as well as Scott Gehlbach (2006) point out that while Hirschman's argument has generated an enormous amount of work in political science and other social science disciplines, only a few studies have extended his argument to formal-modeling analyses. Among the studies using game-theoretic models, the game presented here bears a superficial similarity to that modeled by Clark, Golder, and Golder in that they both explicitly formalize exit, voice, and loyalty as choices for ordinary people to take action against the state. However, it differs from their highly stylized positive model in that the institutional features of the game here are identified through previous studies as well as my field research on rural politics in China.

Based on plausible assumptions in the context of politics in rural China, the game-theoretic model in this chapter derives the following implications:

1. The increased possibility of outbound migration initially gives villagers greater bargaining power with local officials, imposing the implicit threat that they will leave the village if officials do not respond positively to their demands.
2. However, as the fiscal burden caused by responding to popular demands (such as lowering taxes or providing public goods) brings a local government to an undesirable threshold (such as a decrease in tax revenue as a result of lowered taxes or an increase in fiscal expenditure to provide public goods), local officials may endure protests or an exodus of the villagers as a result of not responding to further popular demands.
3. When the locality will reach this undesirable threshold depends on its economic conditions. The localities with high potential for development could postpone this, whereas those with low potential would encounter the threshold sooner.

In the first section of this chapter, I discuss how rural-to-urban migration makes tax resistance easier in rural areas, which I take as a basic assumption of the game-theoretic model. The second section discusses the model and the logic that the model's equilibrium implies. In the third section, I discuss the model's implications for the relaxation of migration regulation. Throughout, I specify theoretical arguments with a simple game-theoretic model and establish plausibility with cases and events identified in previous research.

MIGRATION MAKES TAX RESISTANCE EASIER

Because the purpose of the game-theoretic model is to capture the effects of the central government's migration policies on local governments' fiscal policy decisions, I consider how these policies form the model's basic assumptions about the actors and the nature of local state-society relations and central-local intergovernmental relations in rural China. These assumptions also pose puzzles. Thus, in this section I discuss the assumptions underlying the theory developed here and the puzzles the model might address.

The key assumption of the game-theoretic model is that the increased possibility of outbound migration made it easier for villagers to resist paying taxes. This assumption reflects the empirical observation that local officials found it difficult to collect taxes from those who were absent from the village. Moreover, as more villagers refused to pay taxes, the cost to collect taxes from any given villager was higher because the personnel and financial resources to collect taxes were limited. However, this assumption does not necessarily mean that each villager could easily resist ex post, but means that each villager would find it easier to resist paying taxes ex ante, given that a local government's effort to collect taxes remained unchanged. In fact, as a strategic player, the local government made extra efforts to collect taxes when it faced the difficulty of tax collection. As I discuss later in this chapter, the game-theoretic model predicts that under certain conditions a local government will make increasing efforts to collect taxes and villagers will have to endure tax increases even though outbound migration is easier.

On this point, there is anecdotal evidence both from previous studies and my field research suggesting that local cadres found it more difficult to collect agricultural taxes as outbound migration became easier. For example, Li Changping (2002, chapter 1) describes the situation of Qipan Township in Hubei Province, where he was serving as township party secretary before a series of rural tax reforms started in 2000. Mr. Li Xianjin, his friend and party secretary of Jiaohu Village in the township, complained to him that because many villagers left the village, it was easier for villagers to resist paying taxes and fees while it became more difficult for local cadres to collect them. Moreover, in the late 1980s and the early 1990s it was usually the case that only part of a household left the village; however, in the late 1990s there were more cases of whole families emigrating. The following conversation between Mr. Li Changping (C) and Mr. Li Xianjin (X) shows local governments' fiscal difficulties when villagers are able to migrate to urban areas:

X: They [villagers] had a meeting and decided to insist on abandoning their farmland. Actually they resist us knowing that we will be in trouble if they abandon their farmland. I do not oppose them leaving the village, but they have to pay for the required levies (*chengbao tiliu*) before leaving the village. If they do not pay for them, then how can I pay the remittance to the township government? I will force you [villagers] to pay them today. If you don't pay them, don't leave the village. I want you [Li Changping] to tell them to pay them....

C: Everyone [villagers], please take good care of yourselves. If you cannot find a job, say so to Secretary Li [Xianjin]. We will wait for you with assigned farmland available in case you have to come back to the village. Take care and good luck!...

X: I wanted you to be at my side. But you became a favorite of villagers and made us in the wrong. How can we do the job of village administration?...

C: It is useless to force them to stay in the village. Even if you can stop them from leaving today, you cannot stop them tomorrow. Even if you can stop them during the day, you cannot stop them at night. Even if you can physically keep them in the village, you cannot keep their minds. You will have to let them leave. If they go to cities, they could live better lives. Rather than thinking about how to stop them from leaving, we should think about how to help them go to cities....

X: What you say sounds fine. But if everyone leaves the village, then who will farm land? Who will collect the levies? Does your township government not need money?

C: That's right! If villagers leave the village, how should we deal with the farmland left behind? To think about this issue, I would like you to come to the township government office. (Li C. 2002, 6–8)

My field research also confirmed these anecdotes, in particular that local cadres found it difficult to collect taxes and fees as outbound migration became easier. One of the villagers in Fire Mountain Town of Hebei Province told me:

There are some villagers who have intentionally not been paying levies. They know that the agricultural tax will be abolished soon, so they have stopped paying taxes now. If you don't pay levies, then you will be fined with interest. So you will have to pay more as you don't pay levies. Some villagers' debt from these unpaid levies and interest is so huge that they can no longer pay it. The township government allowed some of them who cannot pay levies not to pay them. However, this deal is unfair. (Interviewee 28)

Another villager said:

Some villagers were not able to pay levies because they were too heavy. Later because of the interests on unpaid levies, they found it even more difficult to pay levies. Then, the township government allowed some of them not to pay them. This is fair. However, some villagers strategically avoided paying levies, expecting that rural taxes and fees will be abolished soon. This is unfair. (Interviewee 29)

What villagers said in my interviews suggested that there were two logically connected reasons outbound migration made it increasingly difficult to collect levies from villagers. First, as more villagers went out to cities to work – especially as more members of each household left – it was easier for migrant villagers to resist paying levies and more difficult for local cadres to collect levies from nonmigrant villagers. Local cadres complained that they had no choice other than collecting levies from those who might pay even if they were not willing to do so, because otherwise cadres would not have funding sources to remit to higher authorities (Interviewees 22, 81). Second, local cadres had to face villagers' complaints that nonmigrant villagers had to pay an equal or larger amount of levies while migrant villagers were earning more than those who remained in the villages (Interviewees 12, 19, 22).

The possibility of outbound migration making tax resistance easier generated a dilemma for local cadres. If they kept pushing nonmigrant villagers to pay for levies, they would be more likely to face tax resistance. However, if they left a shortfall in tax revenue uncovered, they would likely be demoted because a balanced budget was one of the major criteria for the personnel management of local cadres. This dilemma facing local cadres raised an issue for villagers – the choices available for them to resist the levies. Scholars of contemporary China (e.g., Kelliher 1992; Raymond, Selden, and Zhou 2000; Zweig 1997, chapter 5) once focused on what James Scott (1985) defined as "everyday forms of resistance" as a major means for disenfranchised, weak, and unorganized peasants to resist the powerful authority.[1] In contrast, the many provocative and overt acts of collective action in rural areas as reported by recent studies (e.g., Bernstein and Lü 2003; Gilley 2001; O'Brien and Li 2006; Unger 2002) went beyond this everyday resistance and better fit what Kevin O'Brien defined as rightful resistance (O'Brien 1996, 2002). Along with the institutionalization of remonstrative political participation, villagers used rules and laws as a means to express their grievances with their local governments, including their dissatisfaction with taxes.

Economic and political theories since Charles Tiebout's (1956) have emphasized the positive effects of internal migration on the state's behavior and economic development. Tiebout argued that the ease of outbound migration should lead to competition between local governments to attract residents, investors, and taxpayers. Thus, local officials should be motivated to provide public goods cost-effectively and hence behave as agents to efficiently achieve the economic development of the whole nation. Contrary to this expectation of a positive impact on the provision of public goods and development, the empirical record of internal migration in China shows mixed results. On the

[1] Scott identifies the following examples of everyday forms of resistance: foot dragging; dissimulation; false compliance; pilfering; feigned ignorance; slander; arson; and sabotage, which "require little or no coordination or planning[,]...often represent a form of individual self-help[,]...[and] typically avoid any direct symbolic confrontation with authority or with elite norms" (Scott 1985, 29). Thus, everyday forms of resistance are different from rightful resistance in the sense that they do not need collective action and do not use rules or laws as a means for their resistance.

one hand, a body of literature has emphasized the positive roles of local governments on development through the provision of public goods. According to this literature, decollectivization, fiscal decentralization, and the new institutions on property rights gave local officials strong incentives to implement the policies that would promote development (e.g., Montinola, Qian, and Weingast 1995; Oi 1999; Walder 1995; Whiting 2001). On the other hand, another body of literature has painted a disappointing picture, in which local officials personalized their status in the state apparatus to extract existing surplus and to distribute unproductive rents to their favorite groups (e.g., Bernstein and Lü 2003; Lü 1997; Pei 2006; Wedeman 1997). In this chapter, I show how my model might account for these varying impacts of internal migration on local governments' provision of public goods and on local economic development in rural China.

STRATEGIC INTERACTIONS OF THE LOCAL GOVERNMENT AND VILLAGERS

In this section, I explore strategic interactions between the local government and villagers, using a simple game-theoretic model. The game-theoretic analysis discussed here takes the central government as an actor in the position of setting the rules of the game by establishing and changing various institutions. Villagers are taken as a unitary actor. The villagers take actions after the local government has decided how much to spend for providing public goods. When the local government makes a decision on the amount to be spent on the provision of public goods, it takes into consideration how the villagers will react and assumes that the villagers may take different actions depending on the amount spent. A formal description of the model is presented in Appendix 5A.

Strategies and Payoffs of the Local Government

Previous studies suggest that the government's utility functions might be based on two stylized objectives. One is that governments would seek to maximize their revenue surplus (e.g., Levi 1988; North 1981; Olson 1993). Officials could then use this surplus to pursue whatever aims they had, regardless of whether they were public or private, legal or illegal, or appropriate or inappropriate by some criteria. The second objective is that governments would maximize support from citizens (e.g., Ames 1987; Frieden 1991; Geddes 1994). The argument here is that in order to seek maximum revenue surplus, officials would need to stay in power. Even though it is an authoritarian regime, China's local officials in rural areas would also have an incentive to obtain support from villagers to stay in power. Moreover, because of the authoritarian regime, they would be particularly afraid of the public expression of dissatisfaction visible to higher authorities. Thus, local officials would be afraid of protests because they would be punished for failing to maintain social order. Therefore, they would be more interested in defusing discontent than in maximizing popular support. In other words, they would not be primarily interested in responding to popular discontent but might respond just enough to avoid protests. In sum, to maintain the generality of the model, I assume that local officials would maximize their local government's revenue surplus, would minimize their chance of being punished, or would pursue some combination of the two (e.g., Treisman 1999b).

The model assumes that a local government would maximize the revenue surplus that could be used unproductively and often privately, possibly subject to the constraint that the villagers would not leave the village or protest. At one level, public funds would indeed be used for private purposes – for corruption (Lü 2000a; Wedeman 1997). Taking advantage of being in power, local officials could use the revenue surplus for building a fancy office, purchasing a luxury sedan, or capitalizing their private expenses on the government's account (or stated more simply, eating and drinking on the government's dime). However, at another, deeper level, local officials would seek to maximize the revenue surplus for an institutional reason. As local governments faced aggravated funding shortages, local officials would have a strong incentive to maximize the excess revenue and would use it for filling the fiscal gap between the amount they were supposed to collect and the amount they actually collected. This is because the Budget Law requires that local governments make ends meet every year, and higher-level governments often use the achievement of a balanced budget as one of the most important items in the list of criteria for promotion and bonuses (Edin 2003; Wedeman 2000; Whiting 2004).

If villagers migrate and resist paying levies, local officials would find it more difficult to collect taxes than in the case where villagers stayed in the village and complied with taxation. If villagers choose to protest, a local government would have to compromise with the villagers. If a protest occurred, local officials would be punished through the performance evaluation system of local governments. Superior governments have authority and resources to sanction lower governments by granting rewards such as promotions or inflicting punishments such as dismissal or demotion (Landry 2008, 117).[2] The central government, and hence each superior local government, would take social stability as the most important criterion for promotion and bonuses of lower government officials.[3]

[2] Of course, similar to other political systems in China, the actual operation of the cadre evaluation system might be different from what the formal rules say. However, based on his survey on county officials in Jiangsu Province, Pierre Landry (2008, 150) finds: "Local officials believe that formal rules matter ... [and] the cohesion among respondents speaks to the capacity of the Party to instill and maintain formal norms."

[3] In the actual operation of the regime's cadre management, while the regime is successful in promoting a small set of cadres who perform unusually well, it is less able to demote poorly performing cadres (Landry 2008, chapter 3).

Strategies and Payoffs of the Villagers

The villagers' payoffs would be positively related to their disposable income and negatively related to the cost of migration or protest. The model assumes homogeneous villagers. This assumption implies that payoffs from the possible outcomes of the game would have equal value to all the villagers, and benefits and costs would be distributed evenly. In particular, it implies that the model does not specifically define the cost to solve the collective action problem. Obviously, this is not always the case, and a possible extension of this work would be to explore the implications of heterogeneous villagers.

If the villagers choose not to migrate, they could enjoy the fruits of the provided public goods while paying the entire amount of the tax levied by the local government. Zhao Shukai (2010, 196), one of the leading Chinese researchers on rural governance, identifies the following six items as public goods to be provided in rural areas: security (*zhian*), education (*jiaoyu*), public health (*gonggong weisheng*), infrastructure (*jichu sheshi*), social welfare (*shehui jiuzhu*), and environmental protection (*huanging baohu*). In rural areas, it is local governments (especially township governments) that should provide these public goods, and these local governments have had to finance them by themselves. Thus, if villagers stay in their village to pay the levies imposed by the local government *and* the local government spends to provide the public goods from the levies that it has collected, then villagers will enjoy the benefit of the public goods.

However, there is no guarantee that public goods will be provided even if the villager stays in the village. In Fire Mountain Town, while the town party secretary admitted that the town government did not have the money to provide public goods, a villager complained about the lack of public goods, saying: "There is no water in East Gate Canal, and the government has never fixed the problem" (Interviewee 28). Moreover, spending on the provision of public goods does not always improve the quality of rural governance. For example, Zhao (2010, chapter 6) points out the cases where the national goal did not fit the reality of rural villages and hence township governments were forced to spend money on useless hard infrastructure. A typical case is the construction of school buildings, which then end up with empty classrooms later, as I discussed in the last chapter.

The villagers might benefit from migration because they could have access to a larger income by working in a city and could resist paying agriculture-related levies in their local village. At the same time, migration could be costly, especially because, despite three decades of relaxed regulation, it was still restricted. If the villagers choose to protest, their direct negotiation with local officials could induce a certain compromise from them. At the same time, however, protesting could be costly for the villagers, primarily in terms of punishment. Yongshun Cai finds that among the sixty-six cases of collective action in twenty provinces between 1995 and 2006, collective actions for resisting a local government's policy "often violate the law or government regulations" (Cai 2008, 25). Most noninstitutionalized collective actions, including direct negotiation with the targeted local government, can easily be judged illegal because Article 290 of China's Criminal Law stipulates that the action is considered illegal (i.e., committing a crime) if it "prevents the state agency's operation and causes serious losses" (ibid., 29).

Implications of the Model's Equilibria

This section presents implications of the main equilibrium outcomes of the game-theoretic model. Here I explore the implications of whether exit and/or protest are credible options for the villagers to put pressure on the local government. The formal solution to the model is presented in Appendix 5A.

Equilibrium 1: If protest is not a credible option for the villagers and the exit payoff is *lower* than a certain threshold, then the local government will still provide public goods. At the same time, in the range where the local government provides public goods, the local government will *increase* the provision of public goods as the exit payoff *increases*. Thus, this equilibrium outcome implies that the local government will increase the provision of public goods to keep the taxpayers in the village.

Equilibrium 2: However, once the exit payoff reaches a certain threshold, the local government will switch its strategy to the predatory option of not providing public goods and enduring the villagers' migration. When this threshold is reached depends on the local economic conditions. In the areas where the provision of public goods leads to more effective local development, the threshold will be reached later. In the areas with favorable conditions for development, an increase in the provision of public goods as a result of the increase in the exit payoff is less sharp; however, the local government will be less likely to stop providing public goods even if the exit payoff is very high.

Equilibrium 3: If protest is a credible option and the exit payoff is *lower* than a certain threshold, then the local government will *increase* the provision of public goods as the exit payoff *increases*. However, with the other conditions being equal, the local government will provide *less* public goods funding if the villagers have a credible protest option. Moreover, as the villagers' net gain from rebellion increases, the local government will reduce the provision of public goods. In other words, even if the villagers can gain more by direct negotiation in the protest, the local government will cancel it out by reducing the pre-negotiation provision of public goods.

Equilibrium 4: Furthermore, just as in the case where neither a rebellion nor a petition is a credible option, the local government will stop providing public goods once the exit payoff reaches a certain threshold. However, this threshold is reached earlier in the case where protest is a credible option than in the case where it is not.

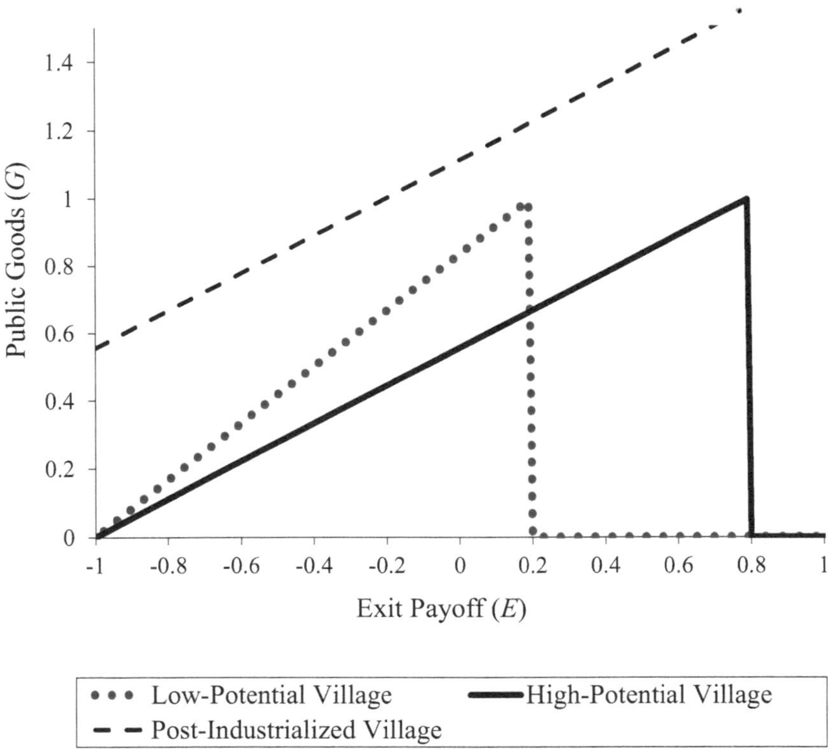

FIGURE 5.1. Effects of Migration on the Provision of Public Goods. *Note*: $T = 1$ and $\delta = 0.2$ for low-potential villages; $T = 1$ and $\delta = 0.8$ for high-potential villages; and $T = 2$ and $\delta = 0.8$ for post-industrialized villages.

MIGRATION AND THE PROVISION OF PUBLIC GOODS

To assess the effect of the relaxation of state migration policies on the provision of public goods and local state-society relations in rural China, one must consider how changes in certain parameters would affect the equilibria. To do this, I assign certain values to the parameters in the game and examine how changes in the values of these parameters would affect the value of the local government's expenditure for public goods at equilibrium.[4]

The relaxation of migration policies could be modeled as an increase in the value of the exit payoff. I examine how the effects of an increase in the exit payoff on the local government's provision of public goods might vary depending on the economic conditions of the locality. Figure 5.1 illustrates the effects, offering a numerical example. In this comparative statics analysis, in order to determine the effects of an increase in the exit payoff I examine

[4] Although altering parameter values changes the numerical results, it does not change the substantive results.

the case where protest is not a credible choice for the villagers to pressure the local government.[5] Before the post-Mao reform started in the early 1980s, rural-to-urban migration had been practically prohibited. Moreover, few villages – if any at all – were industrialized at the beginning of the post-Mao reform.[6]

Figure 5.1 illustrates that an increase in the villagers' exit payoff would increase the local government's expenditure for public goods, suggesting that the local government would be more inclined to assuage the villagers once the *potential* for their ability for migration had increased their leverage vis-à-vis the local government. At this equilibrium, the villagers would comply, satisfied with the local government's provision of public goods. However, as an increase in the expenditure for public goods reaches an undesirable threshold, the local government will stop this spending. Once the local government has stopped providing public goods, the villagers would start migrating. Figure 5.1 also suggests that rural industrialization would have complicated any heterogeneous effects on the local government's provision of public goods. The local government would increase the provision of public goods *more rapidly* in the villages with *lower* potential for industrialization than in the villages with higher potential. However, it would reach the undesirable threshold to stop providing public goods *sooner* in the villages with lower potential than in the villages with higher potential.

Not so coincidentally, this predicted series of events corresponds with what happened in rural China in the 1980s and 1990s. When villagers gained the ability to migrate from villages in the 1980s, they actually *stayed* in the village and worked in local rural factories. In the meantime, local officials started to provide public goods and increased local government entrepreneurship, leading to a rapid upsurge of rural industrialization in the 1980s. Local governments had clear financial incentives and strong interests in the development of rural industry (Montinola, Qian, and Weingast 1995; Oi 1992, 1995; Walder 1995). However, as expenditures for providing public goods to develop the local economy increased, local officials in less developed areas found it difficult to keep their rural industry competitive. As a result of surging competition among rural industrial firms in the 1990s, many local governments in less developed areas were no longer able to expect profit from rural industry and therefore

5 I first assign $T = 1$ to the local government's tax revenue for agricultural villages. I assign $\delta = 0.2$ for the villages with low potential for development and $\delta = 0.8$ for those with high potential for development. Then, to examine the effects of an increase in tax revenue on developed areas, I assign $T = 2$ for the villages that have already been industrialized. I assign $\delta = 0.8$ for the post-industrialized villages.

6 For example, in Water Dragon Village in Guangdong Province, which started industrialization very early compared with other regions, there had been no factories, and fiscal revenue had relied completely on the agricultural levies in the late 1970s. However, in 2004 when I visited Water Dragon Village, the village had forty factories and fiscal revenue relied mostly on the corporate taxes.

had to depend primarily on exactions from villagers for financing their budgets. Then local officials decided not to play entrepreneurial or developmental roles but predatory ones, faced large-scale outbound migration by villagers, struggled to collect taxes and fees from increasingly mobile villagers, and imposed heavier financial burdens on those who remained behind.

Qipan Township in the late 1990s, where Li Changping served as the party secretary, was a typical example of a hinterland agricultural area with a heavy financial burden and no public goods. In Qipan, an average villager had an annual agricultural income of 360 yuan per mu, farming costs of 170 yuan per mu, and a financial burden of 230 yuan per mu (Li C. 2002, 34). Therefore, villagers needed an additional 40 yuan per mu, which they earned by working in a city. In 1999, the township government had debt of 26 million yuan, and it had to pay 4.7 million yuan for debt service with an average annual interest rate of 18 percent. After paying this debt service, the township government had only 3.5 million yuan remaining, from which it spent 3 million yuan for officials' salaries (ibid., 35–36). Needless to say, there was no way for the township government to provide public goods. Li argues that although one of the reasons the township government ended up with such huge debt was because of natural disasters (especially the costs of the Yangtze River flood in 1996 and construction projects against floods in 1998 and 1999), another reason for the debt was that villagers had not paid taxes and fees (ibid., 36). In the 1990s, when an increasing number of villagers left the village to work in cities, local officials in Qipan tried to encourage remaining villagers to farm – so that they could earn sufficient agricultural revenue to pay the levies – by reducing these taxes and fees. However, because the remittance to higher authorities did not change, the local government had to cover the gap between the collected levies and the assigned remittance by imposing capitation levies on the remaining villagers (ibid., 65).

In contrast, tax revenue would increase in relation to rural industrialization because rural industrial enterprises pay corporate taxes. In Figure 5.1, this is represented as the shift from the high-potential village to the post-industrialized village. Once tax revenue has reached a certain level, the local government will never attain the undesirable threshold but will keep increasing the expenditure for public goods as the exit payoff increases. One can interpret the shift to a steady increase in public goods provision, which is what Jean Oi (1999) terms the "takeoff" of rural China. In many villages of the coastal provinces, the local government's initial provision of public goods in the 1980s effectively led to rural industrialization, which provided the local government with sufficient revenue sources to keep increasing public goods and also brought further industrialization and prosperity to the villages. In contrast, the equilibrium at which the local government would stop providing public goods once it has reached the undesirable threshold corresponds with the argument that "only a subset of all townships and villages in rural China were able to 'take off'" (Bernstein and Lü 2003, 70). In the hinterlands of the inland provinces, the initial provision of public goods led to rural industrialization very slowly, if at all. Local officials then lacked financial revenue to increase the pace of modernization and had to squeeze the nonmigrant villagers for financial resources to meet the development program target imposed by higher authorities.

Note that in Figure 5.1, I assume that protest is not a credible option for the villagers to pressure their local government with their demands. Thus, the increase in the provision of public goods by the local government shown in the figure is based solely on the effect of an increase in the exit payoff. In other words, the model's equilibrium outcome suggests that the heterogeneous pattern of local government's behavior observed in rural China in the 1980s and the 1990s can be explained by the ease of outbound migration and varying local economic conditions.

The contrast between migrant-sending hinterland villages with no public goods and migrant-receiving advanced industrialized villages with public goods suggests that a vicious circle emerged in the former case while a virtuous circle emerged in the latter case. Li Changping (2002, 28) summarizes the vicious circle as

> heavy financial burdens on villagers (*nongmin fudan guozhong*) → absence of farmers (*tian wu ren zhong*) → a decrease in actually collected levies (*tian mu fudan jianshao*) → an increase in capitation levies (*rentou fudan zengjia*) → leaving the village while abandoning farmland (*qitian waichu changqi bu guijia*) → difficulty in collecting levies (*fudan shou bu qi lai*) → [local governments] borrowing money with high interest rates, hiring gangsters to collect levies, and paying fees to the gangsters (*kao gaolidai bao yunzhuan, pinqing shehui liumang shoukuan, shoukuan gei huikou*) → increasing levies on villagers (*jiazhong qunzhong fudan*).

Li (2002, 6–8, 28) argues that the solution to this vicious circle should be encouraging villagers to leave the village and then asking them to pay from the money they earn from working in cities, rather than discouraging them from leaving villages and then forcing them to pay from their agricultural incomes. It is interesting that local governments in the agricultural villages that sent migrant workers failed to collect taxes from those migrant villagers.

CONCLUSION

The game-theoretic model suggests that rural-to-urban migration might strengthen the power of villagers vis-à-vis that of local governments by giving local officials an incentive to provide public goods under certain conditions. However, this incentive would be sustained in the long run only in the villages that had high potential for development. Allowing outbound migration would initially give local officials everywhere an incentive to increase the provision of public goods to prevent the villagers from migrating. However, local officials in the villages where public investment did not effectively lead to development would soon be unable to keep up the pace by increasing the provision of public goods. In the villages that did not have high potential for development, outbound migration would decrease the local government's provision of public goods. In sum, the relaxation of migration policies would increase the provision of public goods in the villages with high potential for development while it would decrease the provision of public goods in the villages with low potential.

Political economists have argued that relying on repressive means to collect taxes is an inefficient means of collecting taxes. Instead Margaret Levi (1988) argues that in order to establish efficient taxation with what she conceptualizes as taxpayers' "quasi-voluntary compliance," tax collectors will have to give taxpayers "reassurance" that they will use the collected taxes to provide promised goods and services. In industrialized villages in China, tax collectors (local officials) and taxpayers (villagers) shared common interests in local development, hence taxpayers could be reassured that the levies would be used for the public goods and services that would promote industrialization. In agricultural villages, however, tax collectors found it difficult to give taxpayers reassurance that the levies would be used for public goods and services. Thus, local officials in agricultural areas found it difficult to collect levies from migrant villagers and therefore had to rely on imposing more levies on nonmigrant villagers.

A vicious circle of rural taxation emerged in agricultural villages in the 1990s when migration from rural to urban areas became increasingly less costly. When taxation became unbearable, people migrated out, which made it more difficult for local officials to collect levies and gave officials an incentive to impose capitation levies on remaining villagers. Under the authoritarian regime where the superior government had authority to monitor lower-level governments through the personnel system called the cadre responsibility system (CRS), this occurred because local officials had to send the same remittance even if the amount of levies that they were able to collect from villagers decreased. The redistributive system of fiscal transfers from the central government to local governments did not function to solve this problem, because the central government and each level of local government used fiscal transfers as a reward for local economic development, and hence richer local governments received more fiscal transfers in the 1990s. As a result, the CCP had a greater stake in providing public goods to industrialized areas than agricultural areas, and greater predatory state tendencies occurred in the hinterland regions in the 1990s. In short, the CRS constrained available alternatives for the central government's strategy of rural development, and the relaxation of migration restrictions – the policy needed for national economic development under the market system – ended up fostering fiscal crises in agricultural areas.

APPENDIX 5A: FORMAL DESCRIPTION AND SOLUTION TO THE GAME OF MIGRATION AND TAXATION

Figure A5.1 shows the sequential, noncooperative game of migration and taxation in extensive form. Assume that all information about the payoffs and structure of the game are common knowledge.

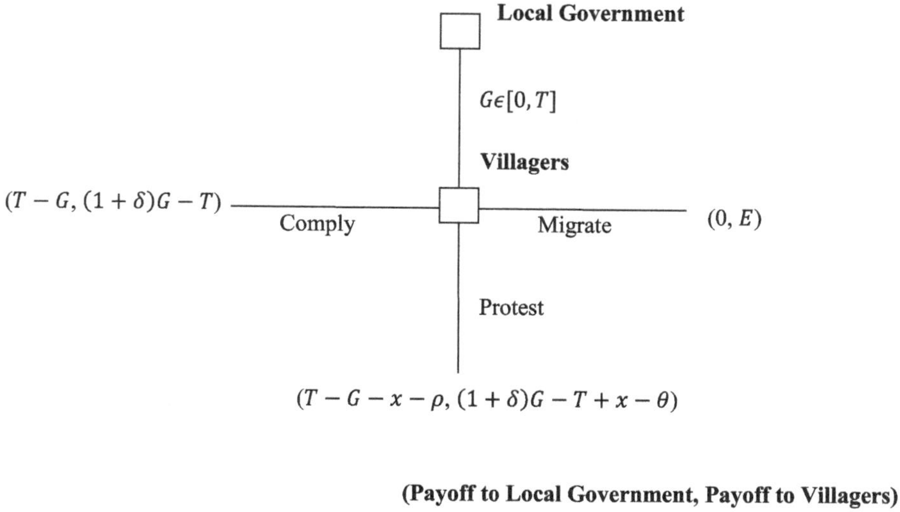

FIGURE A5.1. Extensive Form of the Game of Migration and Taxation.

Sequence of Moves

The game begins with the local government's decision to set a fixed amount to be spent on providing public goods, G. The model assumes that the amount to be spent cannot exceed the tax revenue, T (i.e., $0 \leq G \leq T$). Following the local government's move, the villagers choose a response. They select to stay in the village to pay taxes (Comply), leave the village (Migrate), or directly rebel against the local government to resist paying taxes (Protest). Notice that the local government cannot decide the amount of T because the superior government sets it. This assumption implies that the local government chooses the amount for public goods expenditure within the budget constraint given by its superior government. Whereas the tax revenue to be collected is exogenously determined by higher authorities, the amount to be directed to public goods and the amount to be skimmed as rents are subject to local government control.

Strategies and Payoffs of the Local Government

The model normalizes the local government's payoff from the villagers' migration as zero. This normalization does not mean that the local government will completely lose their revenue source, but implies that it will not have sufficient revenue to generate the surplus that can be used for officials' private purposes. I assume that the direct negotiation between local officials and villagers when villagers choose to protest should be a zero-sum game. Thus, the model assumes that if villagers protest, the local government will lose x while the villagers will gain x (i.e., $x > 0$). The "pain" that local officials feel from being punished by the superior government for social instability when protest has occurred is measured as ρ (i.e., $\rho > 0$). Note that ρ does not include the financial loss the local officials may suffer – by losing excessive levies that they have kept for private purposes – but only captures the local officials' loss from punishment through the personnel management system.

Strategies and Payoffs of the Villagers

The model defines the benefit of staying in the local village as $(1 + \delta)G$. The value of δ depends on the efficiency of public investment in the village. Thus, a larger value of δ indicates that the village has greater potential for development. Because villagers can enjoy the benefits of public goods while paying the entire amount of the tax if they stay in the village, their utility from staying in the village is $(1 + \delta)G - T$. If villagers choose to migrate, they will receive the exit payoff, E. The model assumes that the exit payoff can be either positive or negative (i.e., $-\infty < E < \infty$). As a result of the zero-sum negotiation with the local government when they protest, they will gain x while the local government will lose x. At the same time, protesting is costly for the villagers. The cost of a rebellion is measured as θ (i.e., $\theta > 0$).

Solution to the Model

This part presents the solution and main results of the model. Solving by backward induction, I first consider the villagers' subgame. There are three strategies available for the villagers. The strategies that can be sustained as equilibrium are different depending on specific conditions. Here I explore the implications of the equilibrium outcomes depending on whether exit and/or protest are credible options for the villagers to pressure the local government.

The Villagers' Node

The villagers will comply if $(1 + \delta)G - T \geq E$ and $(1 + \delta)G - T \geq (1 + \delta)G - T + x - \theta$. Thus, the villagers will comply if $G \geq \frac{E+T}{1+\delta}$ and $\theta \geq x$.

The villagers will migrate if $E \geq (1 + \delta)G - T$ and $E \geq (1 + \delta)G - T + x - \theta$. Thus, the villagers will migrate if $G \leq \frac{E+T}{1+\delta}$ and $G \leq \frac{E+T-x+\theta}{1+\delta}$. Therefore, the villagers will migrate if $G \leq \frac{E+T}{1+\delta}$ and $\theta \geq x$, or if $G \leq \frac{E+T-x+\theta}{1+\delta}$ and $\theta \leq x$.

The villagers will protest if $(1 + \delta)G - T + x - \theta \geq (1 + \delta)G - T$ and $(1 + \delta)G - T + x - \theta \geq E$. Thus, the villagers will protest if $\theta \leq x$ and $G \geq \frac{E+T-x+\theta}{1+\delta}$.

The Local Government's Node

First, if $\theta \geq x$, then the following two strategies will be sustained as equilibrium:

(1) The villagers will comply if $G \geq \frac{E+T}{1+\delta}$.
(2) The villagers will migrate if $G \leq \frac{E+T}{1+\delta}$.

The local government might choose: (1) $G = \frac{E+T}{1+\delta}$ to induce the villagers' compliance; or (2) $G = 0$ enduring the villagers' migration. Substituting the value of G into the utility functions of the local government's payoffs (U_L), we get:

maximum U_L for (1) $= \frac{\delta T - E}{1+\delta}$
maximum U_L for (2) $= 0$

Of these two utility functions: $G = \frac{E+T}{1+\delta}$ if $E \leq \delta T$; and $G = 0$ if $E \geq \delta T$.

Second, if $\theta \leq x$, then the following strategies will be sustained as equilibrium:

(1) The villagers will protest if $G \geq \frac{E+T-x+\theta}{1+\delta}$.
(2) The villagers will migrate if $G \leq \frac{E+T-x+\theta}{1+\delta}$.

The local government might choose: (1) $G = \frac{E+T-x+\theta}{1+\delta}$ enduring the villagers' protest; or (2) $G = 0$ enduring the villagers' migration. Substituting the value of G into the utility functions of the local government's payoffs (U_L), we get:

maximum U_L for (1) $= \frac{\delta(T-x)-E-\theta}{1+\delta} - \rho$
maximum U_L for (2) $= 0$

Of these two utility functions, $G = \frac{E+T-x+\theta}{1+\delta}$ if $E \leq \delta(T - x) - (1 + \delta)\rho - \theta$; and $G = 0$ if $E \geq \delta(T - x) - (1 + \delta)\rho - \theta$.

Summary

Equilibrium 1: $G = \frac{E+T}{1+\delta}$ and the villagers will comply, if $\theta \geq x$ and $E \leq \delta T$.
Equilibrium 2: $G = 0$ and the villagers will migrate, if $\theta \geq x$ and $E \geq \delta T$.
Equilibrium 3: $G = \frac{E+T-x+\theta}{1+\delta}$ and the villagers will protest, if $\theta \leq x$ and $E \leq \delta(T - x) - (1 + \delta)\rho - \theta$.
Equilibrium 4: $G = 0$ and the villagers will migrate, if $\theta \leq x$ and $E \geq \delta(T - x) - (1 + \delta)\rho - \theta$.

6

Voice Strategies of Villagers

Petitions and Taxation in Rural China

In this chapter, I explore how the institutionalization of remonstrative political participation affected relations between villagers and local governments in rural China. The explanation in this chapter builds on the assumption that even authoritarian regimes are concerned with popular support to remain in power. As a result, almost all authoritarian regimes actually have some forms of democratic institutions. Studies focusing on these elements of authoritarian regimes have argued that democratic institutions such as parties and elections are a central part of the regime's survival strategy (e.g., Blaydes 2010; Brownlee 2007; Gandhi 2008; Geddes 2006; Lust-Okar 2005; Magaloni 2006).

Of course, the institutions are only seemingly democratic, semi-democratic, or pseudo-democratic under such regimes. Moreover, previous studies on democratic institutions in authoritarian regimes have agreed that the main function of these institutions is to strengthen authoritarian rule; as Barbara Geddes (2006) notes, democratic institutions help the regime conduct well-institutionalized authoritarian rule. Moreover, Jason Brownlee argues that democratic institutions, especially one-party ruling political parties, "have been the root cause of regime persistence in much of Africa, the Middle East, and Asia" (Brownlee 2007, 3). Jennifer Gandhi also contends that nominally democratic institutions are "a way in which opposition demands can be contained and answered without appearing weak," and hence they are "instruments of co-optation" (Gandhi 2008, xviii).

In this chapter, in order to explore the roles of democratic institutions in the context of authoritarian politics, I focus on one of the important channels for political participation in rural China: petitions.[1] Instead of elections, I

[1] Strictly speaking, petitioning is different from what Albert Hirschman (1970) defines as "voice." Hirschman looks at voice as the action of constituents or customers communicating with the principal or the firm. In petitioning, participants lodge their complaints about a local government

select the petition system for emphasis for the following reasons: (1) petitions have been widely used in rural China to express popular grievances against various levels of local governments while elections have been limited to the village level; (2) ordinary villagers have often found that elections have not solved their grievances but in fact generated them; and (3) instead of seeking solutions by electing representatives, people apparently have preferred solving their specific grievances directly. In short, Chinese villagers arguably have found the petition system a more effective means than elections to make their demands known.

This chapter introduces a game-theoretic model, building on the model discussed in the previous chapter. I explore the impact of the availability of institutionalized channels for protest by adding petitioning to the available alternatives from which villagers may choose when they are not satisfied with their local government's behavior. Based on plausible assumptions in the context of politics in rural China, the model in this chapter derives the following implications:

1. The institutionalization of the petition system has different consequences for the local government's responsiveness to popular preferences, depending on the local economic conditions and the effectiveness of the exit option.
   (a) When local conditions are favorable for development, both the exit option (potential migration) and the voice option (potential petitions) may work to pressure officials to respond to popular preferences under certain conditions.
   (b) When local conditions are not favorable for development, neither the exit option nor the voice option works to prevent officials from predatory behavior, for they would have neither an incentive nor the capacity to respond to popular demands.
2. Regardless of economic conditions, as long as local cadres perceive petitions and riots (noninstitutionalized protests) equally as indictments of social instability, villagers will choose to negotiate directly with the targeted local government even when they have petitioned. If local cadres perceive that a rebellion is problematic but a petition is not, the local government will provide more public goods and the villagers will comply even when they have petitioned. In short, the real institutionalization of the petition system will give substantive legitimacy to petitions, which in turn will bring social stability and good governance to rural China.

In the first section of this chapter, I introduce the petition system as a semi-institutionalized channel for political participation, which I take as a basic

to its superior government. The logic of petitioning here captures that element of Hirschman's theory regarding the upward communication of information about customer satisfaction and the organization's problems.

assumption of the game-theoretic model. The second section discusses the model and the logic that the model's equilibrium implies. In the third section, I discuss the model's implications for the institutionalization of the petition system. As in the previous chapter, I specify theoretical arguments with a simple game-theoretic model and establish plausibility with cases and events discussed in earlier research.

THE PETITION SYSTEM IS SEMI-INSTITUTIONALIZED

The key assumption of the game-theoretic model in this chapter is that the petition system is semi-institutionalized – neither fully institutionalized nor noninstitutionalized. The petition system is institutionalized in the sense that it makes protesters "work within constraints built into existing channels and . . . refrain from direct action" (X. Chen 2008, 56). Once a petition is submitted and reviewed, higher authorities send a delegation to investigate the locality where the petition originated. Then, if higher authorities conclude that the levies were too high, the local government's revenue was spent inappropriately, and/or the local governments committed some other misconduct, they punish the local officials and perhaps demote them.

At the same time, the petition system is not fully institutionalized. First, petitioning has not been differentiated from noninstitutionalized protests such as riots in the perception of local cadres. When villagers submit a petition, formal rules state that local officials should be punished for the accusers' claim only when it is judged that they have committed an inappropriate act such as corruption. In reality, however, most of the local cadres I interviewed believed that petitions were just as serious an indictment on their performance as public demonstrations (Interviewees 4, 14–15, 17–19, 22–23, 27, 30, 50, 52–54, 65–66, 78–82, 87, 100–101, 103). The central government placed a premium on social stability; signs of instability were treated as just cause for punishment in the cadre responsibility system (CRS) (Edin 2003; Whiting 2004; Zhan 2006).

Second, although petitioning is legal, targeted local officials might retaliate against petitioners in illegal ways.[2] Thus, this semi-institutionalized characteristic of the petition system imposes additional costs on petitioners. Petitions are not anonymous and local officials have been known to exact retribution on informants. For example, a group of petitioners from Anhui Province went to Beijing to bring their complaints about taxation to the central government, but when they returned home local officials beat them (Chen and Wu 2004,

[2] The most extreme way of retaliating against petitioners is sending them to "black jails," where they might face rapes and other abuses, according to the report of Human Rights Watch released in November 2009 (Human Rights Watch 2009). In December 2009, the central government acknowledged that there were at least seventy-three black jails in Beijing alone. For one of the few media reports on the black jails issue, see a report in the *Los Angeles Times* on January 11, 2010 (Glionna 2010).

chapter 4).[3] Indeed, Lianjiang Li's (2008, 216) survey research on 1,314 petitioners finds that more than 60 percent of petitioners suffered from some kind of local repression.

Third, as a result of the semi-institutionalized characteristic of the petition system, villagers often combine petitioning with noninstitutionalized methods of protest to pursue their goals. Xi Chen (2009), based on his research on the official petition records in Y Prefecture of Hunan Province, finds that petitioners used petitioning as part of their protest tactics to compel the government's response. His statistical analysis of 644 petition cases suggests that a petition would be more likely to receive a substantive government response if the petition was combined with tactics disrupting social order or government operation. In Y Prefecture, petitioners physically assaulted government officials or blocked traffic to make their voice be heard. When petitioners did not receive a satisfactory response from local government officials, they might refuse to leave the government office (creating a disturbance) and/or block the gate of the governmental buildings or the parking lot. Kevin O'Brien and Lianjiang Li (2006, chapter 4) also show that disgruntled villagers started negotiating directly with their targeted local officials once they found that their petitioning had not solved their problem, a strategy they conceptualize as "tactical escalation." Why petitioners did not follow the petition rules but engaged in disruptive tactics or direct negotiation with the targeted local government is not puzzling. Given the lack of mechanisms that held officials accountable to ordinary people, the strategy to simply follow the petition rules might be quite costly – including not only the direct costs incurred from petitioning but also opportunity costs. However, the fact that people used the petition system before engaging in other less institutionalized methods is puzzling.

In this chapter, I examine how these semi-institutionalized characteristics of the petition system affected villagers' strategies, local officials' behaviors, and overall local state-society relations. Did the petition system make local governments more responsive to popular preferences? Did this remonstrative institution help bring social stability to the Chinese countryside? Using a formal model, I answer these questions.

MIGRATION, PARTICIPATION, AND TAXATION AS A GAME

The game-theoretic model discussed in this chapter uses the same setup as the model discussed in the previous chapter. Most importantly, the central government is an actor in the position of setting the rules of the game. Thus, the model assumes that only the central government can decide the extent to which the petition system is institutionalized (or semi-institutionalized).

[3] More examples are reported on the Internet. One of the cases is a petitioner from Sichuan Province who was beaten by local officials after he returned from petitioning in Beijing. See http://www2.chinesenewsnet.com, accessed November 21, 2004.

Moreover, villagers are taken as a unitary actor, and they take actions after the local government has decided how much to spend on public goods. The local government takes into consideration what modes are available for villagers to respond to the local government's policy and to what extent the petition system is institutionalized as such a mode of expressing their grievances to the local government. A formal description of the model is presented in Appendix 6A.

Under China's authoritarian regime where higher authorities monitor local officials through the CRS, local officials might be afraid of petitions if petitions are considered a sign of social instability. The following scenario is what a formal institution (i.e., relevant law) says. Of course, it would be utopian if formal institutions were implemented as they literally say, especially in an authoritarian regime. Later in this chapter, after setting up the game following formal institutions, I will establish the logic that may account for why actors do not follow what formal rules dictate in everyday politics in rural China.

According to the formal institution of the petition system, once a petition is reviewed, higher authorities send a delegation to investigate the locality where the petition originated. Then, if higher authorities conclude that levies were too high and/or the local government's revenue was spent inappropriately, they do two things. First, they punish the local officials through the CRS. Second, higher authorities order the local government to return the excess amount to the villagers. Thus, if the petition is reviewed, the local government loses the amount of the revenue not spent on public goods and suffers from the pain of punishment by higher authorities, which is a negative payoff. When the villagers write a petition, formal rules state that local officials should be punished for the accuser's claim only when it is determined that the officials have been engaged in an inappropriate act such as corruption. In reality, however, local cadres believe that petitions are just as serious an indictment on their performance as riots.

Similar to noninstitutionalized means of protest, petitioning is also costly for the villagers. One of the primary costs associated with petitioning is the possibility that a local government would retaliate. Although petitioning is a more institutionalized means of protest, its semi-institutionalized characteristics put petitioners in a weak legal position. Petitioning with more than five participants would be illegal under the current law (Cai 2008, 29). This restriction on the number of participants joining a petition poses a dilemma for protesters. On the one hand, a larger number of participants would be more likely to induce substantial responses from the local government (Chen 2009). On the other hand, a petition with more than five participants would be ruled illegal. Moreover, as I discussed, local cadres often perceived petitioning as the same indictment of social instability as rioting. In fact, local cadres have an even stronger incentive to suppress petitioning than rioting because they are concerned more with protesters approaching higher authorities than protesters rioting in the village

(Cai 2008, 36). If the petition were to be reviewed, higher authorities would rule that the local government should return to the villagers the excess amount of tax revenue that was not spent on providing public goods. If the petition were to be ignored, the villagers would have the option of complying, migrating, or rioting.

Implications of the Model's Equilibria

In this part, I explore the implications of the main equilibrium outcomes of the game-theoretic model depending on whether exiting, rioting, and/or petitioning are credible options for the villagers to pressure the local government. In the following nine equilibrium outcomes, the first four equilibria have the same outcome as the four equilibria in the previous chapter, as they are the equilibria under the conditions where petitioning is not a credible option. In the next section, when assessing the effect of the institutionalization of the petition system on the provision of public goods and local state-society relations in rural China, I compare the first four equilibria and the latter five equilibria. The formal solution to the model is presented in Appendix 6A.

Equilibrium 1: If riot and petition are both so costly that neither is a credible option for the villagers, and the exit payoff is *lower* than a certain threshold, then the local government will still provide public goods. As in Equilibrium 1 in the previous chapter, in the range where the local government provides public goods, the local government will *increase* the provision of public goods as the exit payoff *increases*, and hence this equilibrium outcome implies that the local government will increase the provision of public goods to keep taxpayers in the village.

Equilibrium 2: If neither riot nor petition is a credible option, and the exit payoff is *higher* than a certain threshold, then the local government will stop providing public goods. As in Equilibrium 2 in the previous chapter, when this threshold is reached will depend on the local economic conditions. The threshold will be higher (thus reached later) in well-endowed areas while lower (thus reached earlier) in poorly endowed areas.

Equilibrium 3: Just as the case where neither rebellion nor petition is a credible option, if riot is a credible option but petition is not, and the exit payoff is *lower* than a certain threshold, then the local government will *increase* the provision of public goods as the exit payoff *increases*. As in Equilibrium 3 in the previous chapter, the local government will provide *less* public goods funding if the villagers have a credible riot option, and as the villagers' net gain from rioting increases, the local government will cancel it by reducing the pre-negotiation provision of public goods.

Equilibrium 4: If riot is a credible option but petition is not, and the exit payoff is *higher* than a certain threshold, then the local government will stop providing public goods – just as in the case where neither a riot nor a petition is a credible option. As in Equilibrium 4 in the previous chapter, this threshold will be reached earlier in the case where riot is a credible option than in the case where it is not.

Equilibrium 5: If riot is not a credible option but petition is, and the exit payoff is *lower* than a certain threshold, then the local government will provide public goods, but the villagers will petition at their first node and then comply at their second node.

Equilibrium 6: Meanwhile, if riot is not a credible option but petition is, and the exit payoff is *higher* than a certain threshold, then the local government will provide public goods, and the villagers will comply at their first node, responding to the provision of public goods.

Equilibrium 7: If riot and petition are both credible options, and the exit payoff is *lower* than a certain threshold, then the local government will *increase* the provision of public goods as the exit payoff *increases* and as the villagers' net gain from riot *decreases*. In this situation, the local government will provide the same amount of public goods as the case where riot is a credible option but petition is not (i.e., Equilibrium 3).

Equilibrium 8: When the cost the local officials will pay from the punishment for social instability is *lower* than a certain threshold, if riot and petition are both credible options, and the exit payoff is *higher* than the threshold, then the local government will *increase* the provision of public goods as the villagers' net gain from riot *decreases* and as the cost of petitioning *decreases*.

Equilibrium 9: When the cost from the punishment for social instability is *higher* than a certain threshold, if riot and petition are both credible options, and the exit payoff is *higher* than the threshold, then the local government will stop providing public goods – unlike the case where the cost from the punishment for social instability is lower than the threshold. Moreover, the threshold regarding the exit payoff will be reached earlier in the case where riot and petition are both credible options than in the case where only riot is a credible option. In short, making petition a credible option will *decrease* the provision of public goods if riot is also a credible option, as long as the cost from the punishment for social instability is high.

PETITIONING AND THE PROVISION OF PUBLIC GOODS

In this section, I assess the effect of the institutionalization of the petition system on the provision of public goods and local state-society relations in rural China. Similar to the analysis in the previous chapter, I assign certain values to the parameters in the model and examine how changes in the values of the parameters would affect the value of the local government's expenditure for public goods at equilibrium.

The petition system was in a state of flux at the outset of the post-Mao reform in 1978. As a result of instability and social chaos, the organizations supporting the petition system did not function properly during the Cultural

Revolution. Formal complaint bureaus and specialized offices were later rebuilt and reconstituted in each local government (Luehrmann 2003). Although petitioning is a relatively institutionalized means of collective action, it is at best semi-institutionalized. Although petitioning is a legal means of protest, local officials perceive petitions as at least equally problematic signs of social instability as riots and as the same indictment against them as noninstitutionalized means of protest.

Here I examine the influence of this semi-institutionalized characteristic of the petition system on the local government's responsiveness to popular preferences. The institutionalization of the petition system could be modeled as a reduction in the value of the villagers' cost of petitioning.[4] Here I first analyze the case where riot is a credible option for the villagers to pressure the local government. Then I analyze the case where riot is not a credible option. In this way, I examine how the availability of a noninstitutionalized means of protest would affect the effectiveness of a relatively institutionalized means of protest. Figure 6.1 illustrates how the effect a decrease in the villagers' cost of petitioning on the local government's provision of public goods might vary depending on economic conditions and the ease of outbound migration, offering a numerical example.[5]

Figure 6.1 shows that a decrease in the cost of petitioning might increase the local government's expenditure for providing public goods under certain conditions. The local government in a rich village *without* a credible exit option would increase expenditure for providing public goods as the villagers' cost of petitioning decreases. Overall, the local government in a rich village with a credible exit option would provide more public goods than that in a rich village without a credible exit option, but its provision of public goods would be mostly not responsive to the decrease in the villagers' cost of petitioning. However, in a rich village with a credible exit option, the local government would decide to stop providing public goods if the cost of petitioning is lower than a certain threshold. Meanwhile, in a rich village without a credible exit option, the local government will not stop providing public goods even if the cost of petitioning is lower than that threshold. In sum, a decrease in the villagers' cost of petitioning and the availability of a credible exit option would

[4] Alternatively, one can assume that the probability that higher authorities review a petition should increase with institutionalization of the petition system. Formally, this could be modeled as an increase in the value of q. However, this assumption is less plausible than the interpretation here that the cost that villagers have to pay when they petition would drop with institutionalization of the petition system. It is not plausible to assume that higher authorities could control the number of petitions; hence q might drop even when higher authorities increased the *number* of petitions to be reviewed, because they might face a flood of petitions.

[5] I assign $T = 1$ and $\delta = 0.2$ for poor villages, and $T = 2$ and $\delta = 0.8$ for rich villages. Moreover, to distinguish whether villagers have a credible exit option to pressure the local government, I assign $E = 0.5$ for the villages with a credible exit option and $E = -0.5$ for the villages without it. For other parameters, I assign $x = 0.3$, $\rho = 0.3$, $\theta = 0.1$, and $q = 0.5$.

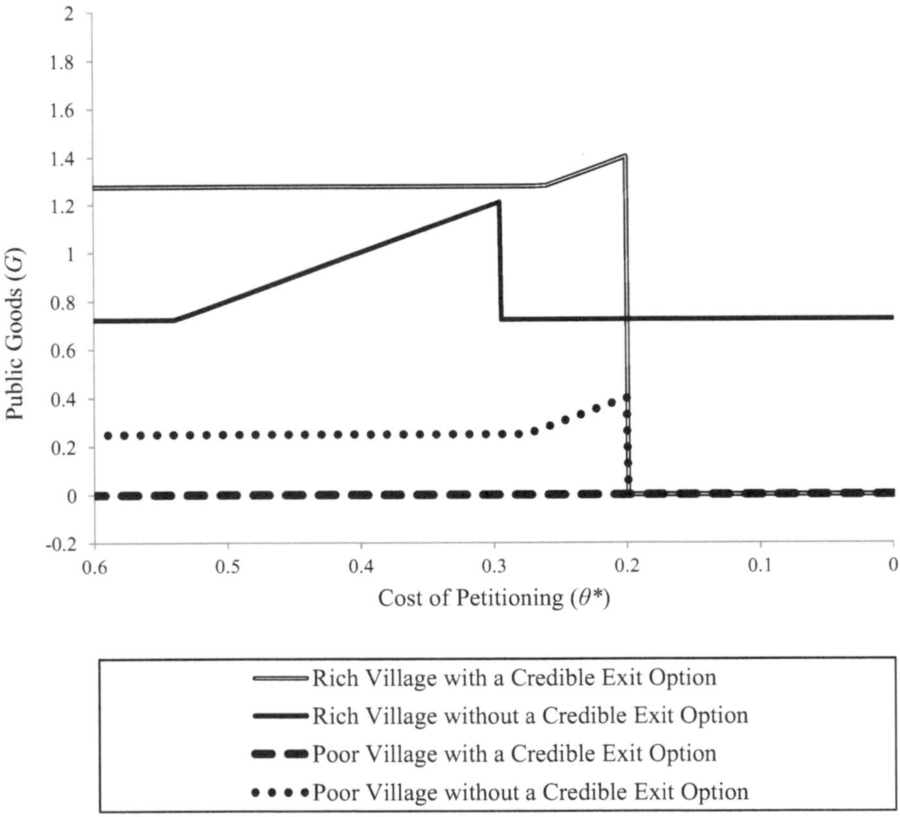

FIGURE 6.1. Effects of Petitions on the Provision of Public Goods (If Riot Is a Credible Option). *Note:* $T = 2$ and $\delta = 0.8$ for rich villages; and $T = 1$ and $\delta = 0.2$ for poor villages. $E = 0.5$ for villages with a credible exit option; and $E = -0.5$ for villages without a credible exit option. $x = 0.3$, $\rho = 0.3$, $\theta = 0.1$, and $q = 0.5$ for all villages.

have a positive impact on the local government's provision of public goods in rich villages. In other words, if riot is a credible option, the institutionalization of the petition system and the relaxation of the migration regulation would give local officials in rich villages an incentive to provide public goods.

In poor villages, not surprisingly, the local government would provide less in public goods funding, if any, than in rich villages, because the local government's available tax revenue is lower. Moreover, unlike in rich villages, a decrease in the cost of petitioning would not increase the provision of public goods in poor villages. Interestingly, in poor villages the local government will spend more on providing public goods in the case where villagers do *not* have a credible exit option than in the case where they do. The local government would provide a small amount of public goods in a poor village without a credible exit option, while it would not provide public goods at all in a poor village with a credible exit option. Where the villagers do not have a credible exit option, the amount of public goods needed to keep the villagers in the village would be smaller and within the ability of the local government to finance these public goods, even with a smaller amount of available tax revenue. Thus, the local government would spend at least some portion of its available tax revenue on public goods, so that it could keep taxpayers in the locality. As a response to the provision of public goods, the villagers would stay in the village. Under the condition that riot is a credible option to pressure the local government, the villagers would riot if the cost of petitioning is higher than a certain threshold, while they would petition and subsequently start direct negotiation with the targeted local government if the cost of petitioning is lower than a certain threshold.[6]

Both the local government's behavior in providing public goods and the villagers' reactions at equilibrium are interesting. Not surprisingly, the villagers would stay in the village if the local government provides public goods, whereas they would migrate otherwise. When staying in the village, as long as riot is a credible option, they would choose to negotiate directly with the targeted local government. Interestingly, they would not choose to petition when the local government increases the provision of public goods as the petitioning cost decreases. In the only case where the villagers would petition – in a rich village without a credible exit option – they would petition because the cost of petitioning is low and the exit payoff is low; however, the low cost of petitioning would result in a *drop* in the provision of public goods. In this case, the villagers would negotiate directly with the local government after they found that their petitioning did not solve their problem, the situation Kevin O'Brien and Lianjiang Li (2006, chapter 4) conceptualize as tactical escalation.

In sum, did the petition system make local governments more responsive to popular preference? Did this remonstrative institution help bring social stability to the Chinese countryside? The model's equilibrium outcomes imply that *potential* petitions might give local officials an incentive to *increase* the provision of public goods under certain conditions while *actual* petitions would result in a decrease in the provision of public goods. In a rich village without a credible exit option, the institutionalization of the petition system would increase the provision of public goods in the way that potential petitions give local officials an incentive to avoid petitions by providing public goods. However, as long as riot is a credible option for the villagers to pressure the local government, the villagers would choose to negotiate directly with the targeted local government.

[6] In many ways, the logic here is equivalent to the theory developed in the model by William Clark, Matt Golder, and Sona Golder (2007, 27), implying "dictatorships where citizens have no credible exit threat should perform relatively well since citizens have little option but to continue investing, making the best of what they have and hoping that the state does not predate too much. In contrast, dictatorships where citizens have credible exit threats will perform poorly since the citizens will redeploy their assets elsewhere to avoid state predation."

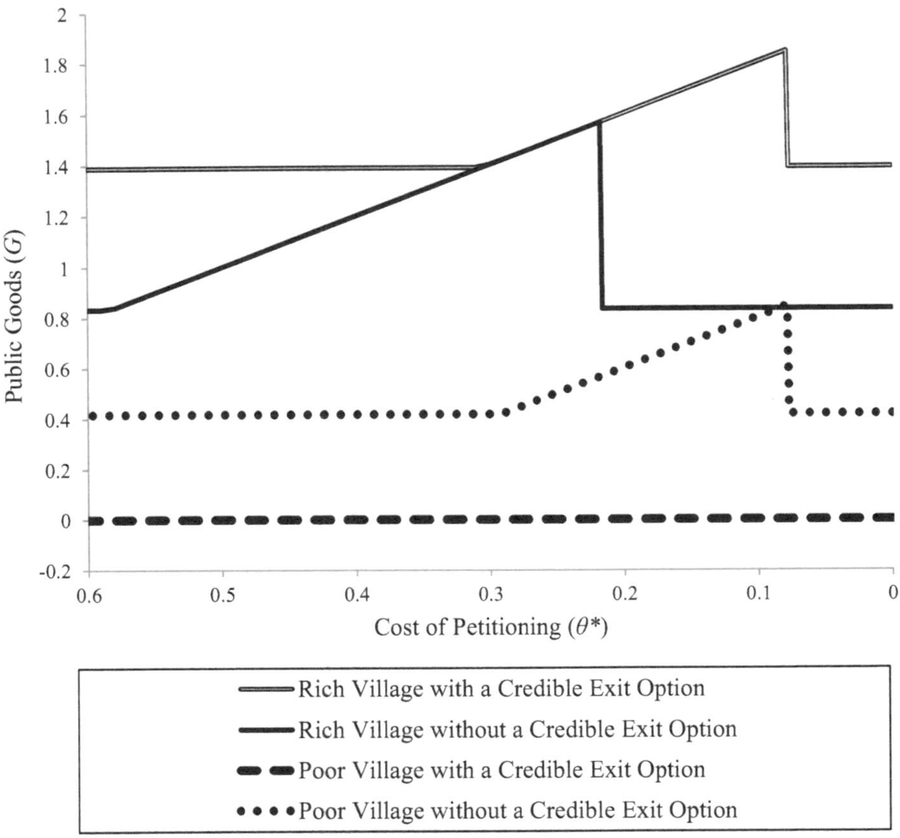

FIGURE 6.2. Effects of Petitions on the Provision of Public Goods (If Riot Is Not a Credible Option). *Note:* $T = 2$ and $\delta = 0.8$ for rich villages; and $T = 1$ and $\delta = 0.2$ for poor villages. $E = 0.5$ for villages with a credible exit option; and $E = -0.5$ for villages without a credible exit option. $x = 0.3$, $\rho = 0.3$, $\theta = 0.5$, and $q = 0.5$ for all villages.

Even when the villagers petitioned, they would riot after the petitioning was unsuccessful. In this sense, the petition system would not reduce the villagers' use of noninstitutionalized means of protest as long as villagers expect the net gain of direct negotiation with the targeted local government to be high.

Then how would the effect of the petition system on social stability in the Chinese countryside change if direct negotiation with the local government is not beneficial for the villagers? Figure 6.2 shows the effect a decrease in the cost of petitioning has on the provision of public goods in the case where riot is not a credible option.[7]

[7] To illustrate this case, I assign $\theta = 0.5$ instead of $\theta = 0.1$. For all the other parameters, I use the same numerical example as the one used in Figure 6.1.

Figure 6.2 illustrates that, ceteris paribus, the local government would spend more on public goods when riot is not a credible option than when it is a credible option. Moreover, a decrease in the cost of petitioning would increase the local government's expenditure for public goods in rich villages, regardless of whether the villagers have a credible exit option, once riot is not a credible option. Although the local government in a rich village would be responsive to the institutionalization of the petition system, the local government in a poor village with a credible exit option would not. Moreover, similar to the case where riot is a credible option, the local government would spend more on public goods in a poor village without a credible exit option than in a poor village with a credible exit option. In a rich village, by contrast, the local government would spend more on public goods in a village with a credible exit option than in a village without a credible exit option.[8]

Unlike the case where riot is a credible option, the villagers would choose to comply as long as public goods are provided if riot is not a credible option. Similar to the case where riot is a credible option, they would not choose to petition when the local government increases the provision of public goods as the petitioning cost decreases. When the petitioning cost is lower than a certain threshold, the villagers would petition and subsequently comply. In a sense, in the same logic of the credible riot case, the low petitioning cost would result in a *drop* in the provision of public goods. However, unlike the credible riot case, the villagers would comply after petitioning if riot is not a credible option.

In sum, the examination of the hypothetical case where riot is not a credible option suggests that the real institutionalization of the petition system would bring social stability and good governance to rural China. Distinguishing petition from riot by giving a high cost to riot and a low cost to petition would lead to villagers' compliance and the local government's increasing the provision of public goods. The model's equilibrium outcomes imply that as long as local officials perceive that petitioning is equally problematic to (or even more problematic than) rioting as a sign of social stability, villagers would choose to negotiate directly with the targeted local government once petitioning did not solve their problem. In contrast, if local officials perceive that rioting is problematic but petitioning is not, villagers would comply even if petitioning did not solve their problem, because the local government would provide more public goods to induce the villagers' compliance.

CONCLUSION

The game-theoretic model suggests that similar to the impact of rural-to-urban migration, the petition system might strengthen the power of villagers vis-à-vis

[8] Strictly speaking, the local government would spend at least the same amount (if not more) on public goods in a village with a credible exit option as in a village without it.

that of local governments by giving local officials an incentive to provide public goods under certain conditions. However, this incentive would be sustained in the long run only in the villages with high potential for development. The petition system would give local officials an incentive to increase the provision of public goods in the villages where officials would benefit from local development. In sum, the combination of the relaxation of migration policies and the institutionalization of the petition system would increase the provision of public goods in the villages with high potential for development while it would decrease the provision of public goods in the villages with low potential.

The model's equilibrium outcomes imply that the petition system would not give local officials strong incentives to be responsive to popular preferences. In reality, the petition system instead apparently helped the central government strengthen its control over local governments. Indeed, the fact that local governments in agricultural areas, which used to rely on revenue from the agricultural taxes, faced the problem of inadequate revenue implies that local officials complied with the implementation of a series of rural tax reforms that began in 2000 and led to the complete abolition of the agricultural tax.

Through the introduction of the petition system, the Chinese central government allowed ordinary people to raise their demands against local governments. The game-theoretic model suggests why the introduction of a remonstrative institution did not necessarily make local governments accountable to villagers. Local governments in agricultural areas failed to provide public goods, and by allowing villagers to petition against local governments, the central government succeeded in castigating these local officials for this failure. Villagers had favorable views of the central government and blamed local governments. The state media actively reported these policies as favorable to villagers – such as the relaxation of migration policies, the appreciation of people's use of the petition system, and the abolition of the agricultural taxes. These policies, which were favorable for villagers, brought negative effects on local governments and rural governance in agricultural areas. In sum, the petition system helped the central government strengthen its authority and gain popular support at the cost of the local government's capacity for governance.

If the central government's policy had negative effects in agricultural villages in interior rural areas, such as a lack of public goods and burdens on local officials with its unfunded mandates, then why did villagers have more positive views of the central government than of local governments? Xiaolin Guo (2001) argues that villagers had a bifurcated perception of the state – distinguishing the central government from local governments. Lianjiang Li (2004, 2008, 2010, 2011, 2013) has also wrestled with this question in his serial works based on his survey research in rural China. Li contends that villagers "'disaggregate[d]' the state . . . into a trustworthy Center and untrustworthy grassroots authorities or, more broadly, into trustworthy 'higher levels' (*shangji* or *shangmian*) and untrustworthy 'lower levels' (*xiaji* or *xiamian*)" (Li 2004, 231–32). However, villagers did not trust the central government's ability to enforce its policies (ibid., 238), and they turned their more peaceful, institutionalized petitions into more violent, noninstitutionalized riots once they found local officials had failed to meet their demands (ibid., 248). Li (2008, 222) further argues that the villagers' experience of the failure to achieve their petitioned demands, the repression by the targeted local government, and the cost to petition to higher authorities (especially when they went to Beijing) weakened petitioners' trust in the central government.

Did villagers demand not only the state's rule enforcement but also their participation in rule making? Lianjiang Li (2010) defines the demand for the state's rule enforcement as "rules consciousness" and the demand for participation in rule making as "rights consciousness," and argues that increasing rights-conscious resistance took place during the 1990s in rural China. In rights-conscious resistance, villagers formed a bifurcated view of the central government. They maintained their trust in the central government's ability and intention to make rules – such as the institutionalization of the petition system – while they did not have trust in its ability and capacity to enforce rules – such as solving the problems that they petitioned (Li 2004, 2013). Moreover, Li (2013) finds that the petitioners that he interviewed in Beijing trusted only one or a few leaders in the central leadership, although they did respond affirmatively to the survey question of whether they trusted the central government. Therefore, combining the findings from a series of surveys by Li, one can conclude that the reason people had negative views of local governments and positive views of the central government was: they had positive views of particular leaders (especially President Hu Jintao and Premier Wen Jiabao); they were skeptical about the central government's ability to implement the well-intended policy to solve actual problems, even though they were confident in the leadership's intentions to solve the problems; and villagers were hence skeptical about the state's capacity to solve the problems in rural governance. By introducing a series of rural tax reforms that began in 2000 under the CRS, the central government attributed the problems of rural governance to local governments. Although this strategy of co-opting villagers' interests seemingly maintained villagers' trust in central leaders, it also sowed the seeds for riots and resistance against local officials.

Finally, the Chinese central government's introduction of the two policies that are discussed in the previous chapter and this chapter – the relaxation of migration policies and the institutionalization of the petition system – is consistent with its goal of regime survival. It is conventional wisdom that the authoritarian regime needs popular support to stay in power. However, the popular support an authoritarian regime needs is not limited to the votes required to stay in office as in a democratic regime. Indeed, an authoritarian regime often seeks an electoral victory by huge margins, much larger than the margin needed to win the majority of the parliamentary seats. Beatriz Magaloni (2006) argues that this is because, as in the case of the Mexican Institutional Revolutionary Party, the electoral result of the overwhelming majority discourages opponents from organizing against the regime. China's central leaders were haunted by the fear that they were losing popular support and that their days in power were numbered, especially after the 1989 pro-democracy protests in Tiananmen Square and the fall of communism in the Soviet Union (Shirk 2007). The analysis in these two chapters suggests that allowing villagers to migrate to urban areas and to petition against local governments strengthened popular support for the regime at the cost of support for local governments, especially in agricultural areas. This arguably alleviated the Chinese leadership's fear of being ousted from power.

APPENDIX 6A: FORMAL DESCRIPTION AND SOLUTION TO THE MIGRATION, PARTICIPATION, TAXATION GAME

Figure A6.1 shows the sequential, noncooperative game of migration, participation (including both petitions and riots), and taxation in extensive form. Assume that all information about the payoffs and structure of the game are common knowledge. The game in this chapter makes most of the assumptions that were made in the game in the previous chapter. However, it adds the petition node to the villagers' choice set. Petitions may be reviewed or ignored. The probability that petitions are reviewed is common knowledge but neither the local government nor the villagers can control it.[9]

Just as in the game in the previous chapter, the game begins with the local government's decision to set G, assuming $0 \leq G \leq T$. Following the local government's move, the villagers choose a response. In addition to Comply and Migrate, villagers have two more choices: directly protesting against the local government with noninstitutionalized means (Riot) and submitting a petition to the superior government (Petition). If the villagers choose to comply, migrate, or riot, then the game ends. In the event of petitioning, the superior government may review or ignore the petition, and the probability that higher authorities respond to the petition in favor of the villagers is q. If the petition is reviewed (Successful), then the game ends with the tax reduced to the amount spent on providing public goods. In other words, the successful petition implies that the local government cannot enjoy revenue surplus to be spent for private purposes. If the petition is ignored (Not Successful), then the villagers have to choose among compliance, riot, and migration.

[9] In its basic structure, the model presented here is similar to that of Clark, Golder, and Golder (2007). In their model, citizens have three choices – exit, voice, and loyalty – and the state will choose to respond to their voice or ignore it. In their model the state that is the target of citizens' actions decides to respond or ignore, while in my model whether the petition (voice) is reviewed or ignored is determined by nature, incorporating various factors that may influence the probability that petitions are reviewed. Moreover, in my model villagers have two choices for voice: petitioning (institutionalized) and rioting (noninstitutionalized).

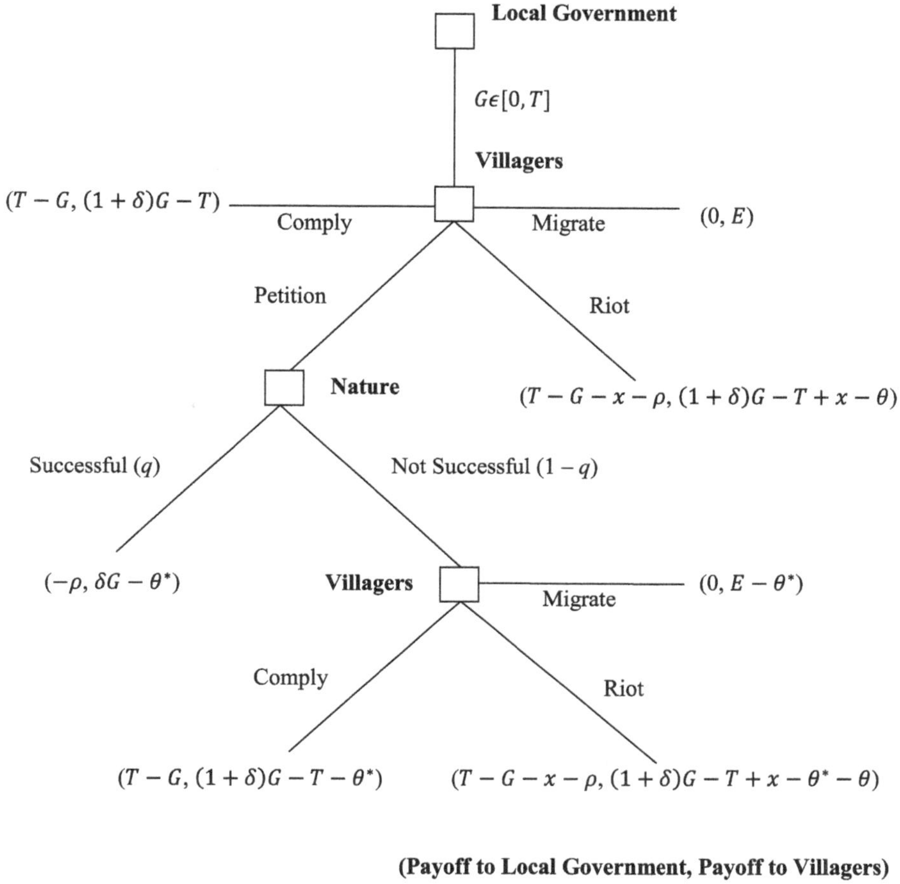

FIGURE A6.1. Extensive Form of the Migration, Participation, Taxation Game.

If petitioning is successful, the local government's payoff will be $-\rho$ (i.e., $T-G-\rho=-\rho$ when $T=G$). The cost of petitioning for villagers is measured as θ^* (i.e., $\theta^*>0$). If the petition is reviewed, the villagers will get δG (i.e., $(1+\delta)G-T=\delta G$ if $T=G$) minus θ^*. If the petition is ignored, the villagers will have the option of complying, migrating, or rebelling. If the petition is ignored and the villagers comply, their payoff will be $(1+\delta)G-T-\theta^*$. If the petition is ignored and the villagers exit, their payoff will be $E-\theta^*$. If the petition is ignored and the villagers riot, their payoff will be $(1+\delta)G-T+y-\theta^*-\theta$.

Solution to the Model

Solving by backward induction, I first consider the villagers' subgame. There are six strategies available for the villagers. The strategies that can be sustained as equilibrium are different depending on specific conditions. Here I explore the implications of the equilibrium outcomes depending on whether exit, riot, and/or petition are credible options for the villagers to pressure the local government.

The Villagers' Second Node

The villagers will comply if $(1+\delta)G - T - \theta^* \geq E - \theta^*$ and $(1+\delta)G - T - \theta^* \geq (1+\delta)G - T + x - \theta^* - \theta$. Thus, the villagers will comply at their second node if $G \geq \frac{E+T}{1+\delta}$ and $\theta \geq x$.

The villagers will migrate if $E - \theta^* \geq (1+\delta)G - T - \theta^*$ and $E - \theta^* \geq (1+\delta)G - T + x - \theta^* - \theta$. Thus, the villagers will migrate if $G \leq \frac{E+T}{1+\delta}$ and $G \leq \frac{E+T-x+\theta}{1+\delta}$. Therefore, the villagers will migrate at their second node if $G \leq \frac{E+T}{1+\delta}$ and $\theta \geq x$, or if $G \leq \frac{E+T-x+\theta}{1+\delta}$ and $\theta \leq x$.

The villagers will riot if $(1+\delta)G - T + x - \theta^* - \theta \geq (1+\delta)G - T - \theta^*$ and $(1+\delta)G - T + x - \theta^* - \theta \geq E - \theta^*$. Thus, the villagers will rebel in their second node if $\theta \leq x$ and $G \geq \frac{E+T-x+\theta}{1+\delta}$.

The Villagers' First Node

The villagers' utility from petitioning $(U_V(P))$ is as follows:

$U_V(P) = \delta G + (1-q)(G-T) - \theta^*$, if $\theta \geq x$ and $G \geq \frac{E+T}{1+\delta}$

$U_V(P) = q\delta G + (1-q)E - \theta^*$, if $\theta \geq x$ and $G \leq \frac{E+T}{1+\delta}$, or if $\theta \leq x$ and $G \leq \frac{E+T-x+\theta}{1+\delta}$

$U_V(P) = \delta G + (1-q)(G-T+x-\theta)$, if $\theta \leq x$ and $G \geq \frac{E+T-x+\theta}{1+\delta}$

If $\theta \geq x$ and $G \geq \frac{E+T}{1+\delta}$, then the following strategies will be sustained as equilibrium: (1) the villagers will comply at their first node if $(1+\delta)G - T \geq \delta G + (1-q)(G-T) - \theta^*$; and (2) the villagers will petition at their first node and comply at their second node if $\delta G + (1-q)(G-T) - \theta^* \geq (1+\delta)G - T$. Thus, the villagers will comply at their first node if $\theta \geq x$, $G \geq \frac{E+T}{1+\delta}$, and $G \geq T - \frac{\theta^*}{q}$. Meanwhile, the villagers will petition at their first node and comply at their second node if $\theta \geq x$, $G \geq \frac{E+T}{1+\delta}$, and $G \leq T - \frac{\theta^*}{q}$. Therefore, the villagers will comply at their first node if $\theta \geq x$, $G \geq \frac{E+T}{1+\delta}$, and $\theta^* \geq \frac{q(\delta T - E)}{1+\delta}$; or if $\theta \geq x$, $G \geq T - \frac{\theta^*}{q}$, and $\theta^* \leq \frac{q(\delta T - E)}{1+\delta}$. Meanwhile, the villagers will petition at their first node and comply at their second node if $\theta \geq x$, $\frac{E+T}{1+\delta} \leq G \leq T - \frac{\theta^*}{q}$, and $\theta^* \leq \frac{q(\delta T - E)}{1+\delta}$.

If $\theta \geq x$ and $G \leq \frac{E+T}{1+\delta}$, or if $\theta \leq x$ and $G \leq \frac{E+T-x+\theta}{1+\delta}$, then the following strategies will be sustained as equilibrium: (1) the villagers will migrate at their first node if $E \geq q\delta G + (1-q)E - \theta^*$; and (2) the villagers will petition at their first node and migrate at their second node if $q\delta G + (1-q)E - \theta^* \geq E$. Thus, the villagers will migrate at their first node if $\theta \geq x$, $G \leq \frac{E+T}{1+\delta}$, and $G \leq \frac{qE+\theta^*}{q\delta}$; or if $\theta \leq x$ and $G \leq \frac{E+T-x+\theta}{1+\delta}$, and $G \leq \frac{qE+\theta^*}{q\delta}$. Meanwhile, the villagers will petition at their first node and migrate at their second node if $\theta \geq x$, $G \leq \frac{E+T}{1+\delta}$, and $G \geq \frac{qE+\theta^*}{q\delta}$; or if $\theta \leq x$, $G \leq \frac{E+T-x+\theta}{1+\delta}$, and $G \geq \frac{qE+\theta^*}{q\delta}$. Therefore, the villagers will migrate at their first node if $\theta \geq x$, $G \leq \frac{E+T}{1+\delta}$, and $\theta^* \geq \frac{q(\delta T-E)}{1+\delta}$; if $\theta \geq x$, $G \leq \frac{qE+\theta^*}{q\delta}$, and $\theta^* \leq \frac{q(\delta T-E)}{1+\delta}$; if $\theta \leq x$, $G \leq \frac{E+T-x+\theta}{1+\delta}$, and $\theta^* \geq \frac{q(\delta T-E-\delta x+\delta\theta)}{1+\delta}$; or if $\theta \leq x$, $G \leq \frac{qE+\theta^*}{q\delta}$, and $\theta^* \leq \frac{q(\delta T-E-\delta x+\delta\theta)}{1+\delta}$. Meanwhile, the villagers will petition at their first node and migrate at their second node if $\theta \geq x$, $\frac{E+T}{1+\delta} \geq G \geq \frac{qE+\theta^*}{q\delta}$, and $\theta^* \leq \frac{q(\delta T-E)}{1+\delta}$; or if $\theta \leq x$, $\frac{E+T-x+\theta}{1+\delta} \geq G \geq \frac{qE+\theta^*}{q\delta}$, and $\theta^* \leq \frac{q(\delta T-E-\delta x+\delta\theta)}{1+\delta}$.

If $\theta \leq x$ and $G \geq \frac{E+T-x+\theta}{1+\delta}$, then the following strategies will be sustained as equilibrium: (1) the villagers will riot at their first node if $(1+\delta)G - T + x - \theta \geq \delta G + (1-q)(G - T + x - \theta)$; and (2) the villagers will petition at their first node and riot at their second node if $\delta G + (1-q)(G-T+x-\theta) \geq (1+\delta)G - T + x - \theta$. Thus, the villagers will rebel at their first node if $\theta \leq x$, $G \geq \frac{E+T-x+\theta}{1+\delta}$, and $G \geq T - x + \theta - \frac{\theta^*}{q}$. Meanwhile, the villagers will petition at their first node and riot at their second node if $\theta \leq x$, $G \geq \frac{E+T-x+\theta}{1+\delta}$, and $G \leq T - x + \theta - \frac{\theta^*}{q}$. Therefore, the villagers will riot at their first node if $\theta \leq x$, $G \geq \frac{E+T-x+\theta}{1+\delta}$, and $\theta^* \geq \frac{q(\delta T-E-\delta x+\delta\theta)}{1+\delta}$; or $\theta \leq x$, $G \geq T - x + \theta - \frac{\theta^*}{q}$, and $\theta^* \leq \frac{q(\delta T-E-\delta x+\delta\theta)}{1+\delta}$. Meanwhile, the villagers will petition at their first node and riot at their second node if $\theta \leq x$, $\frac{E+T-x+\theta}{1+\delta} \leq G \leq \frac{E+T-x+\theta}{1+\delta}$, and $\theta^* \leq \frac{q(\delta T-E-\delta x+\delta\theta)}{1+\delta}$.

The Local Government's Node

The local government's utility from petitioning ($U_L(P)$) is as follows:

$$U_L(P) = (1-q)(T-G) - q\rho, \text{ if } \theta \geq x \text{ and } G \geq \frac{E+T}{1+\delta}$$
$$U_L(P) = -q\rho, \text{ if } \theta \geq x \text{ and } G \leq \frac{E+T}{1+\delta}, \text{ or if } \theta \leq x \text{ and } G \leq \frac{E+T-x+\theta}{1+\delta}$$
$$U_L(P) = (1-q)(T-G-x) - \rho, \text{ if } \theta \leq x \text{ and } G \geq \frac{E+T-x+\theta}{1+\delta}$$

First, if $\theta \geq x$ and $\theta^* \geq \frac{q(\delta T-E)}{1+\delta}$, then the following two strategies will be sustained as equilibrium:

(1) The villagers will comply at their first node if $G \geq \frac{E+T}{1+\delta}$.
(2) The villagers will migrate at their first node if $G \leq \frac{E+T}{1+\delta}$.

The local government might choose: (1) $G = \frac{E+T}{1+\delta}$ to induce the villagers' compliance; or (2) $G = 0$ enduring the villagers' migration. Substituting the value of G into the utility functions of the local government's payoffs (U_L), we get:

$$\text{maximum } U_L \text{ for (1)} = \frac{\delta T-E}{1+\delta}$$
$$\text{maximum } U_L \text{ for (2)} = 0$$

Of these two utility functions, $G = \frac{E+T}{1+\delta}$ if $E \leq \delta T$; and $G = 0$ if $E \geq \delta T$.

Second, if $\theta \leq x$ and $\theta^* \geq \frac{q(\delta T - E - \delta x + \delta\theta)}{1+\delta}$, then the following strategies will be sustained as equilibrium:

(1) The villagers will riot at their first node if $G \geq \frac{E+T-x+\theta}{1+\delta}$.
(2) The villagers will migrate at their first node if $G \leq \frac{E+T-x+\theta}{1+\delta}$.

The local government might choose: (1) $G = \frac{E+T-x+\theta}{1+\delta}$ enduring the villagers' riot; or (2) $G = 0$ enduring the villagers' migration. Substituting the value of G into the utility functions of the local government's payoffs (U_L), we get:

maximum U_L for (1) $= \frac{\delta(T-x)-E-\theta}{1+\delta} - \rho$
maximum U_L for (2) $= 0$

Of these two utility functions, $G = \frac{E+T-x+\theta}{1+\delta}$ if $E \leq \delta(T-x) - (1+\delta)\rho - \theta$; and $G = 0$ if $E \geq \delta(T-x) - (1+\delta)\rho - \theta$.

Third, if $\theta \geq x$ and $\theta^* \leq \frac{q(\delta T - E)}{1+\delta}$, then the following strategies will be sustained as equilibrium:

(1) The villagers will comply at their first node if $G \geq T - \frac{\theta^*}{q}$.
(2) The villagers will petition at their first node and then comply at their second node if $T - \frac{\theta^*}{q} \geq G \geq \frac{E+T}{1+\delta}$.
(3) The villagers will petition at their first node and then migrate at their second node if $\frac{E+T}{1+\delta} \geq G \geq \frac{qE+\theta^*}{q\delta}$.
(4) The villagers will riot at their first node if $G \leq \frac{qE+\theta^*}{q\delta}$.

The local government might choose: (1) $G = T - \frac{\theta^*}{q}$ to induce the villagers' compliance; (2) $G = \frac{E+T}{1+\delta}$ to induce the villagers' compliance if the petition is ignored; (3) $G = \frac{qE+\theta^*}{q\delta}$ expecting the villagers to migrate if the petition is ignored; or (4) $G = 0$ enduring the villagers' migration. Substituting the value of G into the utility functions of the local government's payoffs (U_L), we get:

maximum U_L for (1) $= \frac{\theta^*}{q}$
maximum U_L for (2) $= \frac{(1-q)(\delta T - E)}{1+\delta} - q\rho$
maximum U_L for (3) $= -q\rho$
maximum U_L for (4) $= 0$

Of these four utility functions, the local government will never select (3) or (4) under any condition because $-q\rho$ and zero are always smaller than $\frac{\theta^*}{q}$. Thus, the local government will make a decision between (1) and (2). Of these two utility functions, $G = T - \frac{\theta^*}{q}$ if $E \geq \delta T - \frac{(1+\delta)(\theta^* + q^2\rho)}{q(1-q)}$; and $G = \frac{E+T}{1+\delta}$ if $E \leq \delta T - \frac{(1+\delta)(\theta^* + q^2\rho)}{q(1-q)}$.

Fourth, if $\theta \leq x$ and $\theta^* \leq \frac{q(\delta T - E - \delta x + \delta\theta)}{1+\delta}$, the following strategies will be sustained as equilibrium:

1. The villagers will riot at their first node if $G \geq T - x + \theta - \frac{\theta^*}{q}$.
2. The villagers will petition at their first node and then riot at their second node if $T - x + \theta - \frac{\theta^*}{q} \geq G \geq \frac{E+T-x+\theta}{1+\delta}$.

3. The villagers will petition at their first node and then migrate at their second node if $\frac{E+T-x+\theta}{1+\delta} \geq G \geq \frac{qE+\theta^*}{q\delta}$.
4. The villagers will migrate at their first node if $G \leq \frac{qE+\theta^*}{q\delta}$.

The local government might choose: (1) $G = T - x + \theta - \frac{\theta^*}{q}$ enduring the villagers' riot; (2) $G = \frac{E+T-x+\theta}{1+\delta}$ expecting the villagers to riot if the petition is ignored; (3) $G = \frac{qE+\theta^*}{q\delta}$ expecting the villagers to migrate if the petition is ignored; or (4) $G = 0$ enduring the villagers' migration. Substituting the value of G into the utility functions of the local government's payoffs (U_L), we get:

maximum U_L for (1) $= \frac{\theta^*}{q} - \theta - \rho$
maximum U_L for (2) $= \frac{(1-q)(\delta T - E - \delta x - \theta)}{1+\delta} - \rho$
maximum U_L for (3) $= -q\rho$
maximum U_L for (4) $= 0$

Of these four utility functions, the local government will never select (3) under any condition (because $-q\rho$ is always smaller than zero). The local government will make a decision between (1) and (2) if $\rho \leq \frac{\theta^*}{q} - \theta$ and between (2) and (4) if $\rho \geq \frac{\theta^*}{q} - \theta$. Thus, $G = T - x + \theta - \frac{\theta^*}{q}$ if $\rho \leq \frac{\theta^*}{q} - \theta$ and $E \geq \delta(T-x) - \frac{q(2-q)\theta + (1+\delta)\theta^*}{q(1-q)}$; $G = \frac{E+T-x+\theta}{1+\delta}$ if $\rho \leq \frac{\theta^*}{q} - \theta$ and $E \leq \delta(T-x) - \frac{q(2-q)\theta + (1+\delta)\theta^*}{q(1-q)}$; $G = \frac{E+T-x+\theta}{1+\delta}$ if $\rho \geq \frac{\theta^*}{q} - \theta$ and $E \leq \delta(T-x) - \frac{(1+\delta)\rho}{1-q} - \theta$; and $G = 0$ if $\rho \geq \frac{\theta^*}{q} - \theta$ and $E \geq \delta(T-x) - \frac{(1+\delta)\rho}{1-q} - \theta$.

Summary

Equilibrium 1: $G = \frac{E+T}{1+\delta}$ and the villagers will comply at their first node, if $\theta \geq x$, $\theta^* \geq \frac{q(\delta T - E)}{1+\delta}$, and $E \leq \delta T$.

Equilibrium 2: $G = 0$ and the villagers will migrate at their first node, if $\theta \geq x$, $\theta^* \geq \frac{q(\delta T - E)}{1+\delta}$, and $E \geq \delta T$.

Equilibrium 3: $G = \frac{E+T-x+\theta}{1+\delta}$ and the villagers will riot at their first node, if $\theta \leq x$, $\theta^* \geq \frac{q(\delta T - E - \delta x + \delta\theta)}{1+\delta}$, and $E \leq \delta(T-x) - (1+\delta)\rho - \theta$.

Equilibrium 4: $G = 0$ and the villagers will migrate, if $\theta \leq x$, $\theta^* \geq \frac{q(\delta T - E - \delta x + \delta\theta)}{1+\delta}$, and $E \geq \delta(T-x) - (1+\delta)\rho - \theta$.

Equilibrium 5: $G = \frac{E+T}{1+\delta}$ and the villagers will petition at their first node and comply at their second node, if $\theta \geq x$, $\theta^* \leq \frac{q(\delta T - E)}{1+\delta}$, and $E \leq \delta T - \frac{(1+\delta)(\theta^* + q^2\rho)}{q(1-q)}$.

Equilibrium 6: $G = T - \frac{\theta^*}{q}$ and the villagers will comply at their first node, if $\theta \geq x$, $\theta^* \leq \frac{q(\delta T - E)}{1+\delta}$, and $E \geq \delta T - \frac{(1+\delta)(\theta^* + q^2\rho)}{q(1-q)}$.

Equilibrium 7: $G = \frac{E+T-x+\theta}{1+\delta}$ and the villagers will petition at their first node and riot at their second node, if $\theta \leq x$, $\theta^* \leq \frac{q(\delta T - E - \delta x + \delta\theta)}{1+\delta}$, and

$E \leq \delta(T - x) - \frac{q(2-q)\theta+(1+\delta)\theta^*}{q(1-q)}$ (if $\rho \leq \frac{\theta^*}{q} - \theta$) or $E \leq \delta(T - x) - \frac{(1+\delta)\rho}{1-q} - \theta$ (if $\rho \geq \frac{\theta^*}{q} - \theta$).

Equilibrium 8: $G = T - x + \theta - \frac{\theta^*}{q}$ and the villagers will riot at their first node, if $\theta \leq x$, $\theta^* \leq \frac{q(\delta T - E - \delta x + \delta\theta)}{1+\delta}$, $E \geq \delta(T - x) - \frac{(1+\delta)\rho}{1-q} - \theta$, and $\rho \leq \frac{\theta^*}{q} - \theta$.

Equilibrium 9: $G = 0$ and the villagers will migrate at their first node if $\theta \leq x, \theta^* \leq \frac{q(\delta T - E - \delta x + \delta\theta)}{1+\delta}$, and $E \leq \delta(T - x) - \frac{(1+\delta)\rho}{1-q} - \theta$, or if $\theta \leq x, \theta^* \leq q(\rho + \theta)$, and $\delta(T - x) - (1 + \delta)\rho - \theta \geq E \geq \delta(T - x) - \frac{(1+\delta)\rho}{1-q} - \theta$.

7

Village Elections and Authoritarian Rule in Rural China

From the perspective of good governance, a competitive election is considered better than a noncompetitive election. Competition brings the uncertainty of an electoral result. Each candidate, assuming that he or she might have a chance to win, should outline policy positions in a campaign to sway voters and win the election. Moreover, if elected, then the candidate has an incentive to deliver on proposed policies or to represent constituents' interests because the candidate would not be reelected in a subsequent election if he or she failed to do so. In this way, electoral competition creates an incentive for each candidate to campaign. More importantly, elected leaders are held accountable to the electorate through campaigning, because they are forced to make policy pledges during the campaign and would be sanctioned in future elections if they do not keep their pledges after being elected.

The topic of village elections in China has received special attention in light of the limited political reforms introduced during the past three decades of the post-Mao era.[1] In this chapter, I explore the effects of electoral competition and the size of the electorate on the outcomes of grassroots elections, examining China's village elections. In a Chinese village community, every villager knows each other, therefore voters and candidates have perfect information about each other. Under the condition of perfect information, candidates could easily determine what private goods (not public goods) they should provide to each voter to buy his or her votes. Thus, electoral contestation would negatively affect electoral outcomes unless voters reach a pre-electoral consensus

[1] For the most comprehensive empirical analysis of China's village elections, see the works by Baogang He (2007) and John James Kennedy (2002a). For reviews of the recent debates, see the articles in a special edition of the *Journal of Contemporary China* (2009) edited by Kevin O'Brien (i.e., the articles by Alpermann, Kennedy, Manion, O'Brien and Han, Schubert, and Tan).

on competent leadership. Whether voters could reach a pre-electoral consensus would depend on the village's economic conditions. In industrialized villages, voters could more easily reach a pre-electoral consensus on voting for local entrepreneurs, and hence good governance by economic elites might emerge through village elections. In the meantime, in agricultural villages, because of the absence of economic elites, good governance would emerge only if political or social elites in the village succeed in coming to a pre-electoral consensus on a competent candidate among the villagers.

In this chapter, I merge the arguments on village elections with one of the main topics of this book, democratic institutions and authoritarian rule in rural China. The politics of authoritarian rule have been largely understudied, compared with the politics of democratic rule, although most human beings have lived under authoritarian regimes for much of human history (Geddes 2003, chapter 2). However, the literature on the politics of nondemocracies has been growing recently (e.g., Blaydes 2010; Brownlee 2007; Gandhi 2008; Geddes 2006; Lust-Okar 2005; Magaloni 2006). Moreover, this research has departed from the traditional assumption that dictatorship is a political regime in which a single dictator rules without external constraint or influence. Recent studies have focused on institutions typically associated with democracy, such as elections and legislatures, but frequently established in dictatorships. My analysis in this chapter fits into this growing body of literature concerned with democratic institutions in nondemocratic regimes.

The institutional development of village elections within China's authoritarian regime is an excellent case for examining this issue. China's authoritarian regime hoped that village elections would improve local governance in its vast countryside – where the majority of the Chinese population resides even after large-scale migration from rural to urban areas over the past three decades – by disciplining local officials and preventing massive rural unrest (L. Li 2003; Li and O'Brien 1999; O'Brien 1994b; Shi 1999). Some empirical findings suggest the positive effects the regime hoped for: villages with elected cadres were more likely to have leaders receptive to popular preferences (Alpermann 2001; Chen 2005a; Kennedy, Rozelle, and Shi 2004; Manion 1996, 2006; Wang 1997), and the implementation of village elections arguably reduced the likelihood of mass uprising (Howell 1998; L. Li 2001; O'Brien and Li 2001; Pastor and Tan 2001; Schubert and Chen 2007).

Democratic institutions in authoritarian regimes function primarily as an important part of a survival strategy of the regime. An authoritarian regime is responsive to popular preferences through democratic institutions only when the regime's survival strategy coincides with the functions of the democratic institutions. In this chapter, I use a simple game-theoretic model to account for whether and how village elections are consistent with the CCP's goal of the regime's survival. The model's equilibrium shows that the probability a vote-buying candidate wins an election would increase as the size of the electorate decreases. It also shows that if voters have collectively decided which candidate they plan to elect prior to the election, then the probability that a vote-buying candidate wins would be lower. These results of the model's equilibrium have two implications: (1) vote buying would be less likely in small electorates – such as those in China's village elections – if citizens are able to arrive at a pre-electoral consensus; and (2) elections of this type could work to stabilize and strengthen the Chinese authoritarian regime.

What is common in the examples of studies on authoritarian elections is that democratic institutions might solve intraregime conflict that would otherwise undermine the regime's stability and jeopardize its survival. The key for the regime's survival strategy is to use elections to strengthen the ruling party while deterring the formation and growth of opposition parties. In line with the argument that authoritarian regimes use elections to solve intraregime conflict and constrain potential organized challenges from opponents, this chapter focuses on one of the factors unique to China's village elections: the size of the electorate. China's authoritarian regime established an electoral institution at the village level, but not at higher levels. I argue that the regime has found these elections to be useful for its survival as long as elections are limited to the grassroots level, which is why the CCP leadership has hesitated to introduce elections for higher-level authorities.

Alexis de Tocqueville ([1835 and 1840] 2000) praised grassroots elections as deserving principal credit for the effective democratic government of America in the early nineteenth century. However, after Tocqueville left America, grassroots politics became less important, elections at higher levels became more important, major mass parties developed, and the two-party system was established by the 1860s (Aldrich 1995, chapter 5; Charles 1956). Moreover, studies on electoral institutions have found that grassroots elections are prone to corruption, because the constituencies in elections with small-sized electorates tend to vote on the basis of personal patronage. For example, Morgan Kousser (1974) argues that in the post–Civil War American South, restrictions on African Americans' suffrage made candidates rely on personal patronage from small-sized constituencies, which caused the one-party rule of the Southern states.

Regarding the argument about the effects of constituency size on vote buying, Gary Cox (1987) and other scholars who study the decline of electoral corruption in nineteenth-century England have found that a small constituency size would cause vote buying (e.g., Hanham 1968, 1978; McKenzie 1963; Wald 1983). There had been "a sizable personal vote in the constituencies" in the British parliamentary elections until the mid-nineteenth century and "the politics of avoiding or of winning a contest often involved reliance on influence, patronage, and bribery" (Cox 1987, 169–70). Interestingly, though, candidates started stressing policy in their electoral campaigns in the late nineteenth century, when they had to appeal to the larger electorate that developed as a result of the extension of suffrage. Vote buying persisted even after the 1872 Ballot Act, which had introduced the secret ballot, and "the election of 1880 was considered particularly corrupt by contemporaries" (ibid., 10). However, the 1884 Third Reform Act and the 1885 Redistribution of Seats Act reduced corruption by increasing the size of voting districts, which "completely disfranchised 79 and partially disfranchised 36 of the smaller constituencies in the process of a comprehensive restructuring of the electoral system" (ibid., 11).

Historical observation of the United States and England seems to suggest that it is inevitable for grassroots elections to be corrupt, contrary to what Tocqueville thought. In a grassroots election, candidates would appeal to a small constituency and voters would vote for a person, not for a party. Previous studies of other democratic countries have suggested that a "personal vote" would generate less accountability and more corruption by encouraging candidates and voters to form a patronage relationship (e.g., Cain, Ferejohn, and Fiorina 1987; Carey and Shugart 1995; Golden and Chang 2001). For example, Miriam Golden (2003) suggests that institutional incentives for candidates to search for personal votes caused extensive political corruption and ineffective democratic government in postwar Italy.

However, a survey of rural China reveals that some village elections are corrupt and others are not. In this chapter I suggest that during official enforcement of electoral contestation, a pattern of "consensual elections" emerged as villagers reached a consensus on certain competent candidates before the election. In the sixty-two village elections I discuss in this chapter, twenty-one elections were consensual. Moreover, among the twenty-one consensual elections, in twenty elections the elected village cadres provided public goods after they had been elected. In the consensual elections, the candidates were elected in a contested but noncompetitive election and voters nevertheless felt satisfied with the electoral outcome and the elected representatives. In the meantime, in the villages that had failed to reach a pre-electoral consensus, elections were competitive and corrupt.

Based on assumptions that incorporate the institutional setting of village politics and the characteristics of the village community in rural China, the model's equilibrium derives the following implications:

1. Overall, the probability of a vote-buying candidate winning an election would increase as the size of the electorate decreases.
2. At the same time, if voters have a consensus on which candidate they will elect, and one candidate is significantly stronger than another candidate, then the probability of a vote-buying candidate winning would be lower. In other words, elections would be more likely to be clean if voters have reached a pre-electoral consensus on whom to vote for, which might deter vote buying in grassroots elections.
3. However, if the size of the electorate is more than a certain threshold, then electoral competition, not a pre-electoral consensus, might lower the probability of a vote-buying candidate winning. Once the size of the electorate has reached a certain level, vote buying would become a

> costly strategy to win an election; hence candidates would rely more on electoral campaigns stressing their policy proposals and appeal to the larger electorate with relatively low costs.

This chapter begins by introducing consensual elections, identifying the institutions of China's village elections and their unique characteristics. It then introduces examples of how a pre-electoral consensus may be formed in China's village elections. The third section generalizes my argument on the pattern of consensual elections based on an analysis of sixty-two cases of village elections that occurred in twelve provinces between 1995 and 2004.[2] The fourth section lays out a game-theoretic model and solves it. The fifth section shows how electoral competition and the size of the electorate may influence electoral outcomes, applying a numerical example to the model's equilibrium. This chapter concludes by discussing the model's implications for China's authoritarian regime.

COMPETITION, CORRUPTION, AND CONSENSUAL ELECTIONS

In 1980, eighty-five households in Hezhai Village, Guangxi Province, participated in a landmark event: the first popular election for a villagers' committee (VC: *cunmin weiyuanhui*) in China.[3] The Chinese government institutionalized the elections of VC members by the Organic Law of Villagers' Committees (hereafter the Organic Law) in 1988, revising it in 1998. Article 14 of the revised Organic Law specified that each election ought to be *contested*.[4] A contested election is one in which the number of candidates exceeds the seats available (*cha'e xuanju*). Beginning in 1998, contested village elections spread throughout China (Kennedy 2002b).[5] However, contested elections are not always *competitive*. A competitive election is one in which the race between candidates is so close that one cannot easily predict who will win. In rural China, as well as in other countries, some elections were competitive and

[2] See Appendix C for the sources.

[3] Strictly speaking, it was one of the natural villages (*ziran cun*) of Hezhai Village. Although the first popular election for a VC was held in a natural village, village elections are now held at administrative villages (*xingzheng cun*). Administrative villages are usually equivalent to the production brigades of the commune era under the Maoist command economy. Most administrative villages are natural villages, although a large natural village is sometimes divided into several administrative villages, while several small natural villages can be combined into one administrative village. Hezhai Village belongs to Bingnan Township, Yishan County (now County-Level City: *Xian-Ji Shi*), Yizhou Prefecture, Guangxi Zhuang Zu Autonomous Region. For a detailed account of the first village election in Hezhai Village, see the work by Xu Yong (2003, 3–14).

[4] I cite the revised Organic Law from the book by Hu Rong (2001, 206–11).

[5] Although the revised Organic Law required an election to be contested, John James Kennedy's (2002b) survey in 2000 in Shaanxi Province finds that an election was not contested in six of the thirty-four villages.

others were not. Moreover, I define consensual elections as the ones where (1) voters reached pre-electoral consensus on which candidate(s) to vote for; (2) the elections were not competitive although they were contested; and (3) voters were satisfied with the performance of the elected VCs. The following two examples show how villagers talked about public goods: the need for them before, during, and after an election.

When an election took place in East Gate Village of Hebei Province in May 2003, the then village party secretary was elected VC chief in a consensual election. When interviewing the elected VC chief, I asked: "How was the last election for you? How did you appeal to villagers during the election?" He answered: "I did nothing during the last election. I felt that I did not have to be VC chief as I had already been village party secretary. But villagers nominated me for candidacy and I was elected" (Interviewee 20). His answer is interesting, because under normal circumstances if a candidate does nothing, the candidate would lose the election. In fact, he thought that there was no need to campaign at all.

Two villagers in East Gate Village said that they were satisfied with the job the VC chief did when he was village party secretary and thus they had no reason to nominate someone else as a candidate for VC chief (Interviewees 28–29).[6] After he was elected, he was committed to providing public goods to a significant extent. In 2004, the village governmental office spent 60,000 yuan for repairing or constructing roads, developing wells, and covering social welfare expenditures. Moreover, this village office earned 100,000 yuan from managing a street market, where many small shops were selling clothes, repairing agricultural machines, and opening other retail stores from the rents they paid. Although the villagers I interviewed had some minor complaints, overall they were satisfied with the village office's management of the market both before and after the election, and they considered it as the village office's provision of public goods (Interviewees 28–29).

In another example of a consensual election, villagers in Highland Park Village of Zhejiang Province elected Mr. Shi, a then thirty-six-year-old entrepreneur managing a successful apparel factory, to be VC chief in 1995 (Interviewees 103–105). The election was a landslide as most of the villagers expected him to use his talent as an entrepreneur for village governance – making policies to promote rural industrialization. Originally, Highland Park Village had not been as wealthy as surrounding affluent villages because of its unfavorable geographic conditions, and thus villagers recognized that policies to promote industrialization would be the necessary public goods provision. After Mr. Shi became VC chief, he used his entrepreneurial talent to provide public goods. First, the VC invested in infrastructure to attract factories to the village and to provide many employment opportunities for villagers. Then,

[6] Institutionally, candidates in village elections do not decide to run themselves but are nominated by villagers, village cadres, or township cadres (Kennedy 2002b).

those factories paid corporate taxes to the village, so the village offices had sufficient revenue for the provision of other public goods, such as social welfare and improved hygiene conditions. Thus, villagers were satisfied with the village office's provision of public goods. Now, Highland Park Village is one of the wealthiest villages in Zhejiang, the province with the highest rural per capita income in the nation.

Among the many features that characterize village elections in rural China, two factors in particular make this electoral institution unique. First, even though the Organic Law stipulates that the elected VC is the village's highest decision-making organization, the nonelected village party branch (VPB: *cun dang zhibu*) is apparently more powerful and influential in village politics than the VC.[7] These two organizations are vested with the authority to make policy decisions in every Chinese village. However, the VPB is often at an advantage over the VC because the township government supports the VPB as part of the CCP's vertical organization. Moreover, the CCP organizations (both the VPB and the township government) control villagers' major real property: land. Therefore, the implementation of village elections may be difficult as it "often involves a struggle between villagers who demand improved accountability and township leaders who, initially at least, refuse to cede their authority to appoint village cadres" (Li and O'Brien 1999, 143). Nonelected party officials at the township and county levels have many opportunities to use a strategy of "feigned compliance" to resist holding village elections (Kelliher 1997, 84). Furthermore, there are reported cases of a CCP-supported candidate failing to be elected and nonelected township officials subsequently declaring that these nonelected CCP cadres should be in charge of all administrative responsibilities, with the elected cadres simply empowered to follow the CCP cadres' decisions (Liu 2000). Thus, John James Kennedy (2009) argues that the key to a successful village election is removing township officials from the process of electing village leaders.

Second, the unique characteristics of the village community influence voters' behavior, candidates' strategies, and electoral outcomes. For example, when interviewing the vice-secretary of Rose Town in Hunan Province, who was in the position of monitoring implementation of village elections in his town, I asked: "How do candidates conduct a campaign during the village election?" He proudly responded: "Candidates in the village elections in our town never carry on a campaign. So we don't have a problem of 'buying votes.' No campaign, no corruption" (Interviewee 53). His answer was interesting, because he assumed that campaigning and vote buying should be closely related, and hence if there was campaigning, the elections would be tainted by corruption.

This anecdote suggests that those who are involved in village elections perceive that a campaign is not necessary to win an election. A Chinese village

[7] For a detailed discussion about the institutional features of the relationship between the VC and the VPB, see the book by Jing Yuejin (2004).

is small enough that each villager knows all the other villagers in the community in person as they interact with each other on a daily basis. This not only applies to Water Dragon Village in Guangdong Province, a small village with a population of 309, but also to Bird Town Village in Hebei Province, a big village with a population of more than 5,000. In Bird Town Village, I asked three villagers whether they know everyone in their village. They all responded along the lines of: "Yes, I know everyone. Of course, I know some of them better than others, and I'm not familiar with some of the villagers. But I can recognize all the villagers. We usually go to the same elementary school if we live in the same hamlet and all the villagers go to the same junior high school" (Interviewees 35–37). In a Chinese village, it is rare for someone to immigrate from outside the village; thus, it is easy to maintain affinities formed during the school period.

The fact that villagers in the community know each other highlights a significant difference between grassroots elections such as China's village elections and an election with large electorates. In a grassroots election, it would be easy for voters to acquire personal information about the candidates. Thus, policy proposals that candidates state in their campaigns would not change voters' information about the candidates. Therefore, in a small electorate, campaigning would not be an effective strategy to win an election. However, vote buying could easily be an effective means to win an election with a small electorate. First, the number of votes needed to win, and hence the number of votes needed to bribe, would ceteris paribus be smaller as the electorate is smaller. Second, and more importantly, a small community would make it easier for a candidate to figure out what each voter personally wants, and candidates could thus promise their favored voters the provision of *private* goods that would exclusively benefit them, instead of promising the constituency the provision of public goods that would benefit the whole electorate. Third, in a small village community, candidates' promises to provide private goods would be deemed credible once they have shown their intention and ability to give personal favors because they would face social sanctions in their daily interactions with villagers if they do not keep their promise. By contrast, in an election with a large electorate, elected leaders would face electoral sanctions by failing to be reelected if they do not fulfill their pledges after election. In this way, candidates would be forced to make policy pledges during the campaigns, to which candidates and elected leaders would be held accountable to the electorate.

In sum, the cost of punishment for the electoral corruption of vote buying would arguably be low in the case of village elections in rural China. On the one hand, the cost of punishment could be measured by the severity of punishment and the possibility of being punished (Becker 1968). On the other hand, the cost depends on whether formally specified punishment would be enforced. Even with formal rules stipulating severe punishment, if people do not believe that cases of vote buying are revealed and formal rules are enforced, the punishment would not be considered a cost of the illegal act and would not deter it (Tsebelis 1989). In village elections, local officials in the position of monitoring village elections did not have a strong incentive to regulate the elections because the implementation of fair village elections was not considered an important criterion for the evaluation of local officials by higher authorities (Edin 2003; O'Brien and Li 1999; but Kennedy 2007). At the same time, the cost of punishment for failing to provide private goods would seemingly be high in the rural community. Strong affinities in the community would make social sanctions effective when a candidate has failed to provide promised private goods when elected.

Therefore, it is not puzzling that candidates competed to buy votes by providing private goods in campaigns for village elections in rural China – and in grassroots elections in general. However, competition for vote buying did not always occur. In some cases, elected cadres succeeded in their efforts to provide *public* goods and voters felt satisfied with these representatives. Because it is easy for both candidates and voters to acquire personal information about each other, reaching a consensus on electing certain competent candidates would be simpler in a small electorate. Whether a grassroots election would be consensual or competitive depends on the distribution of elite competence and intention. In the next section, I discuss how rural elites were involved in village elections.

CONSENSUAL ELECTIONS AND RURAL ELITES

In this chapter, I define three types of elites in rural China: political, economic, and social. They are, respectively, members of the CCP, entrepreneurs in rural industry, and leaders of kinship groups. They have an ability to provide public goods based on the resources they have, such as political authority, economic resources, and social networks. Because of these resources, their commitment to provide public goods would be credible if they have the intention to serve the whole village. In a small community such as a Chinese village, voters could see who has the intention to serve their village.

This section shows how the emergence of consensual elections might account for the pattern of the provision of, or the failure to provide, public goods by VCs. Political, economic, and social elites in the villages would affect the abilities and incentives of the VCs to provide public goods in different ways through consensual elections. Moreover, exploring consensual elections might impart important insights on how differences in the level of economic development across villages impact these abilities and incentives for the provision of public goods. The incidents examined in this section show that if the village has elites on whom voters could reach a consensus regarding competent leadership, the village election would not be competitive but public goods would be provided. Note that I do not claim that village elites always intend to serve as village leaders or provide public goods. Indeed, there are many cases where village cadres were corrupt (Xu F. 2004), where entrepreneurs were apathetic about village politics (Oi and Rozelle 2001), or where kinship leaders did not serve the whole village but their own kinship group (L. Tsai 2007b). However, I suggest that village elites will be in an advantageous position to convince villagers of their competence to provide public goods *if* they profess to be interested in making a commitment to do so.

Political Elites

In addition to the VC, whose members are elected popularly, the VPB is vested with the authority to make policy decisions in every Chinese village. The members of the VC and the VPB are called village cadres (*cun ganbu*). The VC occupies three to seven seats while the VPB has three to five seats, but members may hold positions concurrently on both the VC and the VPB. Thus, theoretically there could be from three to twelve cadres in any given village at any time. The VPB members are not popularly elected but are selected by the party assembly (*danyuan huiyi*) of the village. That is, they are either elected by the village's party members or selected by the township party committee (*xiangzhen dangwei*), a party organization ranked one step up the organizational hierarchy from the VPB. Even though VPB members are in principle *elected* by the party members, most of them are in practice *selected* by the township party committee. Therefore the party members in a village do not have many real choices, as the CCP has "a formal legitimate role in selecting leaders who are formally elected" (Manion 2000, 766).

The selected VPB is generally more powerful than the elected VC even though the Organic Law stipulates that the VC is the village's highest decision-making organization. The legal basis of this distribution of power between the VPB and the VC is the controversial Article 3 of the revised Organic Law, which affirms that the VPB should be the "leadership core" in the village and its villagers' self-governance (Liu 2004, chapters 4–5).[8] However, it is difficult, if not impossible, to "lead" (*lingdao*) village politics without "meddling" (*ganyu*) in the politics. Thus, in reality Article 3 gives the VPB room to meddle in the administration of the VC. Moreover, the VPB has an advantage over the VC because the township government backs up the VPB through the party organization. For example, Xu Fuqun (2004), a well-known Chinese journalist covering rural issues, reports several cases where the township government declared that the VPB should be in charge of all the administrative responsibilities and the VC should simply follow the VPB's decisions. Moreover, Jean Oi and Scott Rozelle (2001) observe that in the thirty-two villages they studied the appointed VPB members were more powerful than the elected VC members. Thus, the VPB is apparently more influential in decision making in village politics than the VC.[9]

[8] Then President Jiang Zemin advocated inserting Article 3 in the revised Organic Law (L. Li 2002, 720–21).

[9] My field research also supports this argument. In the six villages where I interviewed the VC chief and the village party secretary simultaneously, with one exception, it was always the village party secretary who answered the majority of my questions (Interviewees 12–13, 55–56, 58–59, 75–76, 91–92). The only exception occurred when the village party secretary was drunk when I reached the village office and was not able to answer my questions (Interviewee 67).

One of the important (and controversial) institutional features of village elections in rural China is that candidates do not make the decision to run by themselves but are nominated by villagers, village cadres (especially VPB members), or township cadres (Bai 1998). Qingshan Tan (2009) argues that as a result of this rule someone who does not have the intention to serve villagers might be elected a VC cadre. The rule allowing villagers to nominate candidates is also viewed as a way to prevent party officials from intervening in electoral results. However, Kennedy (2002b) observes that in the thirty-four villages of Shaanxi Province he studied, villagers tended to be satisfied with the electoral processes and results when the VPB nominated candidates. There are many cases demonstrating that the VPB nominated and supported non-CCP members. To cite an example from my field interviews, in Water Dragon Village, a wealthy industrialized village in Guangdong Province, the VPB supported incumbent Mr. Ye in the 2002 election, testifying to his ability to promote industrialization of the village even though he was not a CCP member (Interviewee 1). This observation is puzzling, because VPB members are not popularly elected and they do not always have an incentive to nominate the candidates that the villagers would nominate or support.

The concept of consensual elections might provide an explanation for this observation. Suppose that the village party secretary has the intention to serve the whole village. Then, this cadre would have a strong incentive to nominate a candidate who has the ability and intention to provide public goods. An election would not be competitive but consensual because villagers could reach a pre-electoral consensus on electing the VPB-nominated candidate. Moreover, villagers would be satisfied with the electoral process and result because they knew that the VPB-nominated candidate had the ability and intention to provide public goods. A key aspect of this scenario is that the village already has a village party secretary with the intention of serving the whole village. As long as the village party secretary has such an intention, it would not be difficult for him or her to find a competent leader and for villagers to know that the candidate has the intention and ability to provide public goods in a community where villagers have daily interactions with each other. As a result, we would expect to observe that the village would have a consensual election and the elected VC would provide public goods.

However, the VPB would not always nominate a competent candidate. When VPB cadres are corrupt, they would nominate one of their own members for a village election. Then, if a villager-nominated candidate beat a VPB-nominated candidate, VPB cadres would attempt to nullify the elected VC members' authority. The township government would back up the VPB's attempt because township officials would also benefit from the VPB's corrupt practice. For example, in Wugezhuang Village of Shandong Province, after the village party secretary had been defeated in the 2002 election, the township government declared that the VPB should be in charge of all administrative responsibilities and the VC should simply follow the VPB's decisions (Xu F. 2004, 38). Then, the VPB cadres ignored the interests of the majority of villagers and made decisions in favor of those with whom they had special personal relations when they decided on land expropriation – an issue in which villagers had high stakes.

The example of Wugezhuang Village demonstrates the limitations of village elections in rural China for holding cadres and officials accountable to the electorate. The comparison of Wugezhuang Village with Water Dragon Village suggests that the elected VC would provide public goods if and only if non-elected VPB cadres have the intention to serve the whole village. The reason the VC chief was motivated to provide public goods in Water Dragon Village was because of the possibility of rural industrialization. Mr. Shi, the VC chief of Highland Park Village, also had the same motivation, and the VC chief of East Gate Village was motivated by the rural street market. Thus, they all were motivated to provide public goods for economic reasons.

It suggests that electoral contestation itself would not give cadres and officials an additional incentive to provide public goods. VPB-nominated candidates could also be weak, corrupt, incompetent do-nothings, and total lackeys to the township government. On the one hand, if the VPB cadres consider the whole village's interests and nominate a candidate capable of providing public goods, then the villagers would reach a pre-electoral consensus on electing the VPB-nominated candidate. On the other hand, if VPB cadres' interests are in conflict with elected VC members' interests, then villagers could not reach a consensus on electing the VPB-nominated candidate. Even if the villagers reach a consensus on electing someone other than the VPB-nominated candidate, there would be no way for villagers to check the abuse of power by village cadres because the VPB is a more powerful organization than the VC. Such village elections would neither help the villagers monitor the VPB nor contain the village cadres' corruption.

In sum, the selected VPB is more powerful than the elected VC, and hence whether a consensual election is held and public goods are ultimately provided depends on the intention of the VPB. If the VPB has the intention to serve the whole village, then it nominates a competent candidate. A small village size implies that villagers know that the candidate has the intention and the ability to provide public goods. It would result in a consensual election and the provision of public goods. By contrast, if the VPB does not have the intention to serve the whole village but is instead corrupt, it nominates a crony as candidate. A village's small size means that villagers know that the candidate does not have the intention to provide public goods. It would result in a nonconsensual election, and if the VPB-supported candidate loses, then the VPB would nullify the electoral result.

Economic Elites

In many industrialized wealthy villages, often located in the coastal regions, entrepreneurs became VC chief (called *laoban cunzhang*) when they won a village election *and* became village party secretary when they obtained membership in the CCP (Howell 1998; Lang 2003; Odgaard 1992; Unger 2002, chapters 7–8; Wang 1998). Lang Youxing, a prominent Chinese scholar on rural governance, identifies two popular sayings, which are still often heard: "no one will listen to you if you are poor even if you are elected" and "if you don't have money, you will not be elected" (Youxing 2003, 177). In the following examples, the elections that elected entrepreneurs to be VC members were consensual. Villagers saw entrepreneurs' success in business and expected them to use their wealth to provide public goods. The wealth of entrepreneurs made their commitment to the provision of public goods credible.

There are several examples where entrepreneurs were elected to be VC members through consensual elections, public goods were provided, and villagers were satisfied with the processes and results of elections. In the 2002 election of Huaxi Village in Zhejiang Province, Mr. Yu promised to contribute 100,000 yuan out of his own pocket – 80,000 yuan for cleaning the village and 20,000 yuan for a donation to the village's senior association (ibid., 191–92). In another example from the 2002 Zhejiang Province village elections, in Shangyang Village Mr. Yang promised to spend 100,000 yuan out of his own pocket toward payment of the agricultural tax to the town government, so that villagers would not have to pay the agricultural tax. He also promised to donate his three-year salary to the village's senior association (ibid., 192). In Fuyang Village of Zhejiang Province, a wealthy village with a per capita income of 6,000 yuan in 2001, no one ran against incumbent Mr. Zhou in the 2002 village election (ibid., 188–90). If competition is the criterion for success of an election, this election was a failure. However, if the criterion is whether or not the elected village cadre provided public goods – or more generally is committed to good governance – this election was a success. Mr. Zhou was a successful entrepreneur and served as a village cadre for more than twenty years. Villagers knew how he worked as a village cadre, and more importantly, they knew that he had sufficient financial resources to provide public goods.

In Chinese villages, those who are thought to be adept at promoting local economic development and making economic decisions are called "competent leaders" (*nengren*). Mr. Zhou was a competent leader in Fuyang Village. During the imperial period, Chinese villages had competent unofficial leaders – called rural gentry (*xiangshen*) – who acquired the designation because they interpreted the emperor's policies in a way that would benefit the villagers (Duara 1988, chapter 6; Shen and Zhang 2003, 11–15). In contemporary Chinese villages, successful entrepreneurs might play a similar role to that of the rural gentry during the imperial period.

In these examples, in industrialized villages the presence of an entrepreneur started a virtuous circle for providing public goods while elections were not competitive but consensual. Successful entrepreneurs brought prosperity to the village by using their own wealth to provide public goods.[10] Once entrepreneurs

[10] Also see the works by Kennedy (2002b, 474) and Oi (1996, 130).

have the intention of being a competent leader for the whole village, an election would be consensual because an entrepreneur is an attractive candidate for the whole electorate, and public goods would be provided in the village. However, one should note that entrepreneurs might not always have a strong desire to seek office in rich villages. Lily Tsai (2007a, chapter 7) finds that entrepreneurs of rural industries in rich villages often thought that being a village cadre for one or two terms would be good for building and developing connections. Once social networks were extended, however, the opportunity costs of serving as a village cadre would be too high for their business. Thus, their best strategy would typically be to step down after one or two terms. In other words, entrepreneurs would have a stronger incentive to get elected to office for the first term but a weaker incentive to stay in office.

By contrast, a vicious circle might emerge in agricultural villages. If the village did not have an entrepreneur, then villagers could not find candidates attractive to the whole electorate and hence an election would not be consensual, but perhaps competitive.[11] While the village would not have sufficient financial resources to provide public goods for the whole village, incumbent village cadres would have an incentive to distribute the village's scarce financial resources to their favorite group of villagers. Candidates in a competitive election would then compete for vote buying. In the following example, in Chishi Village, a poor village in Inner Mongolia Province, villagers elected someone "clean" to be VC chief in order to curb existing corruption. The elected VC chief promised to reveal the village party secretary's embezzlement (Ako 2003). However, because the incumbent VPB cadres were corrupt and the VPB was more powerful than the VC, the elected VC chief was not able to check the VPB cadres' corruption. Elected VC members gave up holding them accountable to the electorate. To make thing worse, the elected VC chief joined the corrupt practice of the nonelected VPB members and started enjoying the benefits from the embezzlement.

The comparison of the industrialized villages in Zhejiang Province discussed here with Chishi Village suggests how the difference in economic levels might influence the relationship between the VC and the VPB. Although the VPB is generally more powerful than the VC, there are a few exceptions where the elected VC appeared to have more influence on the village's decision-making process than the VPB. For example, Zhenglin Guo and Thomas Bernstein (2004) find that in the villages of Guangdong Province they studied, elected VC members often had more influence on the village's decision making than VPB members. This variation occurred because of the difference in economic levels. In rich villages, villagers would have an opportunity and incentive to elect economic elites, such as successful entrepreneurs, to be VC cadres. Because the VC and the VPB both share the common goal of local economic development, nonelected VPB cadres would likely agree with the elected economic elite on

[11] The definition of a competitive election is a close race. It does not imply fairness or any normative criterion to evaluate an election.

village administration. Therefore, even in the cases where VC members seemed to have influence on decision making, it does not necessarily imply that VPB members' preferences were disregarded. This explanation conforms to the fact that Guo and Bernstein's cases were all from Guangdong, one of the richest provinces in China.

In sum, in the examples discussed in this section, electoral quality and the provision of public goods depend on the village economy. Benevolent elite governance by an entrepreneur might emerge through a consensual election in industrialized wealthy villages. Entrepreneurs would be one pool of competent candidates that might align the interests of the VPB and the whole village in local economic development. If entrepreneurs have the intention to serve the whole village, it would result in a consensual election, because entrepreneurs' wealth would make their commitment to the provision of public goods credible. By contrast, if villagers cannot find a competent candidate who has the intention and ability to serve the entire village, it would result in a competitive election. As a result of a village's small size, a competitive election would easily feature corrupt vote buying that would compete for the provision of private goods, and public goods would not be provided after the election.

Social Elites

Kinship (*zongzu*) is an important element in the daily lives of people, in society, and in politics in rural China.[12] Previous studies have found conflict between kinship groups in villages, consequently villages with multiple kinship groups often had worse village governance performance. For example, Lily Tsai (2007b) finds that villages with multiple lineage groups were less likely to provide public goods than villages with a single lineage group. Moreover, competitive village elections worsen the conflict between kinship groups. Kennedy (2002b, 479–82) observes that villagers were less likely to be satisfied with the electoral process in multisurname villages than in single-surname villages. Furthermore, Melanie Manion (2006) finds that during the period between 1990 and 1996, the villages with more surnames were ceteris paribus more likely to have an increased public trust in local leaders, while the quality of village elections – in terms of electoral contestation and voting procedures – tended to raise public trust in local leaders during the same period of time. Her logic to account for this finding is that the villages with a few clans would experience more intense clan-based politics than the villages with numerous clans.[13]

Contrary to the findings of kinship politics' negative effects on village elections and rural governance, Xiao Tangbiao (2002a), one of the leading Chinese scholars of rural politics and society, argues that in the forty villages of

[12] For a reviews of the roles of kinships in China's rural society and politics, see the works by Xiao Tangbiao and his coauthors (Xiao T. 2001; Xiao et al. 2002).

[13] Her sample did not include single-surname villages.

Jiangxi Province he and his colleagues studied, kinship politics might have had a positive impact on the process of village elections. Among the forty villages, twenty-five felt the influence of kinship politics in the 1999 elections. Of those elections, he concludes, kinship politics had positive effects on the election in eighteen villages, negative effects in twenty-three villages, and both positive and negative effects in sixteen villages (ibid., 31–32).[14] Thus, even though villagers were often dissatisfied with the electoral process in multikinship villages, they were satisfied with the electoral process in at least some of these villages. In other words, there was *variation* in the degree of satisfaction that villagers had with the electoral process among multikinship villages, while there was a *tendency* for a negative relationship between the multiplicity of kinship groups and the villagers' satisfaction with the electoral process. How would this variation be related to consensual village elections?

In some villages, elections indeed exacerbated kinship rivalries. For example, in one of the villages that Kennedy (2002b, 480) studied in Shaanxi Province, there was a long history of conflict between two major kinship groups, but the balance of power was maintained by assigning a village party secretary from one group and a VC chief from the other group. However, in the first contested election, each group nominated a candidate as their representative, the election was intensely competitive, and the candidate from the same group as village party secretary won the election. The elected VC chief used his status to enrich his own group, and members of the other group were dissatisfied with the electoral process and outcome. Kennedy concludes: "In northern China ... multi-surname villages are more prevalent, and large lineage organizations within the village may attempt to use the elections to secure greater gains for their groups" (ibid., 481).

In some other villages, however, kinship politics had positive effects on elections. For example, in You Village of Jiangxi Province, similar to the village previously discussed, the balance of power had been maintained by assigning village party secretary to one kinship group and VC chief to the other group before the first contested election in 1999 (Tong 2004, chapter 2; Tong and Yu 2001). In the 1999 election, just as in the election of the village discussed by Kennedy, each group nominated a candidate, the election was intensely competitive, and the candidate from the same group as village party secretary won the election. However, the subsequent process was different in You Village. Concerned that the electoral result might create a monopoly of power by a certain kinship group, the party secretary of Niuxi Township, which You Village belonged to, intervened in the electoral process. After discussing the matter with village cadres and kinship leaders, the township party secretary decided to hold the election again, referring to the fact that the winner did not have a majority, if invalid ballots were included. The reelection was scheduled for four days later and kinship leaders vigorously discussed this issue. The

[14] Note that the villages where kinship politics had both positive and negative effects are double-counted in the villages with positive effects and those with negative effects.

kinship leaders agreed that the VC chief should be from the other kinship group so that the balance of power between kinship groups would be maintained. They persuaded members of their kinship groups to vote for the candidate they agreed to elect. Thus, the reelection was not intensely competitive but consensual, a candidate from the group other than the village party secretary's group was elected, and villagers were satisfied with the electoral result.

Various case studies suggest that a kinship leaders' agreement can make an election consensual and have positive effects on the result of village elections. For example, in Zhong Village of Jiangxi Province, the village party secretary and the kinship leaders carefully manipulated the election process to ensure that a competent leader would be elected (Wang X. 2001). In this case, villagers identified those who would have an ability to provide public goods through their observations of intrakinship politics; then, through discussions among kinship leaders, villagers reached a consensus about who would be suitable for the village leadership. Although this showed collusion among the elites and the election was consensual, the village had a competent leader as VC chief as a result of the election.

In sum, the cases discussed here suggest that if kinship leaders are in conflict, an election might be competitive and corrupt, and public goods would ultimately not be provided. By contrast, if relations between kinship leaders are cooperative, an election might be consensual and clean, and public goods would ultimately be provided.

GENERALIZATION OF THE ARGUMENT

The cases just discussed show that public goods were provided in some villages. In the case of East Gate Village, the public goods were provided by managing the rural street market. In the case of Highland Park Village, the elected VC chief made policies to promote rural industrialization. From the cases discussed in the last section, we might draw the following argument. First, whether the nature of an election is consensual or competitive depends on the distribution of elite competence and intention. In villages with competent elites with the intention to provide public goods, a village's small size would lead to a consensual election. Meanwhile, in villages without competent elites with the intention to provide public goods, an election might be competitive. Second, competitive elections would be prone to vote buying because of the village's small size. Third, consensual elections might result in the provision of public goods in the village while competitive elections might not. While these arguments are drawn from anecdotal case study evidence based on examples from particular villages, to what extent can we generalize these arguments?

Here I explore the sixty-two cases I collected mostly from secondary literature (mainly from Chinese-language literature but a few from English-language literature) and partly from my field research, and I examine how the arguments fare with these cases. Table 7.1 shows the list of the sixty-two cases of village elections I collected (see also Appendix C). Among the sixty-two cases,

TABLE 7.1. *The Cases of Village Elections*

#	Village	Province	Economy	Year of Election	Nature of Election	Elite	Public Goods
1	Ai	Jiangxi	Agricultural	1999	Consensual	Political/Social	Yes
2	Cao	Jiangxi	Agricultural	1999	Noncompetitive	Social	No
3	Chengfang	Jiangxi	Agricultural	1999	Noncompetitive	None	No
4	Chishi	Inner Mongolia	Agricultural	2000	Competitive	Political	No
5	De	Inner Mongolia	Agricultural	2000	Consensual	Political	Yes
6	Dong	Jiangxi	Agricultural	1999	Noncompetitive	Political	No
7	East Gate	Hebei	Agricultural	2003	Consensual	Political	Yes
8	Fuyang	Zhejiang	Industrial	2002	Consensual	Economic	Yes
9	Gaoping	Jiangxi	Agricultural	1999	Competitive	Political/Social	No
10	Guan	Jiangxi	Agricultural	1996	Competitive	Political	No
11	Guobaozhuang	Shandong	Agricultural	2001	Competitive	Political	No
12	Guowa	Jiangxi	Agricultural	1999	Competitive	Social	No
13	Guozhuang	Shandong	Agricultural	1999	Competitive	Political	No
14	Guping	Jiangxi	Agricultural	1999	Consensual	Political	Yes
15	Hangbu	Jiangxi	Agricultural	1999	Noncompetitive	Social	No
16	Hejiabao	Tianjin	Industrial	2000	Competitive	None	No
17	Hejiang	Jiangxi	Agricultural	1999	Noncompetitive	Political	No
18	Highland Park	Zhejiang	Industrial	1995	Consensual	Economic	Yes
19	Houbu	Fujian	Industrial	1996	Consensual	Political	Yes
20	Hua	Jiangxi	Agricultural	1999	Noncompetitive	Political	No
21	Huaxi	Zhejiang	Industrial	2002	Consensual	Economic	Yes
22	Jianfeng	Jiangxi	Agricultural	1999	Consensual	Social	Yes
23	Kanxia	Jiangxi	Agricultural	1999	Consensual	Social	No
24	Libei	Jiangxi	Agricultural	1999	Competitive	Social	No
25	Lin	Shandong	?	2002	Competitive	Political	No
26	Lishu	Hubei	Industrial	1999	Consensual	Economic	Yes
27	Long	Inner Mongolia	Agricultural	2000	Noncompetitive	Political/Economic	No
28	Long Bridge	Zhejiang	Agricultural	2001	Competitive	None	No

29	Luojia	Jiangxi	Agricultural	1999	Competitive	Social	No
30	Makou	Jiangxi	Agricultural	1999	Consensual	Social	Yes
31	Mao	Shaanxi	Agricultural	1996	Competitive	Social	No
32	Nanmen	Jiangxi	Agricultural	1999	Consensual	Social	Yes
33	Ping	Inner Mongolia	Agricultural	2000	Noncompetitive	Political	No
34	Putian	Jiangxi	Industrial	1999	Noncompetitive	Political	No
35	Quchi	Jiangxi	Agricultural	1999	Competitive	Political/Social	No
36	Qudou	Jiangxi	Agricultural	1999	Competitive	Social	No
37	Shangfu	Jiangxi	Agricultural	1999	Noncompetitive	Social	No
38	Shangyang	Zhejiang	Industrial	2002	Consensual	Economic	Yes
39	Shiqian	Jiangxi	Agricultural	1999	Consensual	Social	Yes
40	Shiqiao	Jiangxi	Agricultural	1999	Competitive	Social	No
41	Taoyuan	Jiangxi	Agricultural	1999	Noncompetitive	Political	No
42	Tie	Jiangxi	Agricultural	1999	Noncompetitive	Political	No
43	Wangshatang	Jiangxi	Agricultural	1999	Noncompetitive	Political	No
44	Wangyue	Hubei	Agricultural	1999	Competitive	Political	No
45	Water Dragon	Guangdong	Industrial	2002	Consensual	Political	Yes
46	Water Wood	Hebei	Agricultural	2002	Consensual	Political	Yes
47	Wufang	Jiangxi	Agricultural	1999	Noncompetitive	Political	No
48	Wugezhuang	Shandong	Agricultural	2002	Competitive	Political	No
49	Xialang	Zhejiang	Industrial	2002	Competitive	Economic	No
50	Xiawei	Jiangsu	Industrial	1999	Competitive	None	Yes
51	Xing	Inner Mongolia	Agricultural	2000	Consensual	Political	Yes
52	Xinping	Jiangxi	Agricultural	1999	Noncompetitive	None	No
53	Xiaoshui	Jiangxi	Agricultural	1999	Competitive	Social	No
54	Xiyantou	Beijing	?	2004	Competitive	Political	No
55	Yongchang	Jiangxi	Agricultural	1999	Noncompetitive	Political/Social	No
56	You	Jiangxi	Agricultural	1999	Consensual	Social	Yes
57	Zhong	Jiangxi	Agricultural	1999	Consensual	Social	Yes
58	Zhong2	Jiangxi	Agricultural	1999	Competitive	Social	No
59	Zhou	Jiangxi	Agricultural	1999	Competitive	Political	No
60	?	Shaanxi	Agricultural	1999	Competitive	None	No
61	?	Shaanxi	Agricultural	1999	Competitive	Social	No
62	?	Shandong	Industrial	1999	Consensual	?	Yes

thirty-four were from Jiangxi Province while the other twenty-eight were from eleven other provinces. Forty elections out of the sixty-two cases were held in 1999. In many villages, the 1999 election was the first contested election because the revised Organic Law implemented in 1998 required every election to be contested. I collected these cases based on the criterion that I could find information about both the nature of the election and the provision of public goods (or the lack thereof). There were many reports on village elections, but the reports that included both of these kinds of information were limited. Most of the examples from the reports are from three edited volumes published in China (i.e., Li, Guo, and Xiao 2001; Xiao 2002b; Xiao, Qiu, and Tang 2001).

In the previous section, I developed the argument based on anecdotes that the VC cadres elected by a consensual election would provide public goods while those elected by a competitive election would not. In East Gate Village, villagers had no reason to nominate any candidate other than the village party secretary because he had provided public goods by managing the rural street market. In Highland Park Village, villagers knew that Mr. Shi had been a successful entrepreneur of a local apparel industry and they were able to form a consensus on voting for him. In both examples, elections became consensual because villagers had reached a consensus on who could manage rural governance to stimulate economic activities.

Could we observe this tendency in other villages? In Table 7.1, I categorize the sixty-two cases of village elections into three types: competitive, noncompetitive, and consensual. In the elections where the VC chief was elected separately from other VC members, I categorize an election as competitive if the elected VC chief received less than 70 percent of the votes. In the elections where the candidate who received the most votes among the elected VC members would be VC chief, I categorize an election as competitive if the votes for the elected VC member with the fewest votes were less than 70 percent of the eligible votes.[15] The election would be categorized as noncompetitive if the winner received more than 70 percent of the votes and the sources showed no evidence that villagers reached a pre-electoral consensus. Meanwhile, the election would be categorized as consensual if the winner received more than 70 percent of the votes and the sources showed that villagers had reached a pre-electoral consensus. Among the sixty-two cases, there were twenty-four competitive elections, sixteen noncompetitive elections, and twenty-one consensual elections.

In the sixty-two cases I collected, we can observe the tendency that public goods would be provided if an election was consensual while they would not be provided if an election was competitive or noncompetitive. Table 7.2 shows that in this dataset, twenty out of the twenty-one consensual elections led to the provision of public goods by the VC, twenty-four out of the twenty-five competitive elections led to a poor provision of public goods by the VC,

[15] In this type of election, each voter could cast the same number of votes as the number of seats available.

TABLE 7.2. *Nature of Elections and the Provision of Public Goods (N = 62)*

	Public Goods Yes	Public Goods No	*Total*
Competitive	1 Case #50	24 Cases #4, 9, 10, 11, 12, 13, 16, 24, 25, 28, 29, 31, 35, 36, 40, 44, 48, 49, 53, 54, 58, 59, 60, 61	*25 Cases*
Noncompetitive	–	16 Cases #2, 3, 6, 15, 17, 20, 27, 33, 34, 37, 41, 42, 43, 47, 52, 55	*16 Cases*
Consensual	20 Cases #1, 5, 7, 8, 14, 18, 19, 21, 22, 26, 30, 32, 38, 39, 45, 46, 51, 56, 57, 62	1 Case #23	*21 Cases*
Total	*21 Cases*	*41 Cases*	*62 Cases*

and all sixteen noncompetitive elections led to a poor provision of public goods.[16]

In the anecdotes introduced in the last section, villagers in industrialized villages could more easily make a pre-electoral consensus on who would have the intention and ability to provide public goods, while they would find it more difficult to make such a consensus in agricultural villages. Can we observe this tendency in the sixty-two cases listed in Table 7.1? Table 7.3 categorizes the cases based on the village's economic conditions (agricultural or industrialized), its elite type (political, economic, social, or none), and the nature of the election (competitive, noncompetitive, or consensual). Three cases were dropped from the original dataset of Table 7.1. In two cases (#25 and #54), the sources do not specify whether the village was agricultural or industrialized; and I could not obtain information about elite type in one case (#62).

Among the fifty-nine cases shown in Table 7.3, forty-eight were from agricultural villages and eleven were from industrialized villages. Thirteen of the forty-eight elections in agricultural villages were consensual and seven of the eleven elections in industrialized villages were consensual. Thus, we can observe that an election was more likely to be consensual in an industrialized village than in an agricultural village. In the seven industrialized villages that

[16] Note that because many of the cases were from the secondary literature, I could not categorize the provision of public goods in a more systematic way. In many cases the judgment of whether public goods were provided was based on whether villagers were satisfied with the provision of public goods.

TABLE 7.3. *Economy, Elites, and Consensual Elections (N = 59)*

Agricultural	**Political**	**Economic**	**Social**	**Political/ Economic**	**Political/ Social**	**None**	***Total***
Competitive	7 Cases #4, 10, 11, 13, 44, 48, 59	–	9 Cases #12, 24, 29, 31, 36, 40, 53, 58, 61	–	3 Cases #9, 28, 35	1 Case #60	*20 Cases*
Noncompetitive	8 Cases #6, 17, 20, 33, 41, 42, 43, 47	–	3 Cases #2, 15, 37	1 Case #27	1 Case #55	2 Cases #3, 52	*15 Cases*
Consensual	5 Cases #5, 7, 14, 46, 51	–	7 Cases #22, 23, 30, 32, 39, 56, 57	–	1 Case #1	–	*13 Cases*
Total	*20 Cases*	–	*19 Cases*	*1 Case*	*5 Cases*	*3 Cases*	*48 Cases*

Industrialized	**Political**	**Economic**	**Social**	**Political/ Economic**	**Political/ Social**	**None**	***Total***
Competitive	–	1 Case #49	–	–	–	2 Cases #16, 50	*3 Cases*
Noncompetitive	1 Case #34	–	–	–	–	–	*1 Case*
Consensual	2 Cases #19, 45	5 Cases #8, 18, 21, 26, 38	–	–	–	–	*7 Cases*
Total	*3 Cases*	*6 Cases*	–	–	–	*2 Cases*	*11 Cases*

held a consensual election, villagers reached a pre-electoral consensus on the economic elites' intention and ability to provide public goods in five villages.

Not surprisingly, none of the forty-eight agricultural villages had economic elites. In the thirteen agricultural villages that held a consensual election, villagers reached a pre-electoral consensus on the political elites' intention and ability to provide public goods in five cases, on the social elites in seven cases, and on the political and social elites in one case. Note that political elites were by definition CCP members. In the twenty-six cases where the political elites were involved in a village election (including the cases where the political elites were also considered the economic or social elites), an election was consensual and public goods were provided in six cases. In the twenty-eight cases where the social elites were involved in a village election, the election was consensual in eight cases and public goods were provided in seven cases.

Overall, while economic elites in industrialized villages provided public goods, political or social elites' involvement in rural politics in agricultural villages did not always lead to good governance. In the twenty-six cases where political elites were involved in rural politics in agricultural villages, villagers were dissatisfied with the provision of public goods in twenty villages. In these twenty villages, the VC cadres had been elected by competitive elections in ten cases and by noncompetitive elections in ten cases. In these cases, political elites did not have the intention to serve the whole village and the result was a nonconsensual election. If political elites were successful in manipulating an election the result would be a noncompetitive election, while if a village-supported candidate could successfully compete with a VPB-backed candidate, the result would be a competitive election. Even if a village-supported candidate won, political elites would nullify the electoral result and undermine the authority of the elected candidate. As a result, public goods would not be provided following a competitive or noncompetitive election in agricultural villages.

Among the twenty-four cases where social elites were involved in rural politics in agricultural villages, the village held a nonconsensual election and villagers were dissatisfied with the provision of public goods in sixteen cases. Twelve of the sixteen nonconsensual elections were competitive. In these cases, kinship leaders failed to solve historical conflicts between kinship groups in a village election, and competition among kinship groups led to intense electoral competition – and hence electoral corruption. As a result, the elected village cadres did not provide public goods to the whole village but instead provided private goods to their own kinship group.

THE MODEL OF VILLAGE ELECTIONS IN RURAL CHINA

The collection of the data discussed in the previous section is constrained by the limited sources that systematically report the processes and outcomes of village elections. Thus, this section develops a game-theoretic analysis to provide more systematic logic to account for how and under what conditions electoral competition might hold officials accountable. A formal description of the model is presented in Appendix 7A.

Basic Assumptions

Because the purpose of the game-theoretic model is to show logic that might account for how an electorate's size would influence electoral outcomes, I first consider the basic form electoral competition takes. The theoretical argument developed here rests on three broad assumptions about the actors (i.e., villagers, village cadres, and a superior government's local officials), the setting of the political institutions, and the nature of the village community.

Candidates Seek Office and the Value of Winning Is Independent of the Electorate Size

The first assumption is that candidates would positively value holding office and therefore choose strategies designed to win the election. Moreover, the value of winning would *not* be a function of the electorate size. The first part of this assumption is straightforward. One body of literature suggests that candidates would seek to win elections by maximizing support from citizens and/or votes (e.g., Ames 1987; Frieden 1991; Geddes 1994; Magaloni 2006; Mayhew 1975). Once the candidate is elected, he or she could use the office to pursue any aims desired. Another body of literature suggests that candidates would seek office because they pursue the benefits of being in office, whether monetary, financial, fiscal, or of another form (e.g., Blaydes 2010; Levi 1988; North 1981; Olson 1993). Once the candidate has access to the benefits, they could be used to pursue desired political aims. For the sake of simplicity, the model assumes that all the candidates would seek to win the election by maximizing the likelihood of winning.[17]

The second part of this assumption might need more justification. I assume that the value of winning an election would *not* increase with the electorate size, while the cost of using vote buying to win would. One might imagine that a leader in a larger village could extract much greater rents (as well as prestige, job satisfaction, and so on) from the job than a leader of a smaller village could. The major reason I assume that the value of winning would be independent of the electorate size is that rents are not related to the electorate size but to economic size. In other words, even in a small village, rents would be greater if it is an industrialized village. Moreover, empirically there was no association between the electorate size and the village's economic prosperity in village

[17] Of course, politicians would pursue some combination of multiple objectives, as Daniel Treisman (1999b) formalizes. However, even if politicians have multiple objectives when entering an election, they would be primarily interested in winning the election because they could not pursue other objectives without winning.

TABLE 7.4. *The Population and Economy (N = 47)*

Population	Agricultural	Industrialized	*Total*
1–999	11 Cases #4, 23, 24, 30, 35, 36, 43, 46, 53, 56, 57	2 Cases #45, 50	*13 Cases*
1,000–1,999	21 Cases #1, 2, 5, 6, 7, 9, 12, 14, 20, 22, 29, 32, 33, 37, 39, 41, 42, 44, 52, 55, 58	2 Cases #26, 62	*23 Cases*
2,000–2,999	6 Cases #3, 17, 40, 47, 51, 59	2 Cases #27, 34	*8 Cases*
3,000–3,999	–	1 Case #19	*1 Case*
4,000+	2 Cases #10, 15	–	*2 Cases*
Total	*40 Cases*	*7 Cases*	*47 Cases*

elections in rural China. Table 7.4 shows no evidence of a positive relationship between the electorate size and industrialization of the village economy.[18]

The assumption that each candidate would seek office does not mean that public office is always a desirable job. Typically, in poor villages, cadres consider a position in public office an undesirable job. Cadres in agricultural areas often struggle to collect levies and achieve a balanced budget while suffering from the burden of repaying substantial debt. To make matters worse, village cadres become the target of villagers' ridicule, because villagers draw sharp distinctions between the local and central levels of government. The villagers thank the central government for introducing beneficent tax policies (Guo 2001; Hu 2007; Li 2004, 2008, 2013).

In the meantime, public office could be lucrative for cadres in rich villages. Cadres might have better access to profits from land expropriation, for instance.[19] Because land is "collectively" owned in rural China, village cadres are the de facto owners of land and the real claimants of the benefits from land deals. They pay a small amount of compensation to villagers as compared with the price at which they sold the expropriated land to outsiders. The difference between the amount gained by the land deal and the amount paid to villagers as compensation becomes their profit. Although this has become a source of

18 Forty-seven cases are examined out of the sixty-two cases listed in Table 7.1 and Appendix 7A. Fifteen cases are eliminated because the sources used to construct the dataset did not provide the population of the villages.

19 Village cadres may also have better access to the benefits of the privatization of township-and-village enterprises (Li and Rozelle 2003).

villagers' complaints and protests, it is difficult to prevent the village cadres' quasi-illegal, corrupt behavior because property rights and land use laws are underdeveloped (Cheng 2005; Guo 2001; Hsing 2006; Li 2009; Paik 2009, chapters 6–8; Zweig 2003).

To incorporate the size of the population in authoritarian politics, the setup of the game here has a similarity to that modeled by Bruce Bueno de Mesquita and his coauthors (Bueno de Mesquita et al. 2003). Their model implies that political leaders overseeing smaller "selectorates" would invest less in public goods and more in private goods, because private goods would be divided by a smaller number of people if selectorates are smaller (ibid., chapter 3). They define the selectorate as "the set of people whose endowments include the qualities or characteristics institutionally required to choose the government's leadership and necessary for gaining access to private benefits doled out by the government's leadership" (ibid., 42). The model in this chapter is different from their model in that I focus specifically on the size of the electorate. Under the condition of a small electorate in the Chinese village community, where voters and candidates know each other in person and interact on a daily basis, electoral competition would encourage candidates to compete to provide private goods (which is indistinguishable from vote buying in my model). They do this not only because the number of recipients of private goods would be small but also because candidates would have perfect information on what private goods each voter wants. However, in a large electorate, where voters and candidates do not know each other in person, electoral competition would encourage candidates to campaign for a larger constituency. In order to appeal to a larger constituency, candidates would organize their efforts to mobilize the voters, and the formation of a party would be an effective strategy for winning an election (Norris 2002, 127). The formation of an opposition party, however, is the worst-case scenario for an authoritarian party – a scenario that the authoritarian party would try to avoid by all means possible.

One Candidate Is Stronger than the Other Candidate

The second assumption is that one candidate would be to some extent stronger than the other candidate at the outset of electoral competition. In other words, one candidate would have an ex ante advantage. This does not mean that this candidate would always be sure to win the election, but it does mean that the probability a certain candidate wins the election would vary in the continuous range between zero and one. Moreover, each candidate might raise the probability of winning the election by the ex post strategy of buying votes. Each candidate would have two strategies: buying votes and not buying votes. If both candidates buy votes or if neither candidate buys votes, then Candidate 1 would win with the probability of p and Candidate 2 would win with the probability of $1 - p$. Because the definition of the competitiveness of an election is the difficulty with which one could predict who would win, the election with the value of p closer to 0.5 should be considered more competitive. Moreover, if p is larger than 0.5, then one could say that Candidate 1 has an ex ante advantage over Candidate 2.

This exogenously fixed probability of p captures one candidate's "valence" advantage (Groseclose 2001; Stokes 1992). The factors that may give a candidate a valence advantage in American politics are "incumbency, greater campaign funds, better name recognition, superior charisma, superior intelligence, and so on" (Groseclose 2001, 862). Meanwhile, the factors that may give a candidate valence advantage in Chinese village politics are the resources that village elites have, such as political authority, economic resources, and social networks. Voters might reach a pre-electoral consensus on a certain candidate regarding competent leadership through a consensual election. In addition to this valence advantage, the value of p also captures how many voters are expected to prefer the exogenously fixed policies that the candidate is expected to implement. For example, the candidate that has economic resources might have an advantage in achieving the exogenously fixed policy of maintaining a balanced budget without increasing villagers' financial burdens, as in the example of Mr. Yang in Shangyang Village of Zhejiang Province, who credibly promised to spend 100,000 yuan out of his pocket for paying the agricultural tax remittance to the town government (Lang 2003, 192).

Candidates Buy Votes by Providing Private Goods

The third assumption is that when candidates buy votes, they do so by providing private goods. Combined with the first assumption, this assumption means that the incentive for a candidate to buy votes would be solely to win the election. Rather than having players choose the number of votes to buy (or the amount of money to be spent on vote buying), the model takes the cost of vote buying as fixed and independent of the other player's level of vote buying. Or, more precisely, if both players choose to buy votes, then the number of votes each candidate buys would not matter because the election would be determined by p – the same outcome as the case where neither candidate spends any money to buy votes. With this setup, the model could avoid the additional complexity of the strategic choice of coalition members, while maintaining the assumption that each player knows that the other player might also buy votes. In this sense, the model developed in this chapter is different from the models developed by other scholars on vote buying, which highlight the strategic choice of coalition members (e.g., Bueno de Mesquita et al. 2003; Groseclose 2001; Groseclose and Snyder 1996).

Solution to the Model

The intuition behind the strategies taken at equilibrium is straightforward. In the villages where each candidate's expected value of winning an election is high, the candidate would be tempted to buy votes. While both candidates would buy votes if the expected value for winning is very high, neither candidate would buy votes if the expected value is very low. In general, the probability that either or both candidates buy votes would be higher and approach the value of one as the expected value for winning an election increases. However, the reason candidates would buy votes is somewhat different depending on the circumstances.

When the expected value for winning an election is very high, both candidates would buy votes. In the elections where candidates would always buy votes, the game would take the form of a Prisoner's Dilemma. In the Prisoner's Dilemma, each player's rational strategy to maximize his or her individual payoff creates a worse outcome than some other possible outcome that might be better for *both* players. In the game of China's village elections with a high expected payoff from winning, each candidate would buy votes to maximize his or her payoff and end up with the outcome of both candidates buying votes; however, the possible outcome that neither buys votes would be a better outcome for *both* candidates than the outcome that both candidates buy votes. Both candidates would buy votes because they would do better to buy votes regardless of whether the other candidate buys votes. If the other candidate does not buy votes, it would be better to buy votes and win the election, taking advantage of the other candidate's noncorrupt practice. If the other candidate buys votes, it would still be better to buy votes and keep the chance of winning the election to be p for Candidate 1 and $1 - p$ for Candidate 2; otherwise, the candidate that buys votes would win the election for sure. Both would use this same reasoning and would take the same strategy of buying votes.

Once the expected value for winning an election is lower than a certain threshold, the *weaker* candidate would stop buying votes while the *stronger* candidate would keep buying votes. The stronger candidate knows that he or she would be likely to win with a higher probability once the strategy of buying votes is chosen, even if the weaker candidate also chooses the strategy of buying votes. If the weaker candidate does not buy votes, the stronger candidate would still find buying votes to be a better strategy to ensure certain victory. Thus, the stronger candidate would have an incentive to buy votes regardless of the strategy the weaker candidate takes. For the weaker candidate, by contrast, the expected value of winning an election would not be high enough to keep the probability of winning to be p by buying votes, given that the other candidate would buy votes. Therefore, the weaker candidate would not take the strategy of buying votes under this condition.

If the expected value for winning an election is even lower, the stronger candidate would not always have an incentive to buy votes. Instead the candidate would prefer not buying votes if the other candidate does not take the strategy of buying votes, because buying votes would be costly relative to the expected value of winning even for the stronger candidate. Conversely, the weaker candidate would have an incentive to take the strategy of buying votes if and only if the stronger candidate does not buy votes, but would prefer not buying votes otherwise. Thus, for each candidate, the best strategy depends on the strategy the other candidate would take. Moreover, both candidates would have an incentive not to let the other candidate know which strategy was taken. With this logic, each candidate *might* buy votes with a certain probability but would *not always* buy votes. Both candidates would take one strategy with a certain probability and the other strategy with another certain probability.

When the expected value of winning an election is very low, neither candidate would buy votes. The cost to buy votes would be so high for both candidates, relative to the benefit from winning an election, that neither candidate would have an incentive to buy votes whatever strategy the other candidate takes.

ELECTORAL COMPETITION, THE ELECTORATE SIZE, AND VOTE BUYING

I will now assess the effect of electoral competition and the size of the electorate on the behavior of vote buying in village elections in rural China. In the following sections I examine how changes in certain parameters would affect the equilibrium outcomes. I assign certain values to the parameters in the game and examine how changes in the values of certain parameters would affect the probability that the candidate who has bought votes would win the election.[20]

Competition in a Grassroots Election

Would electoral competition prevent a vote-buying candidate from being elected? The extent to which the election is competitive can be modeled as the value of p approaches 0.5. In the game, if one candidate buys votes and the other candidate does not, then the candidate who has taken the strategy of buying votes would win. Thus, as long as the expected value of winning an election is higher than a certain threshold, the winner of the election would always be the one who has bought votes. However, once the value of winning an election is lower than this threshold, there would be a possibility that neither candidate chooses the strategy of buying votes. To examine how changes in certain parameters would affect the equilibrium, I offer a numerical example.[21] Figure 7.1 shows how the probability of the election having a vote-buying winner depends on the extent of electoral competition (p) and the expected value of winning an election (W).

When the value of W is small, no candidate would take the strategy of buying votes however competitive the election is, and the winning candidate

[20] Although altering parameter values changes numerical results, it does not change substantive results.

[21] To be specific, I consider an example assigning $\beta = 0.05$, $\varphi = 0.2$, $A = 5$, and $E = 1.5$.

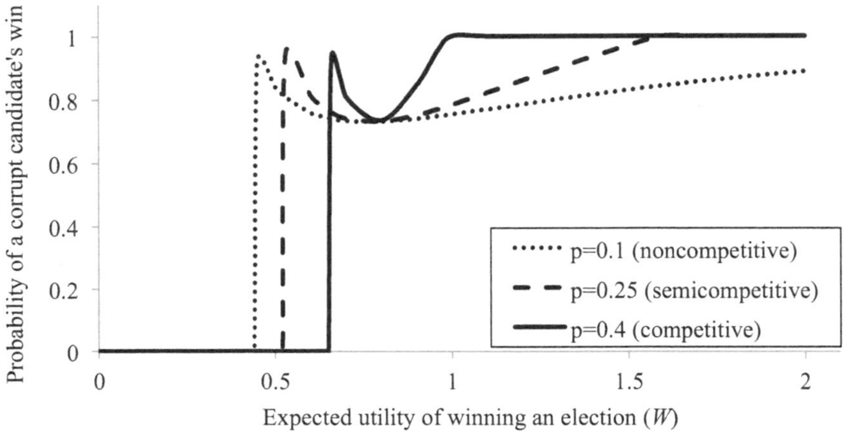

FIGURE 7.1. Probability of a Vote-Buying Candidate's Win for Different Thresholds of Electoral Competition. *Note:* $\beta = 0.05$, $\varphi = 0.2$, $A = 5$, and $E = 1.5$.

would not be a vote-buying one. However, after the value of *W* exceeds a certain threshold, at least one candidate would have an incentive to buy votes with a certain probability, and a winner might be a vote-buying candidate. This threshold would be reached more quickly as the election becomes *less* competitive. When the value of *W* is small, the cost of buying votes would be high enough, compared to the gain from winning an election, to prevent both candidates from buying votes. However, as an election becomes less competitive, the weaker candidate's expected payoff from not buying votes while the stronger candidate does not buy votes would be lower. Thus, the weaker candidate would have more of an incentive to deviate from the strategy of not buying votes to that of buying votes. Knowing that the weaker candidate would have more of an incentive to buy votes, the stronger candidate would also have more of an incentive to buy votes.

Interestingly, after the value of *W* exceeds the threshold, as long as *W* is smaller than 0.78, the probability of a vote-buying candidate's win would *decrease* as *W* increases. As the value of *W* increases, each candidate would primarily have more of an incentive to buy votes to win an election. However, the weaker candidate would prefer the strategy of not buying votes if the stronger candidate buys votes. Moreover, if the weaker candidate does not buy votes, then the stronger candidate would prefer not to buy votes. Thus, both candidates would face the dilemma that the condition that gives them an incentive to buy votes would also give them an incentive not to buy votes. Through this strategic interaction, a larger value of *W* would lower the probability of a vote-buying candidate's win.

However, once the value of *W* exceeds 0.78, the incentive structure of the candidates would be more straightforward. A higher value of *W* would give the

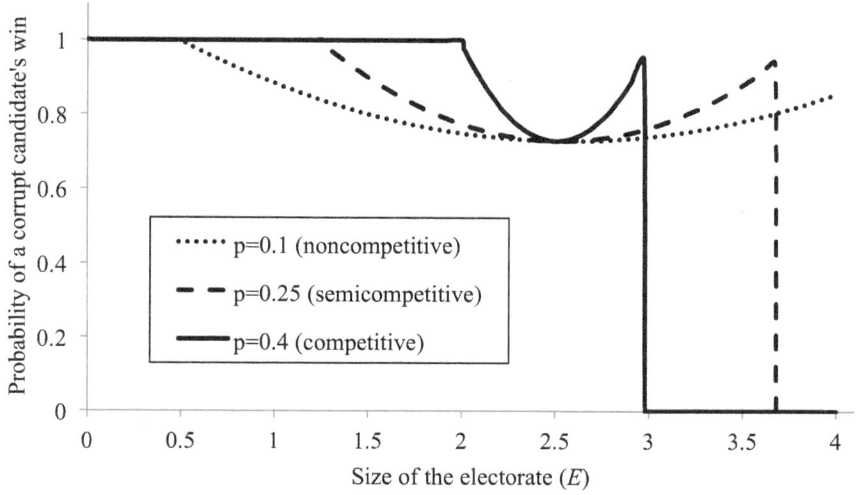

FIGURE 7.2. Probability of a Vote-Buying Candidate's Win Depending on the Electorate's Size. *Note:* $\beta = 0.05$, $\varphi = 0.2$, $A = 5$, and $W = 1.3$.

stronger candidate more of an incentive to ensure victory by buying votes. In a certain range, the stronger candidate would still prefer not buying votes if he or she is not sure whether or not the weaker candidate would buy votes. However, as the value of W is larger, the stronger candidate would be more threatened by the weaker candidate's strategy to buy votes, and hence the election would have a vote-buying winner because the stronger candidate would buy votes and be elected. The stronger candidate would have more of an incentive to ensure victory by buying votes as the election becomes more competitive. Therefore, the probability of a vote-buying candidate's win would be higher as the election becomes more competitive.

The Size of the Electorate

How would the size of the electorate affect candidates' vote-buying behavior? Figure 7.2 examines how the probability of a vote-buying candidate's win would depend on the size of the electorate (E) and the extent of electoral competition (p).[22] Overall, an increase in the value of E would *decrease* the probability that a vote-buying candidate would win. Moreover, electoral competition would make it *more* likely for a vote-buying candidate to win in a *small* electorate, while it might make it *less* likely for a vote-buying candidate to win in a *large* electorate.

If the value of E is small, candidates would always buy votes however competitive the election is. However, an increasing value of E would increase the

[22] I assign $W = 1.3$.

cost to provide private goods, and at a certain threshold the weaker candidate would stop buying votes. Moreover, if the value of E is even larger and exceeds this threshold, then the stronger candidate might also stop buying votes and the probability of a vote-buying candidate's win would be less than one. The value of this threshold would be smaller as the election becomes *less* competitive. After the value of E exceeds the threshold, as long as E is smaller than 2.5, the probability of a vote-buying candidate's win would decrease as E increases. After the value of E exceeds 2.5, the probability of a vote-buying winner would increase as the size of the electorate increases. However, once the value of E reaches a certain threshold, no candidate would buy votes and the probability of a corrupt candidate's win would be zero. The value of this threshold would be *smaller* as the election becomes *more* competitive.

When the electorate is small, the cost to provide private goods would be low, and hence both candidates would have an incentive to buy votes regardless of the other candidate's strategy. However, as the size of the electorate increases, the cost of buying votes would also increase, especially for the weaker candidate. The cost of buying votes for the weaker candidate would increase more steeply along with the increase in the size of the electorate as an election becomes less competitive. Once the weaker candidate's strategy deviates from vote buying, in the new equilibrium both candidates would prefer the strategy of not buying votes if the other candidate does not buy votes. Thus, in this range, a non-vote-buying candidate would win an election with a certain probability, and the increasing size of the electorate would lower the probability of a vote-buying candidate's win. However, once $E > 2.5$, the probability of a vote-buying winner would increase along with the increase in the value of E in a certain range, where the stronger candidate would have more of an incentive to buy votes to ensure victory in case the weaker candidate buys votes to challenge the stronger candidate's advantage. This range would become larger as an election becomes less competitive, because the stronger candidate's cost of buying votes would be lower as the value of p becomes lower. Once the size of the electorate is higher than this threshold, both candidates would find buying votes so costly that neither candidate would buy votes regardless of the other candidate's strategy.

IMPLICATIONS

In sum, the model suggests that electoral competition would increase the probability of a vote-buying candidate's win in a small electorate while it might decrease the probability of vote buying in a large electorate. In other words, it would be pre-electoral consensus that might prevent a vote-buying candidate from winning in a small electorate, while it would be electoral competition that might prevent a vote-buying candidate from winning in a large electorate. Thus, electoral contestation at the grassroots level would not be threatening to the authoritarian regime because it would only lead to competition over the provision of private goods or help villagers elect a competent leader who has an ability and intention to provide public goods. Neither electoral competition over the provision of private goods nor consensual elections for a competent candidate would lead to organizations becoming a threat to the CCP.

The democratic institutional mechanism of elections was promoted by the CCP at the rural grassroots level, but not at higher levels, for two decades. Given the model's equilibrium outcome that electoral competition might decrease the probability of vote buying in an election in a large electorate, one might infer that candidates must compete through organizations and campaign promises to provide public goods. Once candidates have a strong incentive to appeal to larger constituencies, they might form political organizations to mobilize votes. The emergence of party-like political organizations competing with the CCP would be the biggest threat for the survival of China's authoritarian regime. This is arguably the main reason China's authoritarian regime has hesitated to introduce elections to higher levels.

Interestingly, some experiments of electing the chief of a higher local government, especially at the township level, have already been carried out, and in those elections candidates indeed formed organizations they called "think tanks" or "campaign teams" to mobilize votes (L. Li 2002, 715). However, after one or two elections had been held in several places, township elections did not spread beyond these scattered experiments. By contrast, the attempts to allow non-CCP villagers to participate in the election for the post of party secretary, called the two-ballot system, spread widely across the whole nation (Li 1999; Liu 2004, chapter 5). In Sichuan and Liaoning Provinces, the provincial government has even institutionalized the two-ballot system by issuing official documents (Jing 2004, 88–90). Thus, there is apparently a pattern of the two-ballot system at the village level spreading more widely than elections at the township level. In this sense, the model's equilibrium outcome that electoral competition in a larger electorate might decrease the probability of vote buying suggests the logic to account for why the CCP leadership has hesitated to institutionalize elections at higher levels. Village elections only matter a little and do not alter state power because they occur at the village level. Village elections do not change the state power of the township government – the lowest *official* government. However, the introduction of township elections would have different effects. It might threaten the regime's authority and dominance of state power.

Because elections at levels higher than villages have not been institutionalized in China, the model's implication for what would happen if elections are introduced at township levels or higher is more suggestive than conclusive. We cannot examine empirically whether electoral competition at higher levels of government would increase the provision of public goods and make local officials more responsive to popular preferences. Nor can we examine empirically whether candidates in an election at higher levels would be less likely to buy votes and more likely to campaign for their policy proposals. Although we cannot give a conclusive answer to these questions, the model's implication counters what the CCP leadership and officials often claim about the functions of village elections.

The CCP leadership and officials have claimed that the main objective of introducing village elections is to get local leaders to provide public goods. If local governments fail to provide public goods to villagers in rural areas, it would be a crisis for the regime. I agree that the regime ceteris paribus has strong interests in having effective local leadership, with local governments providing public goods and being responsive to popular preferences. However, if the regime's main objective for introducing elections is getting officials to be responsive and provide public goods, why has the regime not introduced elections to higher levels of government? Because of a series of rural tax reforms that began in 2000, lower-level local governments faced fiscal crises and the capacity of grassroots governments to provide public goods declined. Thus, if the main objective of introducing elections was to make the government accountable in providing public goods to villagers, then the regime would have been actively introducing elections to higher levels of local government and spreading township and county elections as well. In reality, the regime was more active in introducing an electoral institution for non-CCP villagers to participate in electing CCP cadres at the village level by the two-ballot system than in spreading the experiment of popularly electing non-CCP cadres (such as township chief) at the township and county levels. Therefore, we can speculate that the reason the regime has hesitated to institutionalize elections at higher levels would be that elections with large electorates would lead to the formation of party-like organizations, which might threaten the survival of the authoritarian regime.

In this chapter, I argue that competitive grassroots elections might encourage electoral corruption because of the small electorate size, unless voters reach a pre-electoral consensus on whom to vote for. I do not argue that corruption is not a serious threat to regime survival. Corruption is one of the most critical issues that China's authoritarian regime is facing in the reform era. Moreover, the CCP leaders have acknowledged the adverse consequences of corruption for the legitimacy of the regime and consider corruption the most serious threat to its survival. The public has also suffered from the effects of corruption, such as the breakdown of political accountability and the distortion of incentives, and the regime has feared that popular dissatisfaction with corrupt officials could become a source of political instability (e.g., Lü 2000b; Manion 2004; Y. Sun 2004; Yang 2004). Furthermore, survey research shows that villagers considered corruption when voting in grassroots elections. Villagers were aware of the quality of elections, including both their processes and outcomes, in their villages and took this into consideration in their responses to surveys when they evaluated rural governance and their village's political leadership (e.g., Chen 2005b; Kennedy 2002b; L. Li 2003; Manion 1996, 2006).

Finally, I should note that my argument developed here is based on the assumption that the CCP would lose control over electoral outcomes once elections are held at higher levels. With other things being equal, increasing the size of the electorate would decrease incentives for competition through vote buying, and instead candidates would have to compete through organization and campaign promises to provide public goods. Competition by candidates through actions that would challenge the authoritarian regime's organizational monopoly on politics would be immensely threatening. In various examples of this from the China Democracy Party to the Falungong, the CCP immediately suppressed such actions, and their organizers and members were severely punished (Tong 2009; Wright 2002). The model suggests that electoral competition in larger electoral districts (which would occur if elections were introduced to higher levels of government) would face an institutional logic of competition through campaigning, organization, and the provision of public goods, which the CCP would find threatening to regime survival.

However, if the CCP is able to intervene in electoral processes and outcomes in some way, such as by influencing who runs for elections or vetoing elected candidates, it might not find those elections at higher levels so threatening. For example, Melanie Manion (2008) finds that the CCP improved the quality of candidates for local people's congresses, and prevented large-scale losses of CCP candidates, when new regulations and laws allowed CCP candidates to lose elections for local people's congress delegates.[23] If elections are held at higher levels, then the CCP would make every effort to have CCP candidates win the elections. However, it is more costly to introduce leadership elections in higher-level governments and make the effort to ensure victory for CCP candidates than to resist the introduction of elections at higher levels altogether.

CONCLUSION

Much of the literature examining China's village elections has evaluated whether and how elections make governments more accountable and responsive to public interests, such as through the provision of public goods (e.g., L. Tsai 2007a). Many of the empirical studies have positively evaluated elections that are so competitive that no one could predict the winner (e.g., Kennedy 2002a). However, the argument in this chapter brings a different perspective to the evaluations of village elections. It suggests that competition is not a good criterion for evaluating the quality of elections if one believes that successful elections make elected cadres serve the whole electorate by providing public

[23] Delegates of Chinese local people's congresses play limited roles in decision making compared with officials in the local government. Thus, one reason the CCP introduced contested elections for delegates of local people's congresses is that the influence of elected delegates would be less than that of the local government's officials.

goods. The game's equilibrium outcomes show that electoral competition in a grassroots election would lead to competition over the provision of private goods, which would not threaten the survival of the authoritarian regime.

In this chapter, I have shown the great difficulty of institutionalizing a state-directed political economy of public goods. The institutionalization of village elections created a virtuous circle in industrialized villages, but created a vicious circle in agricultural villages. This bifurcation of the implications of village elections corresponds with the optimistic and pessimistic views of village elections. The optimistic views suggest that village elections support elected cadres' legitimacy and strengthen the state's authority and capacity. Meanwhile, the pessimistic views suggest that village elections are not useful for villagers to vote incompetent, and often corrupt, candidates out of office. In a sense, the argument presented in this chapter sits in between these optimistic and pessimistic views, although it is closer to the pessimistic ones.

The optimistic scenarios were often observed in the villages with competent leaders. In this kind of village, villagers could easily reach a consensus on who should be elected; the contested elections were not competitive but consensual; the electoral institution gave political legitimacy to the elected cadres; public goods were provided; and villagers were satisfied with the electoral process and result. In other words, in this kind of village, the state collected levies and used them for providing public goods, and the electoral institution helped strengthen the state's authority and capacity by legitimizing elected cadres. In contrast, the pessimistic scenarios were often observed in the villages without competent leaders. In this kind of village, it was difficult for villagers to reach a consensus on who should be elected; the contested elections were not consensual but competitive; the electoral institution gave candidates a strong incentive to compete by distributing scarce economic resources to their favorite groups; competition for providing private goods occurred; and villagers were dissatisfied with the electoral process and result. In other words, in this kind of village, the state did not do anything other than collect levies and the electoral institution did not make the state use the levies for providing public goods.

APPENDIX 7A: FORMAL DESCRIPTION AND SOLUTION TO THE VILLAGE ELECTION GAME

The Candidate's Choice of Strategies and Payoffs

The matrix in Figure A7.1 shows the incentives affecting a candidate in a village election. The utility the candidate would gain from winning the election is denoted W ($W > 0$). Each candidate has two strategies: buying votes (BV) and not buying votes (NBV). The cost of buying votes (C) is the multiplication of the cost to buy one vote (β) and the number of votes needed to buy (V) (i.e., $C = \beta V$). Moreover, the number of votes needed to buy is positively associated with how much the candidate is behind the other candidate (ρ) and the size

		Candidate 2: Buying votes (*BV*)	Candidate 2: Not buying votes (*NBV*)
Candidate 1	Buying votes (*BV*)	Candidate 2: $(1-p)W - C_2$; Candidate 1: $pW - C_1$	Candidate 2: 0; Candidate 1: $W - C_1$
	Not buying votes (*NBV*)	Candidate 2: $W - C_2$; Candidate 1: 0	Candidate 2: $(1-p)W$; Candidate 1: pW

FIGURE A7.1. Payoffs in Village Elections. *Note:* W = the candidate's utility gained by winning the election. C_i = Candidate *i*'s utility lost by buying votes. p = the probability that Candidate 1 wins the election when both candidates take the same strategy. $C_1 = \beta(A+\varphi(1-p))E$ and $C_2 = \beta(A+\varphi p)E$: β = the cost to buy one vote; E = the size of the electorate; φ and A are positive constant numbers.

of the electorate (E) (i.e., $V = \rho E$). Therefore, the cost of buying votes can be written $C = \beta\rho E$.

How much Candidate 1 is behind Candidate 2 is positively associated with $1-p$ while how much Candidate 2 is behind Candidate 1 is positively associated with p (i.e., $\rho_1 = A+\varphi(1-p)$ and $\rho_2 = A+\varphi p$) ($A > 0$ and $\varphi > 0$). Thus, Candidate 1's and Candidate 2's costs of buying votes could be written respectively, $C_1 = \beta(A+\varphi(1-p))E$ and $C_2 = \beta(A+\varphi p)E$. In this model, rather than having players choose the number of votes to buy (or the amount of money to be spent on vote buying), the cost of buying votes (C) is folded into a specific function, $C = \beta\rho E$: where β is the cost to buy one vote; E is the size of the electorate; and ρ is how much the candidate is behind the other candidate, which is hence inversely related to p.

Solution to the Model

This analysis only examines the case of $0 < p \leq 0.5$. In the following section, I write outcomes using the notation: (Candidate 1's strategy, Candidate 2's strategy). Figure A7.2 describes the equilibrium strategies of the two candidates as a set of thresholds along the continuum of possible circumstances.

Equilibrium 1: (BV, BV) will be a pure strategy Nash equilibrium (PSNE) if $pW - \beta(A+\varphi(1-p))E \geq 0$ and $(1-p)W - \beta(A+\varphi p)E \geq 0$. Thus, this PSNE will be sustained if $W \geq \frac{\beta(A+\varphi(1-p))E}{p}$ and $W \geq \frac{\beta(A+\varphi p)E}{1-p}$. Because $\frac{\beta(A+\varphi(1-p))E}{p} \geq \frac{\beta(A+\varphi p)E}{1-p}$ as long as $p \leq 0.5$, (BV, BV) will be a PSNE if $W \geq \frac{\beta(A+\varphi(1-p))E}{p}$.

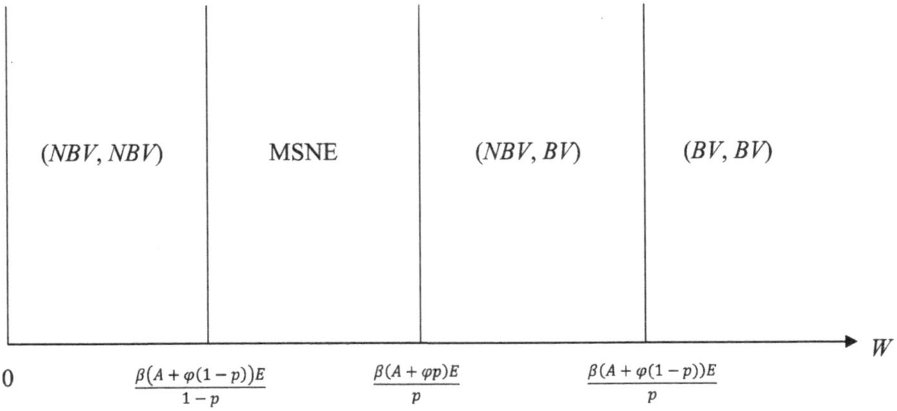

FIGURE A7.2. The Equilibrium Strategies in the Game. *Note:* (*BV*, *BV*) = both candidates buy votes. (*NBV*, *NBV*) = neither candidate buys votes. (*NBV*, *BV*) = Candidate 1 does not buy votes and Candidate 2 buys votes. MSNE = each candidate buys votes with a certain probability.

Equilibrium 2: (*NBV*, *NBV*) will be a PSNE if $pW \geq W - \beta(A+\varphi(1-p))E$ and $(1-p)W \geq W - \beta(A+\varphi p)E$. Thus, this PSNE will be sustained if $W \leq \frac{\beta(A+\varphi(1-p))E}{1-p}$ and $W \leq \frac{\beta(A+\varphi p)E}{p}$. Because $\frac{\beta(A+\varphi p)E}{p} \geq \frac{\beta(A+\varphi(1-p))E}{1-p}$, (*NBV*, *NBV*) will be a PSNE if $W \leq \frac{\beta(A+\varphi(1-p))E}{1-p}$.

Equilibrium 3: (*NBV*, *BV*) will be a PSNE if $0 \geq pW - \beta(A+\varphi(1-p))E$ and $W - \beta(A+\varphi p)E \geq (1-p)W$. Thus, this PSNE will be sustained if $W \leq \frac{\beta(A+\varphi(1-p))E}{p}$ and $W \geq \frac{\beta(A+\varphi p)E}{p}$. Because $\frac{\beta(A+\varphi(1-p))E}{p} \geq \frac{\beta(A+\varphi p)E}{p}$, (*NBV*, *BV*) will be a PSNE if $\frac{\beta(A+\varphi(1-p))E}{p} \geq W \geq \frac{\beta(A+\varphi p)E}{p}$.

Equilibrium 4: No PSNE will exist but a mixed strategy Nash equilibrium (MSNE) will exist if $\frac{\beta(A+\varphi p)E}{p} \geq W \geq \frac{\beta(A+\varphi(1-p))E}{1-p}$. At the MSNE: Candidate 1 will take *BV* with the probability of $\frac{\beta(A+\varphi p)E-pW}{(1-2p)W}$, and *NBV* with $\frac{(1-p)W-\beta(A+\varphi p)E}{(1-2p)W}$; and Candidate 2 will take *BV* with the probability of $\frac{(1-p)W-\beta(A+\varphi(1-p))E}{(1-2p)W}$, and *NBV* with $\frac{\beta(A+\varphi(1-p))E-pW}{(1-2p)W}$. Thus, at the MSNE, (*BV*, *BV*) will occur with the probability of $\frac{(\beta(A+\varphi p)E-pW)((1-p)W-\beta(A+\varphi(1-p))E)}{(1-2p)^2w^2}$, (*NBV*, *NBV*) with $\frac{((1-p)W-\beta(A+\varphi p)E)(\beta(A+\varphi(1-p))E-pW)}{(1-2p)^2w^2}$, (*BV*, *NBV*) with $\frac{(\beta(A+\varphi p)E-pW)(\beta(A+\varphi(1-p))E-pW)}{(1-2p)^2w^2}$, and (*NBV*, *BV*) with $\frac{((1-p)W-\beta(A+\varphi p)E)((1-p)W-\beta(A+\varphi(1-p))E)}{(1-2p)^2w^2}$.

Competition in Grassroots Election

If $W \leq \frac{\beta(A+\varphi(1-p))E}{1-p}$, then (*NBV*, *NBV*) is a PSNE, and hence the probability of a vote-buying candidate's win is zero. If

$\frac{\beta(A+\varphi(1-p))E}{1-p} \leq W \leq \frac{\beta(A+\varphi p)E}{p}$, then at the MSNE the probability of a vote-buying candidate's win is $1 - \frac{(\beta(A+\varphi p)E-pW)((1-p)W-\beta(A+\varphi(1-p))E)}{(1-2p)^2w^2}$; $\frac{\partial}{\partial W}\left(1 - \frac{(\beta(A+\varphi p)E-pW)((1-p)W-\beta(A+\varphi(1-p))E)}{(1-2p)^2w^2}\right) < 0$ if $W < \frac{2\beta(A+\varphi(1-p))(A+\varphi p)E}{(1-p)(A+\varphi(1-p))+p(A+\varphi p)}$; $\frac{\partial}{\partial W}\left(1 - \frac{(\beta(A+\varphi p)E-pW)((1-p)W-\beta(A+\varphi(1-p))E)}{(1-2p)^2w^2}\right) > 0$ if $W > \frac{2\beta(A+\varphi(1-p))(A+\varphi p)E}{(1-p)(A+\varphi(1-p))+p(A+\varphi p)}$; and $\frac{\partial}{\partial W}\left(1 - \frac{(\beta(A+\varphi p)E-pW)((1-p)W-\beta(A+\varphi(1-p))E)}{(1-2p)^2w^2}\right) = 0$ if $W = \frac{2\beta(A+\varphi(1-p))(A+\varphi p)E}{(1-p)(A+\varphi(1-p))+p(A+\varphi p)}$, with which the probability of a vote-buying candidate's win is at a local minimum. If $\frac{\beta(A+\varphi p)E}{p} \leq W \leq \frac{\beta(A+\varphi(1-p))E}{p}$, then (*NBV*, *BV*) is a PSNE, and hence the probability of a vote-buying candidate's win is one. If $W \geq \frac{\beta(A+\varphi(1-p))E}{p}$, then (*BV*, *BV*) is a PSNE, and hence the probability of a vote-buying candidate's win is one.

The Size of the Electorate

If $E \leq \frac{pW}{\beta(A+\varphi(1-p))}$, then (*BV*, *BV*) is a PSNE, and hence the probability of a vote-buying candidate's win is one. If $\frac{pW}{\beta(A+\varphi(1-p))} \leq E \leq \frac{pW}{\beta(A+\varphi p)}$, then (*NBV*, *BV*) is a PSNE, and hence the probability of a corrupt candidate's win is one. If $\frac{pW}{\beta(A+\varphi p)} \leq E \leq \frac{(1-p)W}{\beta(A+\varphi(1-p))}$, then at the MSNE the probability of a vote-buying candidate's win is $1 - \frac{(\beta(A+\varphi p)E-pW)((1-p)W-\beta(A+\varphi(1-p))E)}{(1-2p)^2w^2}$; $\frac{\partial}{\partial W}\left(1 - \frac{(\beta(A+\varphi p)E-pW)((1-p)W-\beta(A+\varphi(1-p))E)}{(1-2p)^2w^2}\right) < 0$ if $E < \frac{\beta(A+\varphi p)pW+\beta(A+\varphi(1-p))(1-p)W}{2\beta^2(A+\varphi p)(A+\varphi(1-p))}$; $\frac{\partial}{\partial W}\left(1 - \frac{(\beta(A+\varphi p)E-pW)((1-p)W-\beta(A+\varphi(1-p))E)}{(1-2p)^2w^2}\right) > 0$ if $E > \frac{\beta(A+\varphi p)pW+\beta(A+\varphi(1-p))(1-p)W}{2\beta^2(A+\varphi p)(A+\varphi(1-p))}$; and $\frac{\partial}{\partial W}\left(1 - \frac{(\beta(A+\varphi p)E-pW)((1-p)W-\beta(A+\varphi(1-p))E)}{(1-2p)^2w^2}\right) = 0$ if $E = \frac{\beta(A+\varphi p)pW+\beta(A+\varphi(1-p))(1-p)W}{2\beta^2(A+\varphi p)(A+\varphi(1-p))}$, with which the probability of a vote-buying candidate's win is at a local minimum. If $E \geq \frac{(1-p)W}{\beta(A+\varphi(1-p))}$, then (*NBV*, *NBV*) is a PSNE, and hence the probability of a vote-buying candidate's win is zero.

Conclusion

SUMMARY OF THE FINDINGS

This book's argument relates to the debates about how authoritarian rulers sustain their regimes. The findings suggest that the Chinese Communist Party (CCP) has placed its own survival ahead of any other problems, such as local fiscal health. To Beijing, local fiscal crises and a lack of public goods were taken less seriously than rural protest caused by heavy financial burdens in rural areas during the 1990s. This survival strategy was possible because the central government, and its strategic agents, controls the personnel system in authoritarian regimes.

To make this argument, I have sought to address the following questions: (1) how China's political institutions and regime affected the quality of rural governance through its system of political participation, taxation, and public goods provision; (2) how the central and local governments implemented and enforced rural reform policies; and ultimately (3) who benefited from and who was harmed by reforms, and how. To answer these questions, I have examined the ways in which, and the extent to which, popular political participation was significant for the central government's implementation of reforms and the local governments' reaction to the reforms. What modes of action, if any, were available to ordinary people in China? Under what circumstances did villagers use those modes of political action – though often ineffective and inefficient – to bring their demands to the regime? What factors constrained and conditioned their choice of strategies and tactics?

As I suggested in Chapters 2 and 3, one of the key differences between post-Mao reform era China and the Maoist history is that villagers are now able to move out of their villages. This change took place without democratization. Because the massive flow of rural migrants to urban areas was a crucial source of cheap labor and an important stimulus for the nation's rapid industrialization and economic growth, Beijing's rulers had to relax migration policies. Apparently, the political ease of outbound migration influenced rural governance under authoritarian rule. In a sense, the increased possibility of outbound migration gave villagers greater bargaining powers with their local governments, making it difficult for the latter to collect taxes and fees. However, in the poorest areas, local officials reacted to the problem by hiring gangsters to coercively and violently collect levies from those who remained in the village. Thus, although villagers had initially gained bargaining power to resist local cadres, many were still vulnerable to caprice and coercion.

The relaxation of migration policies was necessary to pursue the post-Mao market-oriented economic reform, so China's authoritarian regime sought to establish a legitimate tax system within the constraint of the increasing possibility of villagers' outbound migration – and without extending the popular franchise. However, the central government directed rural tax reforms, including the abolishment of the agricultural tax, which left the authoritarian regime without a legitimate tax system in agricultural areas. Thus, this Chinese experience suggests the difficulty that authoritarian rulers face when pursuing market-oriented economic reform and development while maintaining non-democratic regimes.

Chapters 4–6 shed light on why China's authoritarian regime failed to establish legitimate taxation in rural areas. When the ruling CCP faced the choice between establishing efficient taxation with an extension of the popular franchise on the one hand and giving up the attempt to establish efficient taxation while remaining committed to the authoritarian regime on the other hand, it chose the latter. When the central government began implementing rural tax reforms in 2000, it might have recognized that the tax reforms would worsen rural governance in poor areas by depriving local governments of funds needed for public goods and services. However, from the regime's perspective, local fiscal crises and a lack of public goods in agricultural areas were less serious problems than the heavy financial burden and the rural unrest that the local cadres' increasingly predatory extractive behavior had generated in the 1990s. This burden and unrest threatened the ruling party's commitment to market-oriented economic reform, authoritarian rule, and, most importantly, its own survival. In the meantime, local fiscal crises would not threaten authoritarian rule as long as the central government retained authority over the personnel system of local officials.

Moreover, by *appearing* to side with villagers against the predatory agents of the local governments, the central government managed to rechannel the blame for bad governance to local officials – thereby bolstering its image and credibility. Appointed by superiors, local officials had few avenues to articulate their grievances when harmed by the central government's reform policies. The personnel system in which local cadres are not popularly elected but appointed by higher authorities, however, created an institutional incentive for local officials to shirk and disguise accurate information about their locality. Therefore, although the central government succeeded in strengthening its authority, it failed to grasp the reality of local governance in rural areas. However, compared with protest against rural levies, this problem apparently was not a serious threat for regime survival.

With the help of a game-theoretic model, and a series of comparative-static exercises with the simple model, I examine how nationally implemented reform policies influenced the relationship between villagers and local governments depending on preexisting local economic conditions. Evidently, the increased possibility of outbound migration gave villagers substantial bargaining power against their local government in industrialized villages but failed to do the same for villagers in agricultural villages. In the latter, eased outbound migration would strengthen the villagers' bargaining power vis-à-vis their local government up to a point, after which the local government would stop appeasing the villagers and would halt the increase in public goods, triggering popular unrest. Moreover, industrialized villages, benefiting from renewed infrastructure that came with the flow of public goods, would get richer, while agricultural villages would stay poor, locked in the vicious circle of a lack of public goods and poverty. Thus, villagers in richer industrialized villages would be able to find jobs *inside* the village; and local officials would attempt to keep these workers in the village because they would pay taxes as long as they worked in the village. In short, ironically, the local officials would seem less predatory in richer villages even though they had more to exploit. Therefore, they would view their relationship with villagers as a long-term relationship, which would make them think twice about killing the "golden goose of reform," so to speak.

The petition system would not help improve the responsiveness and accountability of local officials in agricultural areas because of its semi-institutionalized nature. Here taxes and fees became a source of contention between villagers and local governments. The central government designed and operated this remonstrative institution to maximize control of local officials, so that the institution could help the central government pursue its strategy of strengthening its regime. However, in the poor areas this came at the cost of the local government's authority and ability to govern rural areas.

The comparative-static analysis showed that the petition system would more or less give local officials an incentive to provide public goods in rich areas but not in poor areas, where villagers would go outside the system to protest against the local government. Believing that being demoted is more costly, local officials in advanced villages would be fearful of potential petitions and hence would more often compromise with villagers' demands. By contrast, in agricultural villages, where local officials had less to lose, the petition system could have little impact on the provision of public goods. Ironically, villagers were more likely to use rioting if local officials perceived petitions as a sign of social instability rather than as legitimate political participation. In other words, local officials' fear of social instability would make villagers' rioting more likely and make officials less responsive to popular preferences. In short, it seems that the petition system did not help improve rural governance. Instead, it helped the central government rechannel the blame for bad governance on local governments and it strengthened the authoritarian regime *at the top* – in the short run.

Village elections, another democratic mechanism introduced by Beijing in rural China during the post-Mao period, allowed villagers to elect cadres, at least in theory. Despite the official requirement that elections were to be contested, however, many of the elections examined in this book were consensual – voters had reached a pre-electoral consensus on which candidates to elect. The village cadres elected by a consensual election were more likely to be committed to the provision of public goods and voters were more likely to be satisfied with their representatives. In the meantime, in the villages where voters had failed to reach a pre-electoral consensus, elections were more likely to be competitive and corrupt. This is counterintuitive because electoral competition is usually considered to bring positive effects, such as good governance, to electoral outcomes.

The different patterns of electoral results were partly dependent on the roles played by the political, economic, and social elites in the village. When a village has elites with the ability and intention to provide public goods, the village tends to have a consensual election and public goods tend to be provided. In this sense, the electoral institution itself does not hold village cadres accountable for providing public goods. The personal qualities of cadres prove to be a crucial factor in determining whether public goods are provided in the village. So it seems that the institution of village elections does not have a decisive effect on rural governance, but it does have a positive effect in that it sometimes enables villagers to reach pre-electoral consensus on competent leadership. Because rich industrialized villages are more likely to have these elites, village elections, much like the petition system, are of little use in delivering public goods to poor agricultural villages. Most importantly, as long as elections remain elite-based, the CCP by and large would not need to worry that the electoral process would create a party-like organization and become a threat to one-party rule.

Using a simple game-theoretic model, I suggest a logic that might account for why electoral competition would give strong incentives for candidates to buy votes, rather than to campaign for votes, in village elections in rural China. At equilibrium, electoral competition would increase the probability of vote buying in a small electorate while it might decrease the probability of vote buying in a large electorate. Electoral competition might exacerbate vote buying in a small electorate because providing private goods would be less costly in an electorate that is smaller. However, an election would be clean in a small electorate if voters reach a pre-electoral consensus on whom to vote, which makes the election not competitive but consensual. By contrast, providing private goods would be more costly if the electorate is larger. Electoral competition might reduce vote buying in a large electorate because candidates would have a strong incentive to campaign on the basis of their policy proposals in order to appeal to larger constituencies. In other words, electoral competition would make candidates accountable to voters through campaigning if the electorate is large. China's authoritarian regime is concerned with the possible emergence of party-like organizations through policy-based campaigning in a large electorate, and this is arguably the reason the regime hesitates to fully introduce an electoral institution at levels higher than villages.

IMPLICATIONS FOR CENTRAL-LOCAL RELATIONS

I have argued that the central government succeeded in strengthening its authority while it failed to grasp the reality of local governance in rural areas. At the same time, however, I have argued that the rural tax reforms that began in 2000 were a conscious trade-off by the central government between fiscal crises and rural instability. For the central leaders, local fiscal crises and public goods deficiencies in rural areas, which occurred as a consequence of the rural tax reforms, were less serious problems than the heavy financial burden and the rural unrest that local cadres' increasingly predatory extractive behavior generated in the 1990s. Thus, it appears that the central government politicians aligned their policy preferences with their interest in regime survival.

Likewise, the rural tax reforms beginning in 2000 were aimed to ensure regime survival. Local officials' behavior in the 1990s was a serious threat to the central government because it led to rural unrest. The central government realized that taxes and fees were a source of popular dissatisfaction, and hence it eliminated the source of this dissatisfaction. To be sure, fiscal crises were exacerbated as a result of these post-2000 rural tax reforms, and the provision of public goods in agricultural areas was not improved, if not worsened. However, tax-based rural uprisings stopped, and, unlike tax resistance riots, local fiscal crises were not a serious threat, at least not an immediate one, to the regime's survival. In short, the regime gave priority to a short-term threat over a long-term threat, and this was perhaps myopic if it was rational.

If the decision was based on myopic rationality, what would be the long-term effect of the rural tax reforms? Moreover, what alternative choice set did the regime have when it decided on the rural tax reforms that ended with the complete abolition of agriculture-related levies? My answer to these questions is that the central government had an alternative choice to the policies implemented through the rural tax reforms, but that the alternative choice contradicted the most important goal: maintaining the authoritarian regime. To conclude this book, I discuss this issue highlighting state-society-market relations in rural China.

IMPLICATIONS FOR LOCAL STATE-SOCIETY-MARKET RELATIONS

The framework of local state-society-market relations is useful for exploring rural governance in post-Mao China. The state and the market have become intertwined at the grassroots level. Property rights institutions, presumably the most fundamental mechanism for the market to work, have been defined by local governments in rural China. In the meantime, the legitimacy of the authoritarian regime is linked to economic development. Local economic development is one of the most important criteria for personnel evaluations of local officials in China and in many other authoritarian regimes.

State-market relations also have a sociological nature. First, people's ability to build trust based on their daily interactions is crucial for property rights institutions and the market mechanism to work. In other words, the state's effort to establish property rights institutions cannot be independent of social networks at the grassroots level (e.g., Oi and Walder 1999). Second, financial institutions cannot work without social networks in the rural community. Because villagers – both farmers and rural entrepreneurs – have had poor access to borrowing from formal lenders, informal lenders have played an important role in rural finance (e.g., Huang 2008; Tsai 2002; Zhou and Takeuchi 2010). Third, a sociological influence has been increasingly evident in policy implementations by local governments. Ironically, given that the central government's authority was strengthened by the 1994 fiscal reform, and was further strengthened by the recent rural tax reforms, local officials have increasingly relied on informal personal ties to overcome pressure from higher authorities (e.g., Zhou 2010).

Since Jean Oi (1992, 1995) introduced the concept of "local state," scholars studying state-society relations in China have disaggregated the concept of the state into the central state and various levels of local states.[1] Among this work, one body of literature has reflected optimistic views of the local state-society-market mixture in rural China. For example, Chinese political scientist Pan Wei (2003) argues that local states not only promoted the development of rural industry by growing township-and-village enterprises (TVEs), but also protected villagers' interests by alleviating the intense competition of a market economy. A different body of work, however, reflects a rather pessimistic view. For example, Minxin Pei (2006) contends that local states colluded with local gangsters and cadres who personalized their official status; hence, local states did not protect the public interest but protected the gangster-related groups' personal interests by sacrificing the interests of the majority of the whole local society.

For the most part, the theoretical argument and empirical findings in this book follow the pessimistic view of Pei (2006) and others, who have argued that severe structural imbalances accumulated in Chinese society and contributed to destabilizing social division in post-Mao China. Resonating with Pei's argument that local states were predatory and colluded with gangsters against the public interest, Sun Liping (2004), a prominent sociologist in China, claims

[1] For reviews of analyses on China's state-society relations disaggregating the concept of the state into central and local, see the works by Richard Baum and Alexei Shevchenko (1999), Kevin O'Brien (2010), Elizabeth Perry (1994), and Elizabeth Remick (2002).

that local elites were detached from the grassroots community and the public interest in agricultural areas, and as a result rural society and the agricultural economy were left behind in the development of the market economy during the post-Mao reform. At the same time, the argument in this book is also consistent with more optimistic arguments about how local states protected and promoted TVEs, set and achieved developmental plans, created unique forms of workable de facto property rights, and managed illegal or quasi-illegal but efficient informal financial institutions (e.g., Oi 1999; Oi and Walder 1999; Pan 2003; Tsai 2002; Walder 1995; Whiting 2001; Zhang 2009). From the optimistic viewpoint, local states not only bridged the gap between villagers' and the central government's interests but also mediated villagers' interests and the market economic system.

Whether the village reflects the optimistic view of local state-society-market relations or the pessimistic view depends in part on the level of rural industrialization in the locality. Although rural tax reforms and other policies for market-oriented reforms were introduced universally in China, their implementation and effects on rural governance varied from area to area. In areas with rural industry, the introduction and implementation of reform policies went more smoothly with fewer serious disruptions; by and large, these local governments had sufficient revenue to cover administrative costs and provide public goods. The provision of public goods, in turn, led to further prosperity of the local economy. Thus, in these well-endowed areas it was rare to witness signs that reforms went awry. By contrast, in areas without rural industry, the introduction and implementation of reform policies unleashed a vicious circle. Local governments lost revenue sources, struggled to cover administrative costs, and were unable to provide public goods. The lack of public goods kept the local economy underdeveloped and in stagnation. More importantly, local governments also lost the authority to govern their localities as villagers blamed *local* governments for the lack of public goods and the declining quality of rural governance.

The theoretical argument and empirical findings in this book are all probabilistic rather than deterministic. The tendency for the rural tax reforms to raise the quality of governance in originally well-endowed, well-run industrialized villages but to lower the quality of governance in badly governed, poor agricultural villages does not mean that rural governance was never improved in agricultural areas or that villages were always well governed in industrialized areas. Moreover, while institutional influences matter in post-Mao governance, none of the arguments in this book dispute that personal elements matter. The importance of local leaders' personal characteristics (i.e., intention and ability) also counts in explaining variations in the quality of local governance. For example, Highland Park Village of Zhejiang Province started to industrialize rapidly after village elections produced a significant change in village leadership. Personal qualities conducive to good governance were the decisive factor in determining whether or not public goods were provided and, more generally, whether good rural governance was achieved. To some extent, therefore, democratic institutions introduced in and by the CCP strengthened the institution-based rule of the authoritarian regime without making the regime accountable to ordinary people. It is important to be cautious here, however, because the evidence suggests that institutional democracy, CCP style, was grafted on a tradition of the "rule of personality" (*renzhi*).

Throughout this book, I have highlighted the negative circumstances of rural tax reforms in contemporary China and the limits of reforms that are subject to an authoritarian regime trying to stay in power. However, I do not mean that the tax reforms and other political and economic reforms in rural China failed. Instead I have shown that my argument is not inconsistent with good governance in some areas of the Chinese countryside. Good governance (i.e., the provision of public goods) was achieved in areas that had favorable conditions for economic development, and, in some cases such favorable conditions might be traced back to the commune and brigade enterprises (*shedui qiye*) that were most favored, and subsidized, by the state during the Maoist era (Pan 2003). In other words, the rich got richer, the poor were left to be poor and to struggle on their own without much state help, after Mao, and so the heritage of socialist development did not serve the poor well under reform.

During the post-Mao era, good governance was achieved in the areas that had capable rural elites with the intention and ability to provide public goods. If local talent appeared in the area, there would be an opportunity for industrialization and development. However, in the areas with a lack of economic or personal foundations, the political and economic institutions and reforms introduced through the post-Mao reforms did not improve the local conditions but rather made them worse. Moreover, even in the areas with local talent, positive roles of the capable rural elites might be crippled by the central government. For example, as Bruce Gilley (2001) describes, Mr. Yu Zuomin in Daqiu Village eventually fell from power, even though he had turned his village into one of the richest villages in China in the 1980s and early 1990s. Once his governance had created tension with the central government, Beijing eventually sent paramilitary police to arrest Mr. Yu and other village leaders.

Then, how serious is the pessimistic view of rural China? A rural crisis is a serious problem for the regime. In this book, I have argued that the CCP's goal of maintaining the authoritarian regime limited the choice set from which the ruling party selected when it implemented tax reforms. Margaret Levi (1988), other political economists, and economic historians have argued that relying on the repressive apparatus to collect taxes is inefficient, and that it is even more inefficient if taxpayers can leave the locality. China's experience with rural taxation confirms Levi's argument. It suggests that once outbound migration was allowed, repressive tax collection became so costly that the ruling party could not establish an efficient tax system in agricultural villages. It is very difficult to collect taxes in agricultural villages once villagers migrate outside of their villages. Political economists and economic historians have suggested that making tax collectors accountable to taxpayers helps collect taxes efficiently, especially when taxpayers are able to move out of the locality (e.g., Hirschman 1970; Hoffman and Norberg 1994b; Levi 1988; Tiebout 1956; Wong 1997). Moreover, the democratic institutions introduced in rural China did not make local officials (tax collectors) accountable to villagers (taxpayers). We saw in Chapter 6 that at equilibrium, the petition system would not give local officials strong incentives to be responsive to popular preferences as long as villagers' submissions of petitions are perceived as a failure of local governance. Although the petition system would not help make local officials accountable to villagers in agricultural areas, it would help make local officials comply with the central government, and hence it would help strengthen the authoritarian regime. We saw in Chapter 7 that at equilibrium, electoral competition would not make candidates accountable to voters in a small electorate, while it would make candidates accountable to voters in a large electorate. Because voters and candidates know each other in person and they have perfect information about each other's demands and preferences, the introduction of an election would not make candidates organize their electoral campaigns. Thus, the regime would not have to worry about the emergence of a potential rival to the CCP – such as a party-like organization – through an election as long as elections are held at the village level.

The equilibrium outcomes shown in this book are not inconsistent with the findings of recent literature on authoritarian politics. By designing democratic institutions to serve the interest of regime survival, China's central government has bought themselves time, and limited popularity. Neither petitions nor village elections are representative institutions that might threaten the ruling party's organizational monopoly. Both have helped strengthen the central government's ability to monitor local governments, to blame bad rural governance on local officials, and to strengthen the central government's legitimacy and the regime's popularity.

When the regime designed rural taxation, it faced a dilemma. Local officials accountable to villagers would help the regime establish efficient taxation by inducing what Levi (1988) terms the taxpayers' quasi-voluntary compliance. However, representative institutions that would make local officials accountable to villagers would cause a threat to regime survival. If the locality has the potential for economic development, local officials would have a strong incentive for investing in public goods for the long-term benefits of development, and villagers could expect that officials would respond to popular preferences as they share the interest in local development. If taxpayers do not have a choice to exit, tax resistance would be costly and threaten their own survival – which in fact occurred during the Great Leap Famine in 1958–60. Although villagers are not able to fully migrate to urban areas under the household registration system, the restriction on rural-to-urban migration has been relaxed for the last three decades. Thus, the political institutions that might help China's authoritarian regime establish efficient taxation would cause a threat to regime survival. In other words, the dilemma that the authoritarian regime faced was the impossibility of making the triad of authoritarian rule, popular mobility, and efficient taxation mutually compatible at any one time. Because population mobility is necessary for market-oriented economic reforms to succeed, this argument could be restated: it is impossible to achieve authoritarian rule, a market economy, and efficient taxation all at once. In this sense, this point fits Pei's argument that "China's closed political system is increasingly becoming an anachronism" (Pei 2006, 206). As a result, the central government has created, and worsened, the problem of local governance. As Gilley's (2001) story about Daqiu Village suggests, the village leaders would be repressed if they created tension with the central government, even if they turned their village into a prosperous one. In other words, whether the central government appreciates or represses local leaders is not based on whether public goods are provided and they are serving villagers but is based on political loyalty to the central government.

The implication of this book's findings is that if the Chinese leadership wants to enjoy political stability in agricultural villages and maintain its authority as a ruling party in the long run, the answer lies not in blaming bad governance on local governments or undermining local authorities' popular legitimacy and administrative capacity, but in expanding true institutions of democratic accountability based on representative institutions. Without competent, empowered, and responsive local leaders, rural governance will continue to be the Achilles' heel of China's authoritarian political system.

APPENDIX

Empirical Sources and Methods

APPENDIX A: INFORMANTS

Guangdong (November 2004)

1. village chief, non-party member.
2. 58-year-old male villager, farmer, land renter.
3. 28-year-old female villager, not farming.

Guizhou (April 2005)

4. township party secretary.
5. 75-year-old male villager, farmer.
6. 73-year-old female villager, farmer.
7. 51-year-old male villager, farmer.
8. 35-year-old male villager, farmer, former village cadre.
9. 33-year-old female villager, farmer.
10. 61-year-old male villager, farmer.
11. 38-year-old male villager, farmer.

Hebei (Zhangjiakou Prefecture) (January 2005)

12. village party secretary.
13. village chief.
14. township official.
15. township official.
16. village party secretary, village chief.
17. township official.
18. township chief.
19. township official.
20. village party secretary, village chief.

21. village cadre.
22. township official.
23. township party secretary.
24. 68-year-old male villager, farmer, plaintiff in administrative litigation.
25. 60-year-old male villager, farmer, plaintiff in administrative litigation.
26. 55-year-old male villager, farmer, plaintiff in administrative litigation.
27. county official.
28. 28-year-old male villager, farmer, clothing salesman.
29. 29-year-old male villager, farmer, dentist.
30. township official.

Hebei (Baoding Prefecture) (April 2005)

31. 63-year-old male villager, farmer.
32. 60-year-old female villager, farmer.
33. 52-year-old female villager, farmer.
34. 35-year-old male villager, farmer.
35. 33-year-old male villager, farmer.
36. 32-year-old male villager, farmer.
37. 32-year-old male villager, farmer.
38. 58-year-old male villager, farmer.
39. 55-year-old female villager, farmer.
40. 67-year-old male villager, farmer, former production brigade party secretary.
41. 65-year-old female villager, farmer.
42. village cadre.
43. 41-year-old female villager, farmer.
44. village party secretary.

Hubei (December 2004)

45. prefectural official.
46. village party secretary.
47. 42-year-old male villager, farmer, factory worker.
48. prefectural official.
49. prefectural official.
50. county party secretary.
51. 50-year-old male villager, former village cadre, farmer.

Hunan (March 2005)

52. township party secretary.
53. township cadre.
54. township cadre.

55. village party secretary.
56. village chief.
57. 68-year-old villager, farmer, social insurance representative, ex-serviceman.
58. village chief.
59. village party secretary.
60. village cadre.
61. village cadre.
62. village party secretary, newly elected village chief.
63. county official.
64. junior high school teacher.
65. township party secretary.
66. township chief.
67. village chief.
68. village party secretary, village chief, president of an enterprise.
69. village cadre.
70. village cadre.
71. village cadre.
72. village cadre.
73. village party secretary, village chief.
74. village cadre.
75. village party secretary.
76. village chief.
77. 78-year-old villager, farmer, chair of the village senior association.

Jiangxi (April 2005)

78. township party secretary.
79. township official.
80. township official, ex-serviceman.
81. township official.
82. township official.
83. 26-year-old male villager, doctor.
84. village party secretary, supermarket manager.
85. village party secretary.
86. 72-year-old male villager, former production brigade chief.
87. township official.
88. 60-year-old male villager, farmer.
89. 58-year-old female villager, farmer.
90. village party secretary.
91. village party secretary.
92. village chief.
93. 55-year-old female villager, farmer.

94. 51-year-old male villager, farmer.
95. village chief.
96. 24-year-old male villager, farmer, barber.
97. 50-year-old male villager, farmer, post officer.
98. 30-year-old female villager, farmer, restaurant manager.
99. 79-year-old male villager, farmer.
100. 70-year-old male villager, farmer, former township official.
101. 73-year-old male villager, farmer, former township official.
102. 78-year-old male villager, farmer, former people's commune party secretary.

Zhejiang (December 2004)

103. county official.
104. village cadre.
105. village cadre.
106. 45-year-old male villager, farmer.
107. 40-year-old male villager, farmer, restaurant manager.
108. 38-year-old female villager, farmer, restaurant worker.

APPENDIX B: INTERVIEW QUESTIONS

For County Cadres

- What is your county's industrial structure? How much does agricultural revenue represent? What is the agricultural population? What is the total population? Where are the products of this county sold? How many townships does this county have? What is the average population of a township? What is the population of the most-populated township and what is the population of the least-populated township? How many officials are there at the county level?
(你们县的产业结构怎么样? 农业收入占多少比例? 农业人口有多少? 总人口有多少? 你们的产品都销往哪里? 全县有多少乡和镇? 平均每个乡(镇)有多少人? 最大的和最小的各有多少? 县级干部有多少人?)
- What is the source of the county's fiscal revenue? What are the county's expenditures for? Does the revenue meet the expenditure? If revenue is not enough, what do you do? Which level of government pays for compulsory education? How much is each level of government paying? Which level of government pays for the wages of county and township officials?
(县的财政收入都从哪里来? 有哪些支出? 你们收支相抵吗? 如果收入不够用怎么办? 县的义务教育费由谁负担? 各占比例多少? 县和乡镇政府的工资由谁负担?)
- Who collects the agricultural tax? How is it collected?
(你们的农业税是由谁收? 怎么收的?)

- How did the tax-for-fee reform affect the county's fiscal revenue? Did it cause difficulty for the county's finances?
  (费改税对县财政收入有什么影响? 会带来财政困难吗?)
- Does the county government have a petition office? How do you deal with petitions? Have you sent people to a lower-level government to investigate? If petitioners are not satisfied with your handling of matters, what do they do?
  (县政府有信访办公室吗? 你们如何处理这些上访? 你们有没有派人去下级调查过? 如果上访者对处理结果不满意, 他们会怎么办?)
- On what topic do villagers petition the most? In general, is it individual petitioning or collective petitioning?
  (农民上访提出最多的问题是什么? 一般是个人上访还是集体上访?)
- How does the county government monitor lower-level governments?
  (县政府如何监督下级政府的工作?)
- Have all the villages in your county held a village election? What role does the county government play in a village election?
  (你们县所有的村都有村委会选举吗? 村委会选举中县政府会发挥什么作用?)

For Township Cadres

- What is your township's industrial structure? How much does agricultural revenue represent? What is the agricultural population? What is the total population? Does your township have township-and-village enterprises? Who is managing the enterprises in your township?
  (你们乡(镇)的产业结构怎么样? 农业收入占多大比例? 农业人口有多少? 总人口有多少? 你们乡(镇)里有没有乡镇企业? 乡(镇)里的企业谁管理?)
- How many officials does the township government have? Which level of government is paying the township officials' wages? Do you have a standard number of township officials? Who decides the number?
  (乡(镇)级干部有多少? 乡(镇)政府的工资由谁负担? 乡(镇)干部的人数有指标吗? 谁定的?)
- What is the source of the township's fiscal revenue? What are the township's expenditures for? Does the revenue meet the expenditure? If revenue is not enough, what do you do? What public goods does the township provide?
  (乡(镇)的财政收入都从哪里来? 有哪些支出? 你们收支相抵吗? 如果收入不够怎么办? 公共建设有哪些项目?)
- Who collects the agricultural tax? How is it collected? Is there any other tax? How are other taxes collected? How are fees collected?
  (农业税是由谁收? 怎么收的? 有其它的税吗? 其它的税怎么收? 费怎么收?)
- How did the tax-for-fee reform affect the township's fiscal revenue? Did it cause difficulty for the township's finances?
  (费改税对乡(镇)财政有什么影响? 会带来财政困难吗?)

- Does the township government have a petition office? How do you deal with petitions? If petitioners are not satisfied with your handling of matters, what do you do? What do they do?
(乡(镇)政府有信访办公室吗? 你们如何处理这些上访? 如果上访者对处理结果不满意, 你们会怎么办? 他们会怎么办?)
- Among the residents of your township, is there anyone who petitioned to the county or higher-level government? If there is, what was the result? Did the county government send someone?
(你们乡(镇)的居民之中, 有没有去县政府或者以上上访过的人? 如果有, 结果怎么样? 县政府有没有派人来?)
- On what topic do villagers petition the most? In general, is it individual petitioning or collective petitioning?
(农民上访提出最大的问题是什么? 一般是个人上访还是集体上访?)
- If your township government sends a report on its administration to the county government, does the county government give you any instruction? What do you usually report?
(如果你们乡(镇)有向县里反映情况, 县政府对你们会有什么指示吗? 你们通常怎么做?)
- Have all the villages in your township held a village election? What role does the township government play in a village election? If some problem appears in a village election, how do you handle it?
(你们乡(镇)里的村都有选举吗? 乡(镇)政府在村民选举中发挥什么作用? 如果村委会选举出现问题, 你们会怎么处理?)

For Village Cadres

- What is your village's economic structure? How much does agricultural revenue represent? How many households does the village have and what is the population? Are there many people who share the same surname/kinship? Is the village's land nationally owned or collectively owned?
(你们村的经济结构怎么样? 从农业来的收入占多大比例? 你们村有多少户, 多少人? 同姓的/一个家族的人多吗? 村里的土地是全民所有还是集体所有?)
- What is the source of the villagers' committee's fiscal revenue? What are the village's expenditures for? Does the revenue meet the expenditure? If revenue is not enough, what do you do? Are you paid wages? Which level of government is paying for the village's compulsory education? How much is each level of government paying?
(你们村村委会的财政收入是从哪里来的? 有哪些支出? 收入够用吗? 如果不够用怎么办? 您拿工资吗? 村的义务教育开支由谁负担? 各占多少比例?)
- What taxes and fees do you collect? Are they easy to collect? Have you faced any resistance?
(你们会收什么样的税和费? 钱好收吗? 会不会遇到什么阻力?)

- Do you have standard amounts of taxes and fees to be collected? Who decides the amounts? If you cannot meet the standard amounts, what do you do?
  (你们收的费或税有什么指标吗? 指标是从哪里下的? 如果达不到指标怎么办?)
- What difficulty does your work have? Do villagers cooperate with your work? If villagers have opinions, what do you do? What do they do? Would villagers petition to a superior government? How would they petition? If villagers petition, what do you do?
  (你们的工作会有什么困难? 村民配合你们的工作吗? 如果村民有意见, 你们会怎么办? 他们会怎么办? 村民会向上级反映吗? 他们怎么向上级反映? 如果村民有问题要上访的话, 你们会怎么办?)
- Has your village held a village election? When was the first village election held? What were the consequences of the last election? How did you win the election? Were the candidates all party members?
  (你们村有村委会选举吗? 最早是从什么时候开始的? 上一次选举时的情况怎么样? 您是什么赢的? 候选人都是党员吗?)
- What is the relationship between the villagers' committee and the village party branch? How do you coordinate your jobs?
  (村委会和村党支部的关系怎么样? 你们的工作是怎么协调的?)
- How often are a villagers' representative assembly (VRA) and a villagers' assembly held? What do they discuss? How many people participate in a VRA? Does your village have villagers' small groups? How often is a villagers' small group assembly (VSGA) held? What does a VSGA discuss? How many people participate in a VSGA?
  (你们村村民代表会议和村民会议隔多久开一次? 讨论什么问题? 村民代表会议由多少人参加? 你们村有村民小组吗? 村民小组会议隔多久开一次? 村民小组会议讨论什么问题? 村民小组会议由多少人参加?)

For Villagers

- What is the source of your revenue? Is it mainly from farming or from nonfarm work? How much does each source represent?
  (你们的收入从哪里来? 种地还是打工? 各占多少比例?)
- What is your major expenditure? How much are you paying in taxes and fees? What kinds of taxes and fees are you paying? Who pays education fees and how much are they? Who collects education fees?
  (主要支出由哪些? 交多少税或者费? 有哪些税和费? 子女教育费由谁出? 交多少钱? 教育费交给谁?)
- Do you feel that the tax you have paid is reasonable? Are taxes and fees too heavy? Why?
  (你们觉得交的税和费合理吗? 税和费太多吗? 为什么?)

- Who collects the taxes and fees you pay? How do you pay them? Are you going to pay them or are you paying them to someone who comes to collect them?
(您交税和费交给谁? 是怎么交的? 是你们自己交还是有人来收?)
- Are you familiar with the township government's job? Do you know the township cadres? How do you feel about their job? Do you have any opinion?
(您了解乡(镇)政府的工作吗? 您认识什么乡(镇)干部吗? 您觉得乡(镇)政府的工作怎么样? 您有什么意见吗?)
- Have you ever petitioned? What was the situation regarding your petition? Which level of government did you petition to? What was the issue? What was the result? What did you do after petitioning? Did you petition again?
(您做过上访吗? 上访的情况怎么样? 给哪级别的政府您上访? 争论的问题是什么? 结果怎么样? 上访了以后做什么? 再来上访吗?)
- How is the villagers' committee (VC) spending the money you have paid? Do you know? Do you feel that it is appropriate? What jobs is the VC doing? Are you satisfied with the VC's job?
(村委会怎么花你们交上的钱? 您知道吗? 您觉得合适吗? 村委会都管哪些事? 你们对村委会的工作满意吗?)
- Has your village held a village election? When was the first village election held? Did you know the candidates? Who won the election? Are you satisfied with the current village chief? What do you think about the election result? Do you have any opinion?
(你们村有村委会选举吗? 选举最早是从什么时候开始的? 隔多久选一次? 您认识候选人吗? 谁当选了? 您对现在的村长满意吗? 您觉得选举的结果怎么样? 您有什么意见吗?)
- What do you think about your village's party secretary? Who is the village party secretary? What jobs is the village party branch doing?
(你们村党支部是什么样的? 党支部书记是谁? 党支部都管哪些事情?)
- Have you ever participated in a villagers' representative assembly? What does it discuss? Have you ever participated in a villagers' small group assembly? What does it discuss?
(您参加过村民代表会议吗? 讨论什么? 您参加过村民小组会议吗? 讨论什么?)
- Who is administrating your land? Have you ever experienced land expropriation? If you have, who came to do that? Did you encounter any problems during the process of land expropriation?
(你们的土地是谁管理的? 你们村有征地建了的吗? 如果有的话, 地是由谁来征的? 征地过程中有什么问题吗?)
- Does your village enforce the family planning regulation? Is it strict?
(你们村现在抓计划生育吗? 管得严吗?)

APPENDIX C: SOURCES OF THE CASES ON VILLAGE ELECTIONS

TABLE A.1. *Sources of the Cases on Village Elections*

#	Village	Province	Population	Sources
1	Ai	Jiangxi	1,695	Tong (2001)
2	Cao	Jiangxi	1,794	Shi (2002)
3	Chengfang	Jiangxi	2,016	Tang, Yang, and Xiao (2002)
4	Chishi	Inner Mongolia	913	Ako (2003)
5	De	Inner Mongolia	1,754	Tong (2002)
6	Dong	Jiangxi	1,437	Zhang F. (2001)
7	East Gate	Hebei	1,200	Interviewees 20, 28–29
8	Fuyang	Zhejiang	?	Lang (2003)
9	Gaoping	Jiangxi	1,316	Dai (2001)
10	Guan	Jiangxi	4,000+	Qiu et al. (2001)
11	Guobaozhuang	Shandong	?	Xu F. (2004)
12	Guowa	Jiangxi	1,765	Chen (2001b)
13	Guozhuang	Shandong	?	Xu F. (2004)
14	Guping	Jiangxi	1,987	Wei (2002)
15	Hangbu	Jiangxi	4,299	Luo (2002)
16	Hejiabao	Tianjin	?	Xu F. (2004)
17	Hejiang	Jiangxi	2,323	Song (2001)
18	Highland Park	Zhejiang	?	Interviewees 103–105
19	Houbu	Fujian	3,456	He Z. (2001)
20	Hua	Jiangxi	1,324	Ju (2002)
21	Huaxi	Zhejiang	?	Lang (2003)
22	Jianfeng	Jiangxi	1,741	Yu and Xiao (2001)
23	Kanxia	Jiangxi	840+	Yi and Xiao (2001)
24	Libei	Jiangxi	617	He and Shi (2002)
25	Lin	Shandong	?	Xu F. (2004)
26	Lishu	Hubei	1,097	Chen (2001a)
27	Long	Inner Mongolia	2,196	Tong (2002, 2004)
28	Long Bridge	Zhejiang	?	Interviewees 106–108
29	Luojia	Jiangxi	1,600+	Yan (2001)
30	Makou	Jiangxi	723	Tang (2001b)
31	Mao	Shaanxi	?	Tong (2004)
32	Nanmen	Jiangxi	1,564	Song (2002)
33	Ping	Inner Mongolia	1,112	Tong (2002, 2004)
34	Putian	Jiangxi	2,400	Wang F. (2001)
35	Quchi	Jiangxi	795	Wang B. (2001)
36	Qudou	Jiangxi	858	Luo (2001)
37	Shangfu	Jiangxi	1,351	Chen (2002)
38	Shangyang	Zhejiang	?	Lang (2003)
39	Shiqian	Jiangxi	1,428	Tang (2001a)

(*continued*)

TABLE A.1 (*continued*)

#	Village	Province	Population	Sources
40	Shiqiao	Jiangxi	2,030	Luo and Xiao (2001)
41	Taoyuan	Jiangxi	1,880	Wei (2001)
42	Tie	Jiangxi	1,720	Qiu (2001)
43	Wangshatang	Jiangxi	853	Yi (2002)
44	Wangyue	Hubei	1,386	He X. (2001)
45	Water Dragon	Guangdong	309	Interviewees 1–3
46	Water Wood	Hebei	595	Interviewees 12–13
47	Wufang	Jiangxi	2,010	Yang (2001b)
48	Wugezhuang	Shandong	?	Xu F. (2004)
49	Xialang	Zhejiang	?	Xu F. (2004)
50	Xiawei	Jiangsu	924	Qian (2001)
51	Xing	Inner Mongolia	2,437	Tong (2002)
52	Xinping	Jiangxi	1,446	Xiao L. (2001)
53	Xiaoshui	Jiangxi	688	Yang (2001a)
54	Xiyantou	Beijing	?	Xu F. (2004)
55	Yongchang	Jiangxi	1,867	Yan and Xiao (2002)
56	You	Jiangxi	900+	Tong (2004); Tong and Yu (2001)
57	Zhong	Jiangxi	702	Wang X. (2001)
58	Zhong2	Jiangxi	1,624	Qiu, Qiu, and Xiao (2002)
59	Zhou	Jiangxi	2,786	Qiu and Xiao (2001)
60	?	Shaanxi	?	Kennedy (2002b)
61	?	Shaanxi	?	Kennedy (2002b)
62	?	Shandong	1,800	Li L. (2001)

References

Adas, Michael. 1980. "'Moral Economy' or 'Contest State'? Elite Demands and the Origins of Peasant Protest in Southeast Asia." *Journal of Social History* 13: 521–46.

———. 1986. "From Footdragging to Flight: The Evasive History of Peasant Avoidance Protest in South and South-east Asia." *The Journal of Peasant Studies* 13: 64–85.

Ako Tomoko. 2003. "Cong 'shangfang' de 'aimeixing' kan Zhongguo nongcun shehui de quanli, liyi he zhixu: Yi Nei Menggu Chishi Cun 'shangfang' yanjiu wei li" (Rights, interests, and order of China's rural society seen from "ambiguity" of "petitioning": A case study of a "petitioning" in Chishi Village in Inner Mongolia), translated by Cheng Yaqin. In Xu Yong (ed.), *Zhongguo Nongcun Yanjiu 2002 Juan* (Chinese Rural Studies 2002). Beijing: Zhongguo Shehui Kexue Chubanshe.

Aldrich, John. 1995. *Why Parties? The Origin and Transformation of Political Parties in America.* Chicago, IL: University of Chicago Press.

Alpermann, Bjorn. 2001. "The Post-Election Administration of Chinese Villages." *The China Journal* 46: 45–67.

———. 2009. "Institutionalizing Village Governance in China." *Journal of Contemporary China* 18: 397–409.

Ames, Barry. 1987. *Political Survival: Politicians and Public Policy in Latin America.* Berkeley: University of California Press.

Arendt, Hannah. [1948] 1973. *The Origins of Totalitarianism.* San Diego, CA: Harcourt Brace & Company.

Aubert, Claude, and Xiande Li. 2002. "'Peasant Burden': Taxes and Levies Imposed on Chinese Farmers." Manuscript. INRA, France.

Bachman, David M. 1991. *Bureaucracy, Economy, and Leadership in China: The Institutional Origins of the Great Leap Forward.* New York: Cambridge University Press.

Bai Gang. 1998. "Zhongguo cunmin zizhi fazhi jianshe pingyi" (Review of the construction of villagers' self-governance and the rule of law in China). *Zhongguo Shehui Kexue* (Chinese Social Science) 3: 88–107.

Barber, Benjamin R. 1984. *Strong Democracy: Participatory Politics for a New Age.* Berkeley: University of California Press.

Bates, Robert H. 1981. *Markets and States in Tropical Africa: The Political Basis of Agricultural Policies*. Berkeley: University of California Press.

______. 1989. *Beyond the Miracle of the Market: The Political Economy of Agrarian Development in Kenya*. New York: Cambridge University Press.

______. 2001. *Prosperity and Violence: The Political Economy of Development*. New York: W. W. Norton & Company.

Bates, Robert H., Avner Greif, Margaret Levi, Jean-Laurent Rosenthal, and Barry R. Weingast. 1998. *Analytic Narratives*. Princeton, NJ: Princeton University Press.

Bates, Robert H., and Anne O. Krueger (eds.). 1993. *Political and Economic Interactions in Economic Policy Reform: Evidence from Eight Countries*. Cambridge, MA: Blackwell Publishers.

Baum, Richard. 1975. *Prelude to Revolution: Mao, the Party, and the Peasant Question, 1962–66*. New York: Columbia University Press.

______. 1994. *Burying Mao: Chinese Politics in the Age of Deng Xiaoping*. Princeton, NJ: Princeton University Press.

______. 1996. "China after Deng: Ten Scenarios in Search of Reality." *The China Quarterly* 145: 153–75.

Baum, Richard, and Alexei Shevchenko. 1999. "The 'State of the State.'" In Merle Goldman and Roderick MacFarquhar (eds.), *The Paradox of China's Post-Mao Reforms*. Cambridge, MA: Harvard University Press.

Bawn, Kathleen. 1997. "Choosing Strategies to Control the Bureaucracy: Statutory Constraints, Oversight, and the Committee System." *Journal of Law, Economics, and Organization* 13: 101–26.

Becker, Gary S. 1968. "Crime and Punishment: An Economic Approach." *Journal of Political Economy* 76: 169–217.

Beik, William. 1985. *Absolutism and Society in Seventeenth-Century France*. New York: Cambridge University Press.

Bernstein, Thomas P. 1999. "Farmer Discontent and Regime Responses." In Merle Goldman and Roderick MacFarquhar (eds.), *The Paradox of China's Post-Mao Reforms*. Cambridge, MA: Harvard University Press.

______. 2006. "Mao Zedong and the Famine of 1959–1960: A Study in Wilfulness." *The China Quarterly* 186: 421–45.

Bernstein, Thomas P., and Xiaobo Lü. 2000. "Taxation without Representation: Peasants, the Central and the Local States in Reform China." *The China Quarterly* 163: 742–63.

______. 2003. *Taxation without Representation in Contemporary Rural China*. New York: Cambridge University Press.

Bianco, Lucien. 1971. *Origins of the Chinese Revolution, 1915–1949*, translated by Muriel Bell. Stanford, CA: Stanford University Press.

Blaydes, Lisa. 2010. *Elections and Distributive Politics in Mubarak's Egypt*. New York: Cambridge University Press.

Bobbio, Norberto. 1987. *The Future of Democracy: A Defense of the Rule of the Games*, translated by Roger Griffin. Cambridge: Polity Press.

Brewer, John. 1989. *The Sinews of Power: War, Money, and the English State, 1688–1783*. New York: Knopf.

Brownlee, Jason. 2007. *Authoritarianism in an Age of Democratization*. New York: Cambridge University Press.

Bueno de Mesquita, Bruce, and Alastair Smith. 2011. *The Dictator's Handbook: Why Bad Behavior Is Almost Always Good Politics*. New York: Public Affairs.
Bueno de Mesquita, Bruce, Alastair Smith, Randolph M. Silverson, and James D. Morrow. 2003. *The Logic of Political Survival*. Cambridge, MA: MIT Press.
Cai, Yongshun. 2006. *State and Laid-Off Workers in Reform China: The Silence and Collective Action of the Retrenched*. New York: Routledge.
———. 2008. "Local Governments and the Suppression of Popular Resistance in China." *The China Quarterly* 193: 24–42.
———. 2010. *Collective Resistance in China: Why Popular Protests Succeed or Fail*. Stanford, CA: Stanford University Press.
Cain, Bruce, John Ferejohn, and Morris Fiorina. 1987. *The Personal Vote: Constituency Service and Electoral Independence*. Cambridge, MA: Harvard University Press.
Caizhengbu (Ministry of Finance). 1993–2008. *Zhongguo Caizheng Nianjian 1992–2007* (China Fiscal Yearbook). Beijing: Zhongguo Caizheng Zazhishe.
———. 1994. *Zhongguo Nongmin Fudan Shi* (History of the Peasant Burden in China), Vol. 2. Beijing: Zhongguo Caizheng Jingji Chubanshe.
Cao Jinqing. 2000. *Huanghebian de Zhongguo: Yi ge Xuezhe dui Xiangcun Shehui de Guancha yu Sikao* (China along the Yellow River: A Scholarly Observation and Reflection on Rural Societies). Shanghai: Shanghai Wenyi Chubanshe.
Carey, John M., and Matthew Soberg Shugart. 1995. "Incentives to Cultivate a Personal Vote: A Rank Ordering of Electoral Formulas." *Electoral Studies* 14: 417–39.
Chan, Anita, Richard Madsen, and Jonathan Unger. 1992. *Chen Village under Mao and Deng*, second edition. Berkeley: University of California Press.
Chan, Sylvia. 1998. "Research Notes on Villagers' Committee Election: Chinese Style Democracy." *Journal of Contemporary China* 7: 507–21.
Chang, Jun, and Jon Halliday. 2005. *Mao: The Unknown Story*. New York: Knopf.
Charles, Joseph. 1956. *The Origins of the American Party System*. Williamsburg, VA: Institute of Early American History and Culture.
Chen, An. 2007. "The Failure of Organizational Control: Changing Party Power in the Chinese Countryside." *Politics and Society* 35: 145–79.
———. 2008. "The 1994 Tax Reform and Its Impact on China's Rural Fiscal Structure." *Modern China* 34: 303–43.
Chen Guidi and Wu Chuntao. 2004. *Zhongguo Nongmin Diaocha* (An Investigation of Chinese Farmers). Beijing: Renmin Wenxue Chubanshe.
Chen, Jie. 2005a. "Popular Support for Village Self-Government in China: Intensity and Sources." *Asian Survey* 45: 865–85.
———. 2005b. "Sociopolitical Attitudes of the Masses and Leaders in the Chinese Village: Attitude Congruence and Constraint." *Journal of Contemporary China* 14: 445–64.
Chen, Jie, and Bruce J. Dickson. 2010. *Allies of the State: China's Private Entrepreneurs and Democratic Change*. Cambridge, MA: Harvard University Press.
Chen Jun. 2003. "Nongcun shuifei zhidu: Lixing fansi yu gaige chonggou" (Rural taxation: Rational reflections and reform restructuring). *Jianghai Xuekan* (Jianghai Academic Journal) 3: 74–79.
Chen Tao. 2001a. "Jingji nengren beijing xia de cunji zhili: Hubei Lishu Cun diaocha" (Rural governance under the economic elite: A study in Lishu Village in Hubei). In

Li Lianjiang, Guo Zhenglin, and Xiao Tangbiao (eds.), *Cunweihui Xuanju Guancha* (Studies on Village Elections). Tianjin: Tianjin Renmin Chubanshe.

______. 2001b. "Zongzu yu diyuan: Guowa Cun xuanju guancha" (Kinships and local networks: A study on the election in Guowa Village). In Xiao Tangbiao, Qiu Xinyou, and Tang Xiaoteng (eds.), *Duowei Shijiao zhong de Cunmin Zhixuan: Dui Shi-Wu ge Cunweihui Xuanju de Guancha Yanjiu* (Village Elections from a Multidimensional Angle: Studies on Fifteen Village Elections). Beijing: Zhongguo Shehui Kexue Chubanse.

______. 2002. "Shangfu Cun xuanju guancha baogao" (A study on the election in Shangfu Village). In Xiao Tangbiao (ed.), *Zongzu, Xiangcun Quanli yu Xuanju: Dui Jiangxi Sheng Shi-Er ge Cunweihui Xuanju de Guancha Yanjiu* (Kinships, Rural Power, and Elections: Studies on Twelve Village Elections in Jiangxi Province). Xi'an: Xibei Daxue Chubanshe.

Chen, Xi. 2008. "Collective Petitioning and Institutional Conversion." In Kevin J. O'Brien (ed.), *Popular Protest in China*. Cambridge, MA: Harvard University Press.

______. 2009. "The Power of 'Troublemaking': Protest Tactics and Their Efficacy in China." *Comparative Politics* 41: 451–71.

______. 2012. *Social Protest and Contentious Authoritarianism in China*. New York: Cambridge University Press.

Chen Yongzheng and Chen Jiaze. 2004. "Lun Zhongguo xiangji caizheng" (Discussing China's township finance). *Zhongguo Nongcun Guancha* (Survey on Rural China) 5: 60–68.

Cheng Jie. 2005. "Caichanquan, xiaoyong yu zhengdang chengxu: Tudi zhengshou zhengyong zhong de chengxu shifan yu chonggou" (Property rights, utilities, and legitimate procedures: Malfunctioning and restructuring of the procedures of land expropriation). Paper presented at Conference on "Rights Advocacy and Legal Reform in China," UCLA Center for Chinese Studies.

Clark, William Roberts, Matt Golder, and Sona Golder. 2007. "The Balance of Power between Citizens and the State: Democratization and the Resource Curse." Manuscript. University of Michigan and Florida State University.

Cox, Gary W. 1987. *The Efficient Secret: The Cabinet and the Development of Political Parties in Victorian England*. New York: Cambridge University Press.

Cui Chuanyi. 2004. *Zhongguo Nongmin Liudong Guancha* (Survey on Migration of Chinese Farmers). Taiyuan: Shanxi Jingji Chubanshe.

Cunningham, Frank. 1987. *Democratic Theory and Socialism*. New York: Cambridge University Press.

Dahl, Robert A. 1989. *Democracy and Its Critics*. New Haven, CT: Yale University Press.

Dai Lichao. 2001. "Gaoping Cun xuanju guancha" (A study on the election in Gaoping Village). In Li Lianjiang, Guo Zhenglin, and Xiao Tangbiao (eds.), *Cunweihui Xuanju Guancha* (Studies on Village Elections). Tianjin: Tianjin Renmin Chubanshe.

de Soto, Hernando. 2000. *The Mystery of Capital: Why Capitalism Triumphs in the West and Fails Everywhere Else*. New York: Basic Books.

Diamant, Neil J. 2000. "Conflict and Conflict Resolution in China: Beyond Mediation-Centered Approaches." *Journal of Conflict Resolution* 44: 523–46.

Dickson, Bruce J. 2003. *Red Capitalists in China: The Party, Private Entrepreneurs, and Prospects for Political Change*. New York: Cambridge University Press.

———. 2008. *Wealth into Power: The Communist Party's Embrace of China's Private Sector*. New York: Cambridge University Press.

Dimitrov, Martin K. 2010. "Building Loyalty: Autocratic Resilience in Communist Europe and China." Manuscript. Tulane University.

Dominguez, Jorge I., and Michael Shifter (eds.). 2003. *Constructing Democratic Governance in Latin America*, second edition. Baltimore, MD: Johns Hopkins University Press.

Duan, Haiyan, and Jing Vivian Zhan. 2009. "Fiscal Transfer and Local Public Expenditure in China: A Cross-County Study of Shanxi Province." Manuscript. Chinese University of Hong Kong.

Duara, Prasenjit. 1987. "State Involution: A Study of Local Finances in North China, 1911–1935." *Comparative Studies in Society and History* 29: 132–61.

———. 1988. *Culture, Power, and the State: Rural North China, 1900–1942*. Stanford, CA: Stanford University Press.

Easterly, William. 2001. *The Elusive Quest for Growth: Economists' Adventures and Misadventures in the Tropics*. Cambridge, MA: MIT Press.

Easterly, William, and Ross Levine. 1997. "Africa's Growth Tragedy: Policies and Ethnic Divisions." *Quarterly Journal of Economics* 112: 1203–50.

Eastman, Lloyd E. 1984. *Seeds of Destruction: Nationalist China in War and Revolution, 1937–1949*. Stanford, CA: Stanford University Press.

Edin, Maria. 2000. "Market Forces and Communist Power: Local Political Institutions and Economic Development in China." Ph.D. dissertation. Uppsala University.

———. 2003. "State Capacity and Local Agent Control in China: CCP Cadre Management from a Township Perspective." *The China Quarterly* 173: 35–52.

Fan, C. Cindy. 1995. "Of Belts and Ladders: State Policy and Uneven Regional Development in Post-Mao China." *Annals of the Association of American Geographers* 85: 421–49.

———. 1997. "Uneven Development and Beyond: Regional Development Theory in Post-Mao China." *International Journal of Urban and Regional Research* 21: 620–39.

Fang, Qiang. 2009. "Hot Potatoes: Chinese Complaint Systems from Early Times to the Late Qing (1898)." *Journal of Asian Studies* 68: 1105–35.

Fewsmith, Joseph. 1994. *Dilemmas of Reform in China: Political Conflict and Economic Debate*. Armonk, NY: M. E. Sharpe.

Frazier, Mark W. 2010. *Socialist Insecurity: Pensions and Politics of Uneven Development in China*. Ithaca, NY: Cornell University Press.

Frieden, Jeffry A. 1991. *Debt, Development, and Democracy: Modern Political Economy and Latin America, 1965–1985*. Princeton, NJ: Princeton University Press.

Friedman, Edward, Paul G. Pickowicz, and Mark Selden. 1991. *Chinese Village, Socialist State*. New Haven, CT: Yale University Press.

———. 2005. *Revolution, Resistance, and Reform in Village China*. New Haven, CT: Yale University Press.

Friedrich, Carl J., and Zbigniew K. Brzezinski. 1965. *Totalitarian Dictatorship and Autocracy*. Cambridge, MA: Harvard University Press.

Gallagher, Mary Elizabeth. 2005. *Contagious Capitalism: Globalization and Politics of Labor in China*. Princeton, NJ: Princeton University Press.

Gandhi, Jennifer. 2008. *Political Institutions under Dictatorship*. New York: Cambridge University Press.

Geddes, Barbara. 1994. *Politician's Dilemma: Building State Capacity in Latin America.* Berkeley: University of California Press.
______. 2003. *Paradigms and Sand Castles: Theory Building and Research Design in Comparative Politics.* Ann Arbor: University of Michigan Press.
______. 2006. "Why Parties and Elections in Authoritarian Regimes?" Manuscript. University of California at Los Angeles.
Gehlbach, Scott. 2005. "Why Don't Predatory Rulers Commit to Non-Predatory Taxes?" Paper presented at the annual meeting of the American Political Science Association, Washington, DC.
______. 2006. "A Formal Model of Exit and Voice." *Rationality and Society* 18: 395–418.
Gilley, Bruce. 2001. *Model Rebels: The Rise and Fall of China's Richest Village.* Berkeley: University of California Press.
______. 2004. *China's Democratic Future: How It Will Happen and Where It Will Lead.* New York: Columbia University Press.
Gimpelson, Vladimir, and Daniel Treisman. 2002. "Fiscal Games and Public Employment: A Theory with Evidence from Russia." *World Politics* 54: 145–83.
Glionna, John M. 2010. "China's 'Black Jails' Shove Complaints into the Dark." *Los Angeles Times*, January 11. (http://articles.latimes.com/2010/jan/11/world/la-fg-china-black-jails11-2010jan11, accessed March 14, 2014).
Gold, Thomas B. 1989. "Guerrilla Interviewing among the Getihu." In Perry Link, Richard Madsen, and Paul G. Pickowitz (eds.), *Unofficial China: Popular Culture and Thought in the People's Republic.* Boulder, CO: Westview Press.
Golden, Miriam A. 2003. "Electoral Connections: The Effects of the Personal Vote on Political Patronage, Bureaucracy and Legislation in Postwar Italy." *British Journal of Political Science* 33: 189–212.
Golden, Miriam A., and Eric C. C. Chang. 2001. "Competitive Corruption: Factional Conflict and Political Malfeasance in Postwar Italian Christian Democracy." *World Politics* 53: 588–602.
Greif, Avner. 2006. *Institutions and the Path to the Modern Economy: Lessons from Medieval Trade.* New York: Cambridge University Press.
Groseclose, Tim. 2001. "A Model of Candidate Location When One Candidate Has a Valence Advantage." *American Journal of Political Science* 45: 862–86.
Groseclose, Tim, and James M. Snyder, Jr. 1996. "Buying Supermajorities." *American Political Science Review* 90: 303–15.
Guo, Gang. 2008. "Vertical Imbalance and Local Fiscal Discipline in China." *Journal of East Asian Studies* 8: 61–88.
______. 2009. "China's Local Political Budget Cycles." *American Journal of Political Science* 53: 621–32.
Guo, Xiaolin. 2001. "Land Expropriation and Rural Conflicts in China." *The China Quarterly* 166: 422–39.
Guo, Zhenglin, and Thomas P. Bernstein. 2004. "The Impact of Elections on the Village Structure of Power: The Relations between the Village Committees and the Party Branches." *Journal of Contemporary China* 13: 257–75.
Guthrie, Doug. 1999. *Dragon in a Three-Piece Suit: The Emergence of Capitalism in China.* Princeton, NJ: Princeton University Press.
Hanham, H. J. 1968. *The Reformed Electoral System in Great Britain, 1832–1914.* London: Historical Association.

———. 1978. *Elections and Party Management: Politics in the Time of Disraeli and Gladstone*, second edition. Hassocks: Harvester Press.
He, Baogang. 2007. *Rural Democracy in China: The Role of Village Elections*. New York: Palgrave Macmillan.
He Qinglian. 1997. "Nongcun jiceng shehui difang e shili de xingqi: Yu Wang Xu shangque" (The rise of local bad power in rural grassroots societies: A debate with Wang Xu). *Ershi-Yi Shiji* (The Twenty-First Century) 41: 129–34.
He Xuefeng. 2001. "Paixing, xuanju yu minzhu guize de minjianhua: Hubei Wangyue Cun diaocha" (Factions, elections, and civilization of democratic rules: A study in Wangyue Village in Hubei). In Li Lianjiang, Guo Zhenglin, and Xiao Tangbiao (eds.), *Cunweihui Xuanju Guancha* (Studies on Village Elections). Tianjin: Tianjin Renmin Chubanshe.
He Xuefeng and Shi Congmei. 2002. "Cunzhuang jingying yu shequ jiyi: Libei Cun xuanju guancha" (The village elite and the community's memory: A study on the election in Libei Village). In Xiao Tangbiao (ed.), *Zongzu, Xiangcun Quanli yu Xuanju: Dui Jiangxi Sheng Shi-Er ge Cunweihui Xuanju de Guancha Yanjiu* (Kinships, Rural Power, and Elections: Studies on Twelve Village Elections in Jiangxi Province). Xi'an: Xibei Daxue Chubanshe.
He Zoengke. 2001. "Cunmin Weiyuanhui xuanju he nongcun fazhan: Xiamen Shi Huli Qi Heshan Zhen Houbu Cun de gean yanjiu" (Village elections and rural development: A case study of Houbu Village, Heshan Town, Huli District, Xiamen City). In Li Lianjiang, Guo Zhenglin, and Xiao Tangbiao (eds.), *Cunweihui Xuanju Guancha* (Studies on Village Elections). Tianjin: Tianjin Renmin Chubanshe.
Held, David (ed.). 1993. *Prospects for Democracy: North, South, East, West*. Stanford, CA: Stanford University Press.
Herbst, Jeffrey. 2000. *States and Power in Africa: Comparative Lessons in Authority and Control*. Princeton, NJ: Princeton University Press.
Hinton, William. 1966. *Fanshen: A Documentary of Revolution in a Chinese Village*. Berkeley: University of California Press.
Hirschman, Albert O. 1970. *Exit, Voice, and Loyalty: Responses to Decline in Firms, Organizations, and States*. Cambridge, MA: Harvard University Press.
Ho, Peter. 2001. "Who Owns China's Land? Policies, Property Rights and Deliberate Institutional Ambiguity." *The China Quarterly* 166: 394–421.
Ho, Samuel P. S., and George C. S. Lin. 2004. "Converting Land to Nonagricultural Use in China's Coastal Provinces: Evidence from Jiangsu." *Modern China* 30: 81–112.
Hoffman, Philip T., and Kathryn Norberg. 1994a. "Conclusion." In Philip T. Hoffman and Kathryn Norberg (eds.), *Fiscal Crises, Liberty, and Representative Government, 1450–1789*. Stanford, CA: Stanford University Press.
——— (eds.). 1994b. *Fiscal Crises, Liberty, and Representative Government, 1450–1789*. Stanford, CA: Stanford University Press.
Hoffman, Philip T., and Jean-Laurent Rosenthal. 1997. "The Political Economy of Warfare and Taxation in Early Modern Europe: Historical Lessons for Economic Development." In John N. Drobak and John V. C. Nye (eds.), *The Frontiers of the New Institutional Economics*. San Diego, CA: Academic Press.
Howell, Jude. 1998. "Prospects for Village Self-Governance in China." *The Journal of Peasant Studies* 25: 86–111.
Hsing, You-tien. 2006. "Brokering Power and Property in China's Townships." *Pacific Review* 19: 103–24.

———. 2010. *The Great Urban Transformation: Politics of Land and Property in China*. Oxford: Oxford University Press.

Hu Rong. 2001. *Lixing Xuanze yu Zhidu Shishi: Zhongguo Nongcun Cunmin Weiyuanhui Xuanju de Gean Yanjiu* (Rational Choice and Institutional Implementation: Case Studies of Chinese Village Elections). Shanghai: Shanghai Yuandong Chubanshe.

———. 2007. "Nongmin shangfang yu zhengzhi xinren de liushi" (Peasants' petitions and the loss of political trust). *Shehuixue Yanjiu* (Sociological Studies) 3: 39–55.

Hu Xingdou. 2004. "Xian xiang jigou gaige po zai meijie" (Administration reforms at the county and township levels as a matter of urgency). (http://www.chinaelections.org, accessed November 4, 2004).

Huang, Philip C. C. 1990. *The Peasant Family and Rural Development in the Yangzi Delta, 1350–1988*. Stanford, CA: Stanford University Press.

Huang Weirong. 2005. "Pochan xiangzhen mianlin de zhuyao wenti ji duice chutan" (A preliminary reflection on the main issues that bankrupt townships are facing and their measures). (http://www.chinaelections.org/NewsInfo.asp?NewsID=41414, accessed September 20, 2009).

Huang, Yasheng. 1996. *Inflation and Investment Controls in China: The Political Economy of Central-Local Relations during the Reform Era*. New York: Cambridge University Press.

———. 2002. "Managing Chinese Bureaucrats: An Institutional Economics Perspective." *Political Studies* 50: 61–79.

———. 2008. *Capitalism with Chinese Characteristics: Entrepreneurship and the State*. New York: Cambridge University Press.

Human Rights Watch. 2009. "An Alleyway in Hell: China's Abusive 'Black Jails.'" (http://www.hrw.org/en/reports/2009/11/12/alleyway-hell-0, accessed July 16, 2010).

Huntington, Samuel P. 1968. *Political Order in Changing Societies*. New Haven, CT: Yale University Press.

Hurst, William. 2009. *The Chinese Worker after Socialism*. New York: Cambridge University Press.

Jennings, M. Kent, and Kuang-Hui Chen. 2008. "Perceptions of Injustice in the Chinese Countryside." *Journal of Contemporary China* 17: 319–37.

Jing Yuejin. 2004. *Dangdai Zhongguo Nongcun "Liangwei Guanxi" de Weiguan Jiexi yu Hongguan Toushi* (Micro Analyses and Macro Perspectives of the "Party-Administration" Relationship in Rural China). Beijing: Zhongyang Wenxian Chubanshe.

Ju Lizhi. 2002. "Chengxu luoshi yu zongzu huodong de hudong: Hua Cun xuanju guancha" (Interactions between implementing procedures and kinship activities: A study on the election in Hua Village). In Xiao Tangbiao (ed.), *Zongzu, Xiangcun Quanli yu Xuanju: Dui Jiangxi Sheng Shi-Er ge Cunweihui Xuanju de Guancha Yanjiu* (Kinships, Rural Power, and Elections: Studies on Twelve Village Elections in Jiangxi Province). Xi'an: Xibei Daxue Chubanshe.

Kelliher, Daniel. 1992. *Peasant Power in China: The Era of Rural Reform, 1979–1989*. New Haven, CT: Yale University Press.

———. 1997. "The Chinese Debate over Village Self-Government." *China Journal* 37: 63–86.

Kennedy, John James. 2002a. "Formal Introductions: Institutional Change and Village Elections in Rural China." Ph.D. dissertation. University of California, Davis.

———. 2002b. "The Fate of 'Grassroots Democracy' in Rural China: Real versus Cosmetic Election." *Asian Survey* 42: 456–82.

———. 2006. "From the Tax-for-Fee Reform to the Abolition of Agricultural Taxes: The Impact on Township Governments in North-west China." *The China Quarterly* 189: 43–59.

———. 2007. "The Implementation of Village Elections and Tax-for-Fee Reform in Rural Northwest China." In Elizabeth J. Perry and Merle Goldman (eds.), *Grassroots Political Reform in Contemporary China*. Cambridge, MA: Harvard University Press.

———. 2009. "Legitimacy with Chinese Characteristics: 'Two Increases, One Reduction.'" *Journal of Contemporary China* 18: 391–95.

Kennedy, John James, Scott Rozelle, and Yaojiang Shi. 2004. "Elected Leaders and Collective Land: Farmers' Evaluation of Village Leaders' Performance in Rural China." *Journal of Chinese Political Science* 9: 1–22.

Kousser, J. Morgan. 1974. *The Shaping of Southern Politics: Suffrage Restriction and the Establishment of the One-Party South, 1880–1910*. New Haven, CT: Yale University Press.

Krueger, Anne O. 1992. *Economic Policy Reform in Developing Countries*. Cambridge, MA: Blackwell Publishers.

———. 1993. *Economic Policies at Cross-Purposes: The United States and Developing Countries*. Washington, DC: Brookings Institution.

Kydd, Andrew H. 2005. *Trust and Mistrust in International Relations*. Princeton, NJ: Princeton University Press.

Landry, Pierre F. 2008. *Decentralized Authoritarianism in China: The Communist Party's Control of Local Elites in the Post-Mao Era*. New York: Cambridge University Press.

Lang Youxing. 2003. "Cong jingji jingying dao zhengzhi guanlizhe: Zhongguo cunmin xuanju yu cunji lingdao de jiti" (From economic elites to political administrators: Village elections in China and succession of the village leadership). In Xu Yong (ed.), *Zhongguo Nongcun Yanjiu 2002 Juan* (Chinese Rural Studies 2002). Beijing: Zhongguo Shehui Kexue Chubanshe.

Lardy, Nicholas R. 1983. *Agriculture in China's Modern Economic Development*. New York: Cambridge University Press.

Lee, Ching Kwan. 2007. *Against the Law: Labor Protests in China's Rustbelt and Sunbelt*. Berkeley: University of California Press.

Levi, Margaret. 1988. *Of Rule and Revenue*. Berkeley: University of California Press.

Levine, Steven I. 1987. *Anvil of Victory*. New York: Columbia University Press.

Levitsky, Steven, and Lucan A. Way. 2002. "The Rise of Competitive Authoritarianism." *Journal of Democracy* 13(2): 51–65.

Li Changping. 2002. *Wo xiang Zongli Shuo Shihua* (Telling the Premier the Truth). Beijing: Guangming Ribao Chubanshe.

———. 2006. "Quxiao nongye shui jiang yinfa yi xilie shenke biange" (Abolition of the agricultural tax has just triggered a series of essential changes). (http://www.usc.cuhk.edu.he/wkgb.asp, accessed January 13, 2006).

Li Changping and Dong Leiming (eds.). 2004. *Shuifei Gaige Beijing xia de Xiangzhen Tizhi Yanjiu* (Studies on the Township Regime under the Influence of the Tax-for-Fee Reform). Wuhan: Hubei Renmin Chubanshe.

Li Deqiang and Lei Xiaojun. 2005. "Nongye shui quxiao hou nongcun xin wenti de duice sikao" (A reflection on measures of the new issues arising after the abolition of the agricultural tax). (http://www.chinaelections.org/NewsInfo.asp?NewsID=40505, accessed September 20, 2009).

Li, Hongbin, and Scott Rozelle. 2003. "Privatizing Rural China: Insider Privatization, Innovative Contracts and the Performance of Township Enterprises." *The China Quarterly* 176: 981–1005.

Li Jiange and Han Jun. 2004. "Jiejue wo guo xin jieduan 'sannong' wenti de silu" (A framework to solve Chinese "agriculture, countryside, and farmers" in the new stage). *Neibu Canyue* (Inside Reference) 695: 2–16.

Li, Lianjiang. 1999. "The Two-Ballot System in Shanxi Province: Subjecting Village Party Secretaries to a Popular Vote." *The China Journal* 42: 103–18.

______. 2001. "Elections and Popular Resistance in Rural China." *China Information* 15(2): 1–19.

______. 2002. "The Politics of Introducing Direct Township Elections in China." *The China Quarterly* 171: 704–23.

______. 2003. "The Empowering Effect of Village Elections in China." *Asian Survey* 43: 648–62.

______. 2004. "Political Trust in Rural China." *Modern China* 30: 228–58.

______. 2008. "Political Trust and Petitioning in the Chinese Countryside." *Comparative Politics* 40: 209–26.

______. 2010. "Rights Consciousness and Rules Consciousness in Contemporary China." *The China Journal* 64: 47–68.

______. 2011. "Distrust in Government Leaders, Demand for Leadership Change, and Preference for Popular Elections in Rural China." *Political Behavior* 33: 291–311.

______. 2013. "The Magnitude and Resilience of Trust in the Center: Evidence from Interviews with Petitioners in Beijing and a Local Survey in Rural China." *Modern China* 39: 3–36.

Li Lianjiang, Guo Zhenglin, and Xiao Tangbiao (eds.). 2001. *Cunweihui Xuanju Guancha* (Studies on Village Elections). Tianjin: Tianjin Renmin Chubanshe.

Li, Lianjiang, Minxing Liu, and Kevin J. O'Brien. 2012. "Petitioning Beijing: The High Tide of 2003–2006." *The China Quarterly* 210: 313–34.

Li, Lianjiang, and Kevin J. O'Brien. 1996. "Villagers and Popular Resistance in Contemporary China." *Modern China* 22: 28–61.

______. 1999. "The Struggle over Village Elections." In Merle Goldman and Roderick MacFarquhar (eds.), *The Paradox of China's Post-Mao Reforms*. Cambridge, MA: Harvard University Press.

Li Lina. 2001. "Shandong mou cun cunji zuzhi jianshe zhuangkuang" (An observation on the construction of a village organization in a certain village in Shandong). In Li Lianjiang, Guo Zhenglin, and Xiao Tangbiao (eds.), *Cunweihui Xuanju Guancha* (Studies on Village Elections). Tianjin: Tianjin Renmin Chubanshe.

Li, Linda Chelan. 2006. "Differentiated Actors: Central-Local Politics in China's Rural Tax Reforms." *Modern Asian Studies* 40: 151–74.

______. 2007. "Working for the Peasants? Strategic Interactions and Unintended Consequences in Chinese Rural Tax Reform." *The China Journal* 57: 89–106.

Li Linda Chelan and Wu Licai. 2005. "'Dao bi' haishi 'fan dao bi': Nongcun shuifei gaige qianhou zhongyang yu difang zhi jian de hudong" (Pressure for changes: Central-local

interactions in the rural tax-for-fee reform). *Shehuixue Yanjiu* (Sociological Studies) 20: 44–63.
Li Rui. 2009. *Shidi Nongmin Quanyi Baozhang* (How to Secure Rights and Interests When Farmers Lose Land). Beijing: Zhishi Chanquan Chubanshe.
Li, Xiande. 2003. "Rethinking the Peasant Burden: Evidence from a Chinese Village." *Journal of Peasant Studies* 30: 45–74.
Lieberthal, Kenneth. 1997. "The Great Leap Forward and the Split in the Yan'an Leadership, 1958–65." In Roderick MacFarquhar (ed.), *The Politics of China: The Eras of Mao and Deng*, second edition. New York: Cambridge University Press.
Liebman, Benjamin. 1998. "Class Action Litigation in China." *Harvard Law Review* 111: 1523–41.
Lin, Justin Yifu, Ran Tao, and Mingxing Liu. 2007. "Rural Taxation and Local Governance Reform in China's Economic Transition: Origins, Policy Responses and Remaining Challenges." Stanford Center for International Development, Working Paper No. 317.
Lin, Justin Yifu, Ran Tao, Mingxing Liu, and Qi Zheng. 2002a. "The Problem of Taxing Peasants in China." Manuscript. Peking University.
———. 2002b. "Urban and Rural Household Taxation in China: Measurement and Stylized Facts." Manuscript. Peking University.
Lin Yifu. 1992. *Zhidu, Jishu yu Zhongguo Nongye Fazhan* (Institutions, Technology, and Agricultural Development in China). Shanghai: Shanghai Sanlian Shudian.
Lin, Yi-min. 2001. *Between Politics and Markets: Firms, Competition, and Institutional Change in Post-Mao China*. New York: Cambridge University Press.
Linz, Juan J. 2000. *Totalitarian and Authoritarian Regimes*. Boulder, CO: Lynne Rienner Publishers.
Liu, Mingxing, Juan Wang, Ran Tao, and Rachel Murphy. 2009. "The Political Economy of Earmarked Transfers in a State-Designated Poor County in Western China: Central Policies and Local Responses." *The China Quarterly* 200: 973–94.
Liu Ya. 2004. *Jieti yu Chonggou: Xiandaihua Jinchengzhong de "Guojia–Xiangcun Shehui"* (Dismantlement and Restructuring: "State–Rural Society" Relations during Modernization). Beijing: Zhongguo Shehui Kexue Chubanshe.
Liu, Yawei. 2000. "Consequences of Villager Committee Elections in China: Better Local Governance or More Consolidation of State Power?" *China Perspectives* 31: 19–35.
Lü, Xiaobo. 1997. "The Politics of Peasant Burden in Reform China." *The Journal of Peasant Studies* 24: 113–38.
———. 2000a. "Booty Socialism, Bureau-preneurs, and the State in Transition: Organizational Corruption in China." *Comparative Politics* 32: 273–94.
———. 2000b. *Cadres and Corruption: The Organizational Involution of the Chinese Communist Party*. Stanford, CA: Stanford University Press.
Lubman, Stanley B. 1999. *Birds in a Cage: Legal Reform in China after Mao*. Stanford, CA: Stanford University Press.
Luehrmann, Laura M. 2000. "Officials Face the Masses: Citizen Contacting in Modern China." Ph.D. dissertation. The Ohio State University.
———. 2003. "Facing Citizen Complaints in China, 1951–1996." *Asian Survey* 43: 845–66.
Luo Xingzuo. 2001. "Haixuan ji qi xiangguan wenti de shizheng fenxi: Qudou Cun zhixuan guancha" (An empirical analysis of direct elections and their relevant issues:

A study on the direct election in Qudou Village). In Xiao Tangbiao, Qiu Xinyou, and Tang Xiaoteng (eds.), *Duowei Shijiao zhong de Cunmin Zhixuan: Dui Shi-Wu ge Cunweihui Xuanju de Guancha Yanjiu* (Village Elections from a Multidimensional Angle: Studies on Fifteen Village Elections). Beijing: Zhongguo Shehui Kexue Chubanse.

———. 2002. "Zongzu geju yu xiangcun xuanju: Hangbu Cun xuanju guancha yu sikao" (Kinship groups and village elections: A study on the election in Hangbu Village). In Xiao Tangbiao (ed.), *Zongzu, Xiangcun Quanli yu Xuanju: Dui Jiangxi Sheng Shi-Er ge Cunweihui Xuanju de Guancha Yanjiu* (Kinships, Rural Power, and Elections: Studies on Twelve Village Elections in Jiangxi Province). Xi'an: Xibei Daxue Chubanshe.

Luo Xingzuo and Xiao Tangbiao. 2001. "Xuanju zhong de jingji yu zongzu yinsu fenxi: Shiqiao Cun di si jie cunwei huanjie xuanju de guancha yu sikao" (An analysis of economic and kinship factors in elections: A study on the fourth village election in Shiqiao Village). In Li Lianjiang, Guo Zhenglin, and Xiao Tangbiao (eds.), *Cunweihui Xuanju Guancha* (Studies on Village Elections). Tianjin: Tianjin Renmin Chubanshe.

Lust-Okar, Ellen. 2005. *Structuring Conflict in the Arab World: Incumbents, Opponents, and Institutions.* New York: Cambridge University Press.

MacFarquhar, Roderick. 1983. *The Origins of the Cultural Revolution 2: The Great Leap Forward 1958–1960.* New York: Columbia University Press.

Magaloni, Beatriz. 2006. *Voting for Autocracy: Hegemonic Party Survival and Its Demise in Mexico.* New York: Cambridge University Press.

Mallee, Hein. 1988. "Rural-Urban Migration Control in People's Republic of China: Effects of the Recent Reform." *China Information* 11(4): 12–22.

———. 1995. "China's Household Registration System under Reform." *Development and Change* 26: 1–29.

Manion, Melanie. 1996. "The Electoral Connection in the Chinese Countryside." *American Political Science Review* 90: 736–48.

———. 2000. "Chinese Democratization in Perspective: Electorates and Selectorates at the Township Level." *The China Quarterly* 163: 764–82.

———. 2004. *Corruption by Design: Building Clean Government in Mainland China and Hong Kong.* New York: Cambridge University Press.

———. 2006. "Democracy, Community, Trust: The Impact of Elections in Rural China." *Comparative Political Studies* 39: 301–24.

———. 2008. "When Communist Party Candidates Can Lose, Who Wins? Assessing the Role of Local People's Congresses in the Selection of Leaders in China." *The China Quarterly* 195: 607–30.

———. 2009. "How to Assess Village Elections in China." *Journal of Contemporary China* 18: 379–83.

Mathias, Peter, and Patrick O'Brien. 1976. "Taxation in Britain and France, 1715–1810: A Comparison of the Social and Economic Incidence of Taxes Collected for the Central Government." *Journal of European Economic History* 5: 601–50.

Mayhew, David. 1975. *Congress: The Electoral Connection.* New Haven, CT: Yale University Press.

McCubbins, Mathew D., and Thomas Schwartz. 1984. "Congressional Oversight Overlooked: Police Patrols versus Fire Alarms." *American Journal of Political Science* 28: 165–79.

McKenzie, Robert Trelford. 1963. *British Political Parties: The Distribution of Power within the Conservative and Labour Parties*, second edition. New York: St. Martin's Press.
Migdal, Joel S. 1988. *Strong Societies and Weak States: State-Society Relations and State Capacities in the Third World.* Princeton, NJ: Princeton University Press.
Montinola, Gabriella, Yingyi Qian, and Barry R. Weingast. 1995. "Federalism, Chinese Style: The Political Basis for Economic Success in China." *World Politics* 48: 50–81.
Mozaffar, Shaheen. 2002. "Patterns of Electoral Governance in Africa's Emerging Democracies." *International Political Science Review* 23: 85–101.
Naughton, Barry. 2007. *The Chinese Economy: Transitions and Growth.* Cambridge, MA: MIT Press.
Norberg, Kathryn. 1994. "The French Fiscal Crisis of 1788 and the Financial Origins of the Revolution of 1789." In Philip T. Hoffman and Kathryn Norberg (eds.), *Fiscal Crises, Liberty, and Representative Government, 1450–1789.* Stanford, CA: Stanford University Press.
Norris, Pippa. 2002. "Campaign Communications." In Lawrence LeDuc, Richard G. Niemi, and Pippa Norris (eds.), *Comparing Democracies 2: New Challenges in the Study of Elections and Voting.* Thousand Oaks, CA: Sage Publications.
North, Douglass C. 1981. *Structure and Change in Economic History.* New York: W. W. Norton & Company.
———. 1990. *Institutions, Institutional Change, and Economic Performance.* New York: Cambridge University Press.
North, Douglass C., and Robert P. Thomas. 1973. *The Rise of the Western World: A New Economic History.* New York: Cambridge University Press.
North, Douglass C., and Barry R. Weingast. 1989. "Constitutions and Commitment: The Evolution of Institutions Governing Public Choice in Seventeenth-Century England." *Journal of Economic History* 49: 803–32.
O'Brien, Kevin J. 1994a. "Agents and Remonstrators: Role Accumulation by Chinese People's Congress Deputies." *The China Quarterly* 138: 359–80.
———. 1994b. "Implementing Political Reform in China's Villages." *Australian Journal of Chinese Affairs* 32: 33–60.
———. 1996. "Rightful Resistance." *World Politics* 49: 31–55.
———. 2002. "Collective Action in the Chinese Countryside." *China Journal* 48: 139–154.
———. 2010. "How Authoritarian Rule Works." *Modern China* 36: 79–86.
O'Brien, Kevin J., and Rongbin Han. 2009. "Path to Democracy? Assessing Village Elections in China." *Journal of Contemporary China* 18: 359–78.
O'Brien, Kevin J., and Lianjiang Li. 1995. "The Politics of Lodging Complaints in Rural China." *The China Quarterly* 143: 756–83.
———. 1999. "Selective Policy Implementation in Rural China." *Comparative Politics* 31: 167–86.
———. 2001. "Accommodating 'Democracy' in a One-Party State: Introducing Village Elections in China." In Larry Diamond and Ramon H. Myers (eds.), *Elections and Democracy in Greater China.* Oxford: Oxford University Press.
———. 2005. "Suing the Local State: Administrative Litigation in Rural China." In Neil J. Diamant, Stanley B. Lubman, and Kevin J. O'Brien (eds.), *Engaging the Law in China: State, Society, and Possibilities for Justice.* Stanford, CA: Stanford University Press.

______. 2006. *Rightful Resistance in Rural China*. New York: Cambridge University Press.
Ocko, Jonathan. 1988. "I'll Take It All the Way to Beijing: Capital Appeals in the Qing." *Journal of Asian Studies* 47: 291–315.
Odgaard, Ole. 1992. *Private Enterprises in Rural China: Impact on Agricultural and Social Stratification*. Brookfield, VT: Ashgate.
Oi, Jean C. 1989. *State and Peasant in Contemporary China: The Political Economy of Village Government*. Berkeley: University of California Press.
______. 1990. "The Fate of the Collective after the Commune." In Deborah Davis and Ezra Vogel (eds.), *Chinese Society on the Eve of Tiananmen: The Impact of Reform*. Cambridge, MA: Council on East Asian Studies, Harvard University.
______. 1992. "Fiscal Reform and the Economic Foundations of Local State Corporatism in China." *World Politics* 45: 99–126.
______. 1995. "The Role of the Local State in China's Transitional Economy." *The China Quarterly* 144: 1132–49.
______. 1996. "Economic Development, Stability and Democratic Village Self-Governance." In Maurice Brosseau, Suzanne Pepper, and Shu-ki Tsang (eds.), *China Review 1996*. Hong Kong: Chinese University Press.
______. 1999. *Rural China Takes Off: Institutional Foundations of Economic Reform*. Berkeley: University of California Press.
______. 2004. "Old Problems for New Leaders: Institutional Disjunctions in Rural China." In Yun-han Chu, Chih-cheng Lo, and Ramon H. Myers (eds.), *The New Chinese Leadership: Challenges and Opportunities after the 16th Party Congress*. Cambridge: Cambridge University Press.
Oi, Jean C., and Scott Rozelle. 2001. "Elections and Power: The Locus of Decision-Making in Chinese Villages." In Larry Diamond and Ramon H. Myers (eds.), *Elections and Democracy in Greater China*. Oxford: Oxford University Press.
Oi, Jean C., and Andrew G. Walder (eds.). 1999. *Property Rights and Economic Reform in China*. Stanford, CA: Stanford University Press.
Oi, Jean C., and Shukai Zhao. 2007. "Fiscal Crisis in China's Townships: Causes and Consequences." In Elizabeth J. Perry and Merle Goldman (eds.), *Grassroots Political Reform in Contemporary China*. Cambridge, MA: Harvard University Press.
Oksenberg, Michel, and James Tong. 1991. "The Evolution of Central-Provincial Fiscal Relations in China, 1971–1984: The Formal System." *The China Quarterly* 125: 1–32.
Olson, Mancur. 1993. "Dictatorship, Democracy, and Development." *American Political Science Review* 87: 567–76.
Ong, Lynette. 2006. "The Political Economy of Township Government Debt, Township Enterprises and Rural Financial Institutions in China." *The China Quarterly* 186: 377–400.
______. 2012. *Prosper or Perish: The Political Economy of Credit and Fiscal Systems in Rural China*. Ithaca, NY: Cornell University Press.
Ostrom, Elinor. 1990. *Governing the Commons: The Evolution of Institutions for Collective Action*. New York: Cambridge University Press.
______. 2005. *Understanding Institutional Diversity*. Princeton, NJ: Princeton University Press.
Paik, Woo Yeal. 2009. "Political Participation, Clientelism, and State-Society Relations in Contemporary China." Ph.D. dissertation. University of California at Los Angeles.

Paik, Wooyeal, and Kihyun Lee. 2012. "I Want to Be Exploited!: The Politics of Xiaochanquanfang Land Development in Suburban China." *Journal of Contemporary China* 21: 261–79.

Pan Wei. 2003. *Nongmin yu Shichang: Zhongguo Jiceng Zhengquan yu Xiangzhen Qiye* (Farmers and the Market: Grassroots Authorities and Township-and-Village Enterprises in China). Beijing: Shangwu Yinshuguan.

Pastor, Robert A., and Qingshan Tan. 2001. "The Meaning of China's Village Elections." In Larry Diamond and Ramon H. Myers (eds.), *Elections and Democracy in Greater China*. Oxford: Oxford University Press.

Pateman, Carole. 1970. *Participation and Democratic Theory*. Cambridge: Cambridge University Press.

Peerenboom, Randall P. 2002. *China's Long March toward Rule of Law*. New York: Cambridge University Press.

Pei, Minxin. 1995. "Creeping Democratization in China." *Journal of Democracy* 6: 65–79.

———. 1997. "Citizens v. Mandarins: Administrative Litigation in China." *The China Quarterly* 152: 832–62.

———. 2006. *China's Trapped Transition: The Limits of Developmental Autocracy*. Cambridge, MA: Harvard University Press.

Peng, Yali. 1996. "The Politics of Tobacco: Relations between Farmers and Local Governments in China's Southwest." *The China Journal* 36: 67–82.

Perry, Elizabeth J. 1980. *Rebels and Revolutionaries in North China, 1845–1945*. Stanford, CA: Stanford University Press.

———. 1985. "Rural Violence in Socialist China." *The China Quarterly* 103: 414–40.

———. 1994. "Trends in the Study of Chinese Politics: State-Society Relations." *The China Quarterly* 139: 704–13.

———. 2002. *Challenging the Mandate of Heaven: Social Protest and State Power in China*. Armonk, NY: M. E. Sharpe.

Powell, G. Bingham, Jr. 1982. *Contemporary Democracies: Participation, Stability, and Violence*. Cambridge, MA: Harvard University Press.

Pye, Lucian W. 1986. "Reassessing the Cultural Revolution." *The China Quarterly* 108: 597–612.

Qian Zhenming. 2001. "Cunweihui de minzhu xuanju ji qi dui cunmin de yingxiang: Suzhou Xiawei Cun de diaocha yu sikao" (Village elections and their effect on villagers: A study in Xiawei Village in Suzhou). In Li Lianjiang, Guo Zhenglin, and Xiao Tangbiao (eds.), *Cunweihui Xuanju Guancha* (Studies on Village Elections). Tianjin: Tianjin Renmin Chubanshe.

Qiu Xinyou. 2001. "Zhengfu zhudao yu liyi qudong: Tie Cun xuanju guancha" (Government's initiative and interest drive: A study on the election in Tie Village). In Xiao Tangbiao, Qiu Xinyou, and Tang Xiaoteng (eds.), *Duowei Shijiao zhong de Cunmin Zhixuan: Dui Shi-Wu ge Cunweihui Xuanju de Guancha Yanjiu* (Village Elections from a Multidimensional Angle: Studies on Fifteen Village Elections). Beijing: Zhongguo Shehui Kexue Chubanse.

Qiu Xinyou, He Xuefeng, Song Zhiyong, and Yi Hui. 2001. "Cunzhuang quanli fenpei geju xia de cunmin xuanju: Guan Cun xuanju guancha" (A village election under the distribution of power in the village: A study on the election in Guan Village). In Xiao Tangbiao, Qiu Xinyou, and Tang Xiaoteng (eds.), *Duowei Shijiao zhong de Cunmin Zhixuan: Dui Shi-Wu ge Cunweihui Xuanju de Guancha Yanjiu*

(Village Elections from a Multidimensional Angle: Studies on Fifteen Village Elections). Beijing: Zhongguo Shehui Kexue Chubanse.

Qiu Xinyou, Qiu Guoliang, and Xiao Tangbiao. 2002. "Xuanju zhong de zongzu yinsu: Zhong Cun xuanju guancha" (The kinship factor in elections: A study on the village election in Zhong Village). In Xiao Tangbiao (ed.), *Zongzu, Xiangcun Quanli yu Xuanju: Dui Jiangxi Sheng Shi-Er ge Cunweihui Xuanju de Guancha Yanjiu* (Kinships, Rural Power, and Elections: Studies on Twelve Village Elections in Jiangxi Province). Xi'an: Xibei Daxue Chubanshe.

Qiu Xinyou and Xiao Tangbiao. 2001. "Minzhu xuanju zhong de qiangren, xiangcun ganbu yu guojia: Zhou Cun xuanju de guancha yu sikao" (Strong people, rural cadres, and the state in democratic elections: A study on the election in Zhou Village). In Li Lianjiang, Guo Zhenglin, and Xiao Tangbiao (eds.), *Cunweihui Xuanju Guancha* (Studies on Village Elections). Tianjin: Tianjin Renmin Chubanshe.

Raymond, Chad, Mark Selden, and Kate Zhou. 2000. "The Power of the Strong? Rural Resistance and Reform in China and Vietnam." *China Information* 14(2): 1–30.

Remick, Elizabeth J. 2002. "The Significance of Variation in Local States: The Case of Local States in Twentieth Century China." *Comparative Politics* 34: 399–418.

Rozelle, Scott. 1991. "The Economic Behavior of Village Leaders in China's Reform Economy." Ph.D. dissertation. Cornell University.

______. 1994. "Decision-Making in China's Rural Economy: The Linkages between Village Leaders and Farm Households." *The China Quarterly* 137: 99–125.

Sacks, David Harris. 1994. "The Paradox of Taxation: Fiscal Crises, Parliament, and Liberty in England, 1450–1640." In Philip T. Hoffman and Kathryn Norberg (eds.), *Fiscal Crisis, Liberty, and Representative Government, 1450–1789*. Stanford, CA: Stanford University Press.

Sartori, Giovanni. 1987. *The Theory of Democracy Revisited*. Chatham, NJ: Chatham House Publishers.

Schatz, Edward. 2006. "Access by Accident: Legitimacy Claims and Democracy Promotion in Authoritarian Central Asia." *International Political Science Review* 27: 263–84.

Schedler, Andreas. 2002. "The Menu of Manipulation." *Journal of Democracy* 13(2): 36–50.

Schubert, Gunter. 2002. "Village Elections in the PRC: A Trojan Horse of Democracy?" Manuscript. Gerhard-Mercator-University Duisburg.

______. 2008. "One-Party Rule and the Question of Legitimacy in Contemporary China: Preliminary Thoughts on Setting Up a New Research Agenda." *Journal of Contemporary China* 17: 191–204.

______. 2009. "Studying 'Democratic' Governance in Contemporary China: Looking at the Village Is Not Enough." *Journal of Contemporary China* 18: 385–90.

Schubert, Gunter, and Xuelian Chen. 2007. "Village Elections in Contemporary China: New Spaces for Generating Regime Legitimacy? Experiences from Lishu County." *China Perspectives* 3: 12–25.

Scott, James C. 1985. *Weapons of the Weak: Everyday Forms of Peasant Resistance*. New Haven, CT: Yale University Press.

______. 1998. *Seeing like a State: How Certain Schemes to Improve the Human Condition Have Failed*. New Haven, CT: Yale University Press.

Shapiro, Ian. 1996. *Democracy's Place*. Ithaca, NY: Cornell University Press.

Shen Yansheng and Zhang Shouli. 2003. "Zizhi yihuo xingzheng: Zhongguo xiangzhi de huigu yu zhanwang" (Self-governance or administration: Retrospection and foresight of rural governance in China). In Xu Yong (ed.), *Zhongguo Nongcun Yanjiu 2002 Juan* (Chinese Rural Studies 2002). Beijing: Zhongguo Shehui Kexue Chubanshe.

Shevchenko, Alexei V. 2002. "Party of Entrepreneurs: The Chinese Communist Party's Survival and Adaptation in the Age of Reform." Ph.D. dissertation. University of California, Los Angeles.

Shi Congmei. 2002. "Qiangshi zongzu beijing xia de guize youxi: Cao Cun xuanju guancha yu sikao" (Playing with rules backed by a strong kinship group: A study on the election in Cao Village). In Xiao Tangbiao (ed.), *Zongzu, Xiangcun Quanli yu Xuanju: Dui Jiangxi Sheng Shi-Er ge Cunweihui Xuanju de Guancha Yanjiu* (Kinships, Rural Power, and Elections: Studies on Twelve Village Elections in Jiangxi Province). Xi'an: Xibei Daxue Chubanshe.

Shi, Tianjian. 1999. "Village Committee Elections in China: Institutional Tactics for Democracy." *World Politics* 51: 385–412.

Shih, Victor, and Qi Zhang. 2007. "Who Receives Subsidies? A Look at the County Level in Two Time Periods." In Vivienne Shue and Christine P. W. Wong (eds.), *Paying for Progress in China: Public Finance, Human Welfare and Changing Patterns of Inequality*. New York: Routledge.

Shirk, Susan L. 2007. *China: Fragile Superpower*. New York: Oxford University Press.

Shue, Vivienne. 1980. *Peasant China in Transition: The Dynamics of Development toward Socialism, 1949–1956*. Berkeley: University of California Press.

______. 1984. "The Fate of the Communes." *Modern China* 10: 259–83.

______. 1988. *The Reach of the State: Sketches of the Chinese Body Politic*. Stanford, CA: Stanford University Press.

Siu, Helen F. 1989. *Agents and Victims in South China: Accomplices in Rural Revolution*. New Haven, CT: Yale University Press.

Solinger, Dorothy J. 1999. *Contesting Citizenship in Urban China: Peasant Migrants, the State, and the Logic of the Market*. Berkeley: University of California Press.

Song Zhiyong. 2001. "Ren zhong er dao yuan: Hejiang Cun xuanju guancha" (A heavy task and a far distance: A study on the election in Hejiang Village). In Xiao Tangbiao, Qiu Xinyou, and Tang Xiaoteng (eds.), *Duowei Shijiao zhong de Cunmin Zhixuan: Dui Shi-Wu ge Cunweihui Xuanju de Guancha Yanjiu* (Village Elections from a Multidimensional Angle: Studies on Fifteen Village Elections). Beijing: Zhongguo Shehui Kexue Chubanse.

______. 2002. "Chuyu minzhu: Nanmen Cun xuanju guancha" (Democracy introduced: A study on the election in Nanmen Village). In Xiao Tangbiao (ed.), *Zongzu, Xiangcun Quanli yu Xuanju: Dui Jiangxi Sheng Shi-Er ge Cunweihui Xuanju de Guancha Yanjiu* (Kinships, Rural Power, and Elections: Studies on Twelve Village Elections in Jiangxi Province). Xi'an: Xibei Daxue Chubanshe.

Steinfeld, Edward S. 1998. *Forging Reform in China: The Fate of State-Owned Industry*. New York: Cambridge University Press.

Stokes, Donald. 1992. "Valence Politics." In Dennis Kavanagh (ed.), *Electoral Politics*. New York: Oxford University Press.

Su Ming. 2002. "Guanyu wo guo nongcun jichu jiaoyu caizheng zhichi de zhengce tansuo" (Search for policies concerning fiscal support for fundamental education in rural China). *Neibu Canyue* (Internal Reference) 616: 2–11.

Sun Liping. 2004. *Zuanxing yu Duanlie: Gaige Yilai Zhongguo Shehui Jiegou de Bianqian* (Transformation and Split: Transition of Social Structure in Reforms). Beijing: Qinghua Daxue Chubanshe.

Sun, Yan. 2004. *Corruption and Market in Contemporary China*. Ithaca, NY: Cornell University Press.

Tan, Qingshan. 2009. "Building Democratic Infrastructure: Village Electoral Institutions." *Journal of Contemporary China* 18: 411–20.

Tang Xiaoteng. 2001a. "Xuanju, gongzheng yu mianzi: Shiqian Cunweihui huanjie xuanju de diaocha" (Elections, justice, and face: A study on the village election in Shiqian). In Li Lianjiang, Guo Zhenglin, and Xiao Tangbiao (eds.), *Cunweihui Xuanju Guancha* (Studies on Village Elections). Tianjin: Tianjin Renmin Chubanshe.

______. 2001b. "Zhengfu de zuoyong ji qi buwanshanxing: Makou Cun diaocha" (Government's functions and their incompleteness: A study in Makou Village). In Xiao Tangbiao, Qiu Xinyou, and Tang Xiaoteng (eds.), *Duowei Shijiao zhong de Cunmin Zhixuan: Dui Shi-Wu ge Cunweihui Xuanju de Guancha Yanjiu* (Village Elections from a Multidimensional Angle: Studies on Fifteen Village Elections). Beijing: Zhongguo Shehui Kexue Chubanse.

Tang Xiaoteng, Yang Da, and Xiao Tangbiao. 2002. "Yingxiang minzhu xuanju de yinsu fenxi: Chengfang Cun xuanju diaocha" (An analysis on the factors influencing a democratic election: A study on the election in Chengfang Village). In Xiao Tangbiao (ed.), *Zongzu, Xiangcun Quanli yu Xuanju: Dui Jiangxi Sheng Shi-Er ge Cunweihui Xuanju de Guancha Yanjiu* (Kinships, Rural Power, and Elections: Studies on Twelve Village Elections in Jiangxi Province). Xi'an: Xibei Daxue Chubanshe.

Tang, Yuen Yuen. 2005. "When Peasants Sue En Masse: Large-Scale Collective ALL Suits in Rural China." *China: An International Journal* 3: 24–49.

Tao, Ran, Mingxing Liu, Fubing Su, and Xi Lu. 2011. "Grain Procurement, Tax Instrument and Peasant Burdens during China's Rural Transition." *Journal of Contemporary China* 20: 659–77.

Teiwes, Frederick C. 1997. "The Establishment and Consolidation of the New Regime." In Roderick MacFarquhar (ed.), *The Politics of China: The Eras of Mao and Deng*, second edition. New York: Cambridge University Press.

Thaxton, Ralph A., Jr. 1997. *Salt of the Earth: The Political Origins of Peasant Protest and Communist Revolution in China*. Berkeley: University of California Press.

______. 2008. *Catastrophe and Contention in Rural China: Mao's Great Leap Forward Famine and the Origins of Righteous Resistance in Da Fo Village*. New York: Cambridge University Press.

Tiebout, Charles M. 1956. "A Pure Theory of Local Expenditures." *Journal of Political Economy* 64: 416–24.

Tilly, Charles. 1990. *Coercion, Capital, and European States, AD 990–1992*. Cambridge, MA: Blackwell.

Tocqueville, Alexis de. [1835 & 1840] 2000. *Democracy in America*, edited and translated by Harvey Mansfield and Delba Winthrop. Chicago, IL: University of Chicago Press.

Tong, James W. 2009. *Revenge of the Forbidden City: The Suppression of the Falungong in China, 1999–2005*. New York: Oxford University Press.

Tong Zhihui. 2001. "'Cunzheng jingying junheng' yu xiangcun minzhu de zhilihua: Ai Cun xuanju guancha" (The balance of village elites and governance of rural democracy: A study on the election in Ai Village). In Xiao Tangbiao, Qiu Xinyou, and Tang Xiaoteng (eds.), *Duowei Shijiao zhong de Cunmin Zhixuan: Dui Shi-Wu ge Cunweihui Xuanju de Guancha Yanjiu* (Village Elections from a Multidimensional Angle: Studies on Fifteen Village Elections). Beijing: Zhongguo Shehui Kexue Chubanse.

______. 2002. *Xiangcun Guanxi Shiye zhong de Cunzhuang Xuanju: Yi Neimenggu Qiao Xiang Cunweihui Huanjie Xuanju wei Gean* (Village Elections in the Perspective of Township-Village Relations: Case Studies from Village Elections in Xiang Township in Inner Mongolia). Xi'an: Xibei Daxue Chubanshe.

______. 2004. *Xuanju Shijian yu Cunzhuang Zhengzhi: Cunzhuang Shehui Guanlian zhong de Cunmin Xuanju* (Elections and Village Politics: Village Elections in Networks in Village Society). Beijing: Zhongguo Shehui Kexue Chubanshe.

Tong Zhihui and Yu Wenhua. 2001. "Xiangcun guanxi, cunzhuang quanli jiegou yu xuanju: You Cun cunweihui xuanju guancha" (Township-village relations, village power structure, and an election: A Study on the village election in You Village). In Li Lianjiang, Guo Zhenglin, and Xiao Tangbiao (eds.), *Cunweihui Xuanju Guancha* (Studies on Village Elections). Tianjin: Tianjin Renmin Chubanshe.

Treisman, Daniel. 1996. "The Politics of Intergovernmental Transfers in Post-Soviet Russia." *British Journal of Political Science* 26: 299–335.

______. 1999a. *After Deluge: Regional Crises and Political Consolidation in Russia*. Ann Arbor: University of Michigan Press.

______. 1999b. "Political Decentralization and Economic Reform: A Game-Theoretic Analysis." *American Journal of Political Science* 43: 488–517.

Tsai, Kellee S. 2002. *Back-Alley Banking: Private Entrepreneurs in China*. Ithaca, NY: Cornell University.

______. 2007. *Capitalism without Democracy: The Private Sector in Contemporary China*. Ithaca, NY: Cornell University Press.

Tsai, Lily L. 2007a. *Accountability without Democracy: Solidary Groups and Public Goods Provision in Rural China*. New York: Cambridge University Press.

______. 2007b. "Solidary Groups, Informal Accountability, and Local Public Goods Provision in Rural China." *American Political Science Review* 101: 355–72.

Tsebelis, George. 1989. "The Abuse of Probability in Political Analysis: The Robinson Crusoe Fallacy." *American Political Science Review* 83: 77–91.

Tsui, Kai-yuan, and Youqiang Wang. 2004. "Between Separate Stoves and a Single Menu: Fiscal Decentralization in China." *The China Quarterly* 177: 71–90.

Unger, Jonathan. 1989. "State and Peasant in Post-Revolution China." *The Journal of Peasant Studies* 17: 114–36.

______. 2002. *The Transformation of Rural China*. Armonk, NY: M. E. Sharpe.

Wald, Kenneth D. 1983. *Crosses on the Ballot: Patterns of British Voter Alignment since 1885*. Princeton, NJ: Princeton University Press.

Walder, Andrew G. 1995. "Local Governments as Industrial Firms: An Organizational Analysis of China's Transitional Economy." *American Journal of Sociology* 101: 263–301.

Wang Bing. 2001. "Cunweihui zhixuan zhong xiangzheng yizhi de kuozhang: Quchi Cun xuanju guancha." (The expansion of political consciousness during a village election: A study on the election in Quchi Village). In Xiao Tangbiao, Qiu Xinyou, and Tang Xiaoteng (eds.), *Duowei Shijiao zhong de Cunmin Zhixuan: Dui Shi-Wu ge Cunweihui Xuanju de Guancha Yanjiu* (Village Elections from a Multidimensional Angle: Studies on Fifteen Village Elections). Beijing: Zhongguo Shehui Kexue Chubanse.

Wang Fei. 2001. "Yi ci jingzhengxing jiaoqiang de xuanju: Putian Cun xuanju jishi" (A relatively competitive election: An observation of the election in Putian Village). In Xiao Tangbiao, Qiu Xinyou, and Tang Xiaoteng (eds.), *Duowei Shijiao zhong de Cunmin Zhixuan: Dui Shi-Wu ge Cunweihui Xuanju de Guancha Yanjiu* (Village Elections from a Multidimensional Angle: Studies on Fifteen Village Elections). Beijing: Zhongguo Shehui Kexue Chubanse.

Wang, Shaoguang. 1995. "The Rise of the Regions: Fiscal Reform and the Decline of Central State Capacity in China." In Andrew G. Walder (ed.), *The Waning of the Communist State: Economic Origins of Political Decline in China and Hungary*. Berkeley: University of California Press.

Wang, Shaoguang, and Angang Hu. 2001. *The Chinese Economy in Crisis: State Capacity and Tax Reform*. Armonk, NY: M. E. Sharpe.

Wang Xiaojun. 2001. "Gezhong liliang jiaozhu xia de minzhu xuanju: Zhong Cun xuanju guancha" (Democratic elections under rivalries of various powers: An observation of the election in Zhong Village). In Xiao Tangbiao, Qiu Xinyou, and Tang Xiaoteng (eds.), *Duowei Shijiao zhong de Cunmin Zhixuan: Dui Shiwu ge Cunweihui Xuanju de Guancha Yanjiu* (Village Elections from a Multidimensional Angle: Studies on Fifteen Village Elections). Beijing: Zhongguo Shehui Kexue Chubanse.

Wang Xu. 1997. "Xiangcun Zhongguo de jiceng minzhu: Guojia yu shehui de quanli huqiang" (Grassroots democracy in rural China: Mutual empowerment of the state and society). *Ershi-Yi Shiji* (The Twenty-First Century) 40: 147–58.

Wang, Yeh-chien. 1971. "The Fiscal Importance of the Land Tax during the Ch'ing Period." *Journal of Asian Studies* 30: 829–42.

Wang, Zhenyao. 1998. "Village Committees: The Basis for China's Democratization." In Eduard B. Vermeer, Frank N. Pieke, and Woei Lien Chong (eds.), *Cooperative and Collective in China's Rural Development: Between State and Private Interests*. Armonk, NY: M. E. Sharpe.

Wank, David L. 1999. *Commodifying Communism: Business, Trust, and Politics in a Chinese City*. New York: Cambridge University Press.

Weber, Max. [1919] 1946. *From Max Weber: Essays in Sociology*, edited and translated by H. H. Gerth and C. Wright Mills. New York: Oxford University Press.

Wedeman, Andrew. 1997. "Stealing from the Farmers: Institutional Corruption and the 1992 IOU Crisis." *The China Quarterly* 152: 805–31.

———. 2000. "Budget, Extra Budgets, and Small Treasuries: Illegal Monies and Local Autonomy in China." *Journal of Contemporary China* 9: 489–512.

———. 2001. "Incompetence, Noise and Fear in Central-Local Relations in China." *Studies in Comparative International Development* 35: 59–83.

Wei Xinghe. 2001. "Cunmin zhixuan de daoru ji qi xiaoying: Taoyuan Cunweihui huanjie xuanju guancha" (The introduction of village elections and its effect: A study on the village election in Taoyuan). In Li Lianjiang, Guo Zhenglin, and Xiao Tangbiao (eds.), *Cunweihui Xuanju Guancha* (Studies on Village Elections). Tianjin: Tianjin Renmin Chubanshe.

———. 2002. "Shequ quanwei lingdao xia de minzhu xuanju: Guping Cun xuanju guancha" (A democratic election under the initiative of community authority: A study on the election in Guping Village). In Xiao Tangbiao (ed.), *Zongzu, Xiangcun Quanli yu Xuanju: Dui Jiangxi Sheng Shi-Er ge Cunweihui Xuanju de Guancha Yanjiu* (Kinships, Rural Power, and Elections: Studies on Twelve Village Elections in Jiangxi Province). Xi'an: Xibei Daxue Chubanshe.

White, Lynn T., III. 1998. *Unstately Power, Volume I: Local Causes of China's Economic Reforms*. Armonk, NY: M. E. Sharpe.

Whiting, Susan H. 2001. *Power and Wealth in Rural China: The Political Economy of Institutional Change*. New York: Cambridge University Press.

———. 2004. "The Cadre Evaluation System at the Grassroots: The Paradox of Party Rule." In Barry J. Naughton and Dali L. Yang (eds.), *Holding China Together: Diversity and National Integration in the Post-Deng Era*. New York: Cambridge University Press.

Whyte, Martin King. 2010. *Myth of the Social Volcano: Perceptions of Inequality and Distributive Injustice in Contemporary China*. Stanford, CA: Stanford University Press.

Will, Pierre-Etienne. 1990. *Bureaucracy and Famine in Eighteenth-Century China*, translated by Elborg Forster. Stanford, CA: Stanford University Press.

Wong, Christine. 1991. "Central-Local Relations in an Era of Fiscal Decline: The Paradox of Fiscal Decentralization in Post-Mao China." *The China Quarterly* 128: 691–715.

———. 1992. "Fiscal Reform and Local Industrialization: The Problematic Sequencing of Reform in Post-Mao China." *Modern China* 18: 197–227.

———. 2009. "Rebuilding Government for the 21st Century: Can China Incrementally Reform the Public Sector?" *The China Quarterly* 200: 929–52.

Wong, Christine P. W., and Richard M. Bird. 2008. "China's Fiscal System: A Work in Progress." In Loren Brandt and Thomas G. Rawski (eds.), *China's Great Economic Transformation*. New York: Cambridge University Press.

Wong, R. Bin. 1997. *China Transformed: Historical Change and the Limits of European Experience*. Ithaca, NY: Cornell University Press.

Wright, Teresa. 2002. "The China Democracy Party and the Politics of Protest in the 1980s–1990s." *The China Quarterly* 172: 906–26.

———. 2008. "State-Society Relations in Reform-Era China: A Unique Case of Post-socialist State-Led Late Development?" *Comparative Politics* 40: 353–74.

———. 2010. *Accepting Authoritarianism: State-Society Relations in China's Reform Era*. Stanford, CA: Stanford University Press.

Xiang Jiquan (ed.). 2004. *Zouchu "Huang Zongxi Dinglü" de Guaijuan: Zhongguo Nongcun Shuifei Gaige de Diaocha yu Yanjiu* (Emerging from the Involution of "Huang Zongxi's Law": Investigation and Research on China's Tax-for-Fee Reform). Xi'an: Xibei Daxue Chubanshe.

Xiao Jin. 2004. "Cong zhenggui jiaoyu de kunjing zou xiang wek shequ jianshe fuwu de jiaoyu peixun" (Moving from the difficulty of formal education to educational training for community building). Paper presented at the Third Conference on Constructing Rural Grassroots Organizations, Chinese University of Hong Kong.

Xiao Lihui. 2001. "Xinping Cun xuanju guancha" (A study on the election in Xinping Village). In Li Lianjiang, Guo Zhenglin, and Xiao Tangbiao (eds.), *Cunweihui Xuanju Guancha* (Studies on Village Elections). Tianjin: Tianjin Renmin Chubanshe.

Xiao Tangbiao (ed.). 2001. *Cunzhi zhong de Zongzu: Dui Jiu ge Cun de Diaocha yu Yanjiu* (Kinships in Village Governance: Studies in Nine Villages). Shanghai: Shanghai Shudian Chubanshe.

______. 2002a. "Daolun" (Introduction). In Xiao Tangbiao (ed.), *Zongzu, Xiangcun Quanli yu Xuanju: Dui Jiangxi Sheng Shi-Er ge Cunweihui Xuanju de Guancha Yanjiu* (Kinships, Rural Power, and Elections: Studies on Twelve Village Elections in Jiangxi Province). Xi'an: Xibei Daxue Chubanshe.

______ (ed.). 2002b. *Zongzu, Xiangcun Quanli yu Xuanju: Dui Jiangxi Sheng Shi-Er ge Cunweihui Xuanju de Guancha Yanjiu* (Kinships, Rural Power, and Elections: Studies on Twelve Village Elections in Jiangxi Province). Xi'an: Xibei Daxue Chubanshe.

Xiao Tangbiao, Qiu Xinyou, and Tang Xiaoteng (eds.). 2001. *Duowei Shijiao zhong de Cunmin Zhixuan: Dui Shi-Wu ge Cunweihui Xuanju de Guancha Yanjiu* (Village Elections from a Multidimensional Angle: Studies on Fifteen Village Elections). Beijing: Zhongguo Shehui Kexue Chubanse.

Xiao Tangbiao, Shi Tianjian, Qiu Xinyou, and Yu Wenhua (eds.). 2002. *Dangdai Zhongguo Nongcun Zongzu yu Xiangcun Zhili: Kua Xueke de Yanjiu yu Duihua* (Kinships and Rural Governance in Contemporary China: Interdisciplinary Studies and Dialogues). Xi'an: Xibei Daxue Chubanshe.

Xu Fuqun. 2004. "Liangwei maodun de chuli: Anzhao tongyi jiepai wudao" (How to solve the Party-administration conflict: Dancing with the same rhythm). Paper presented at the Third Conference on Constructing Rural Grassroots Organizations, Chinese University of Hong Kong.

Xu, Jiang. 2004. "'Rich Brothers' and 'Poor Cousins': The Political Economy of Post-Reform Rural Disparity in a Chinese Township." *Journal of Contemporary China* 13: 801–17.

Xu Yong. 2003. *Xiangcun Zhili yu Zhongguo Zhengzhi* (Rural Governance and Chinese Politics). Beijing: Zhongguo Shehui Kexue Chubanshe.

Yan Jing. 2001. "Zhidu yinru yu xueyuan gongtongti: Luojia Cun xuanju guancha" (Institutional incentives and a kindred community: A study on the election in Luojia Village). In Xiao Tangbiao, Qiu Xinyou, and Tang Xiaoteng (eds.), *Duowei Shijiao zhong de Cunmin Zhixuan: Dui Shi-Wu ge Cunweihui Xuanju de Guancha Yanjiu* (Village Elections from a Multidimensional Angle: Studies on Fifteen Village Elections). Beijing: Zhongguo Shehui Kexue Chubanse.

Yan Jing and Xiao Tangbiao. 2002. "Jingying zhudao yu shequ minzhu: Yongchang Cun xuanju guancha" (The elite initiative and community democracy: A study on the election in Yongchang Village). In Xiao Tangbiao (ed.), *Zongzu, Xiangcun Quanli yu Xuanju: Dui Jiangxi Sheng Shi-Er ge Cunweihui Xuanju de Guancha Yanjiu* (Kinships, Rural Power, and Elections: Studies on Twelve Village Elections in Jiangxi Province). Xi'an: Xibei Daxue Chubanshe.

Yang Da. 2001a. "Xiaoshui di si jie Cunweihui huanjie xuanju guancha" (A study on the fourth village election in Xiaoshui). In Li Lianjiang, Guo Zhenglin, and Xiao Tangbiao (eds.), *Cunweihui Xuanju Guancha* (Studies on Village Elections). Tianjin: Tianjin Renmin Chubanshe.

______. 2001b. "Xuanju beihou de jingji yu shehui tizhi: Wufang Cun xunaju kaocha yu yanjiu" (Economic and social institutions behind elections: A study on the election in Wufang Village). In Xiao Tangbiao, Qiu Xinyou, and Tang Xiaoteng (eds.), *Duowei*

Shijiao zhong de Cunmin Zhixuan: Dui Shi-Wu ge Cunweihui Xuanju de Guancha Yanjiu (Village Elections from a Multidimensional Angle: Studies on Fifteen Village Elections). Beijing: Zhongguo Shehui Kexue Chubanse.

Yang, Dali L. 1996. *Calamity and Reform in China: State, Rural Society, and Institutional Change since the Great Leap Famine*. Stanford, CA: Stanford University Press.

———. 2004. *Remaking the Chinese Leviathan: Market Transition and the Politics of Governance in China*. Stanford, CA: Stanford University Press.

Yep, Ray. 2004. "Can 'Tax-for-Fee' Reform Reduce Rural Tension in China? The Process, Progress and Limitations." *The China Quarterly* 177: 42–70.

Yi Hui. 2002. "Liyi gongtongdi yu xuanju: Wangshatang Cun xuanju guancha" (The interest-based community and an election: A study on the election in Wangshatang Village). In Xiao Tangbiao (ed.), *Zongzu, Xiangcun Quanli yu Xuanju: Dui Jiangxi Sheng Shi-Er ge Cunweihui Xuanju de Guancha Yanjiu* (Kinships, Rural Power, and Elections: Studies on Twelve Village Elections in Jiangxi Province). Xi'an: Xibei Daxue Chubanshe.

Yi Hui and Xiao Tangbiao. 2001. "Ganqun guanxi, zongzu yu xuanju: Kuanxia Cun zhixuan guancha" (Cadre-mass relations, kinships, and elections: An observation of the direct election). In Xiao Tangbiao, Qiu Xinyou, and Tang Xiaoteng (eds.), *Duowei Shijiao zhong de Cunmin Zhixuan: Dui Shi-Wu ge Cunweihui Xuanju de Guancha Yanjiu* (Village Elections from a Multidimensional Angle: Studies on Fifteen Village Elections). Beijing: Zhongguo Shehui Kexue Chubanse.

Ying Xing. 2001. *Dahe Yimin Shangfang de Gushi* (A Story of Migrating Petitioners from a Great River). Beijing: Sanlian Shudian.

Yip, Ngai-ming, and Yihong Jiang. 2012. "Homeowners United: The Attempt to Create Lateral Networks of Homeowners' Associations in Urban China." *Journal of Contemporary China* 20: 735–50.

Yu Jianrong. 2000. "Liyi, quanwei he zhixu: Dui nongcun duikang jiceng zhengfu de quntixing shijian de fenxi" (Interests, authority, and order: An analysis of collective incidents against grassroots governments in rural areas). *Zhongguo Nongcun Guancha* (Survey on Rural China) 4: 70–76.

———. 2001. *Yuecun Zhengzhi: Zhuanxinqi Zhongguo Xiangcun Zhengzhi Jiegou de Bianqian* (Politics in Yue Village: Transformation of the Political Structure during Rural Reforms in China). Beijing: Shangwu Yinshuguan.

Yu Liedong. 2005. "Quanmian quxiao nongye shui dui cunji zuzhi jianshe ji duice: Dui Jiangxi Sheng 31 ge cun de diaocha" (The impact of the complete abolition of the agricultural tax on construction of village-level organizations and their measures: A study of 31 villages in Jiangxi Province). (http://www.chinaelections.org/NewsInfo.asp?NewsID=41754, accessed September 20, 2009).

Yu Liedong and Xiao Tangbiao. 2001. "Jianfeng Cun di si jie Cunweihui xuanju guancha" (A study of the fourth village election in Jianfeng Village). In Li Lianjiang, Guo Zhenglin, and Xiao Tangbiao (eds.), *Cunweihui Xuanju Guancha* (Studies on Village Elections). Tianjin: Tianjin Renmin Chubanshe.

Zelin, Madeleine. 1984. *The Magistrate's Tael: Rationalizing Fiscal Reform in Eighteenth Century Ch'ing China*. Berkeley: University of California Press.

Zhan Chengfu. 2004. *Xiangcun Zhengzhi Ruogan Wenti Yanjiu* (Research on Issues of Rural Politics). Xi'an: Xibei Daxue Chubanshe.

Zhan, Jing Vivian. 2006. "The Logic of Fiscal Reforms: Analysis of Central Control versus Local Discretion in China." Ph.D. dissertation. University of California, Los Angeles.

———. 2009a. "Decentralizing China: Analysis of Central Strategies in China's Fiscal Reforms." *Journal of Contemporary China* 18: 445–62.

———. 2009b. "Undermining State Capacity: Vertical and Horizontal Diffusions of Fiscal Power in China." *Asian Politics and Policy* 1: 390–408.

Zhang Faxiang. 2001. "Xingzheng yizhi zhudao xia de xuanju: Dong Cun xuanju guancha" (An election under the administrative initiative: A study on the election in Dong Village). In Xiao Tangbiao, Qiu Xinyou, and Tang Xiaoteng (eds.), *Duowei Shijiao zhong de Cunmin Zhixuan: Dui Shi-Wu ge Cunweihui Xuanju de Guancha Yanjiu* (Village Elections from a Multidimensional Angle: Studies on Fifteen Village Elections). Beijing: Zhongguo Shehui Kexue Chubanse.

Zhang, Jianjun. 2009. *Marketization and Democracy in China*. New York: Routledge.

Zhang Jing. 2000. *Jiceng Zhengquan: Xiangcun Zhidu Zhu Wenti* (Various Problems of Rural Local Governance in China). Hangzhou: Zhejiang Renmin Chubanshe.

———. 2007. *Jiceng Zhengquan: Xiangcun Zhidu Zhu Wenti* (Various Problems of Rural Local Governance in China), revised edition. Shanghai: Shiji Chuban Jituan Shanghai Renmin Chubanshe.

Zhang Letian. 1998. *Gaobie Lixiang: Renmin Gongshe Zhidu Yanjiu* (Farewell to the Ideal: A Study of the People's Commune Institution). Shanghai: Dongfang Chuban Zhonxin.

Zhang, Li. 2001a. "Migration and Privatization of Space and Power in Late Socialist China." *American Ethnologist* 28: 179–205.

———. 2001b. *Strangers in the City: Reconfigurations of Space, Power, and Social Networks within China's Floating Population*. Stanford, CA: Stanford University Press.

Zhao Shukai. 2010. *Xiangzhen Zhili yu Zhengfu Zhiduhua* (Township governance and the institutionalization of governments). Beijing: Shangwu Yinshuguan.

Zheng Xin. 2005. *Xiangcun Zhengzhi zhong de Boyi Shengcun: Huabei Nongcun Cunmin Shangfang Yanjiu* (Survival Games in Rural Politics: A Study on Rural Petitions in North China). Beijing: Zhongguo Shehui Kexue Chubanshe.

Zhou, Guangyuan. 1993. "Illusion and Reality in the Law of the Late Qing: A Sichuan Case Study." *Modern China* 19: 427–56.

Zhou, Kate Xiao. 1996. *How the Farmers Changed China: Power of the People*. Boulder, CO: Westview Press.

Zhou, Li, and Hiroki Takeuchi. 2010. "Informal Lenders and Rural Finance in China: A Report from the Field." *Modern China* 36: 302–28.

Zhou Qingzhi. 2004. *Zhongguo Xianji Xingzheng Jiegou ji Qi Yunxing: Dui W Xian de Shehuixue Kaocha* (China's County Government and Its Administration: A Sociological Study of W County). Guiyang: Guizhou Renmin Chubanshe.

Zhou, Xueguang. 2010. "The Institutional Logic of Collusion among Local Governments in China." *Modern China* 36: 47–78.

Zhu, Jiangnan. 2012. "The Shadow of the Skyscrapers: Real Estate Corruption in China." *Journal of Contemporary China* 21: 243–60.

Zhu, Keliang, and Roy Prosterman. 2007. "Securing Land Rights for Chinese Farmers: A Leap Forward for Stability and Growth." Cato Institute Center for Global Liberty and Prosperity, Development Policy Analysis. (http://ssrn.com/abstract=1066812, accessed June 27, 2010).

Zhu Shouyin, Zhang Haiyang, and Yan Hui. 2004. "Nongcun shuifei gaige shidian he xiangcun guanli tizhi gaige genzong yanjiu baogao" (A research report following the testing points of rural reforms). In Li Changping and Dong Leiming (eds.), *Shuifei Gaige Beijing xia de Xiangzhen Tizhi Yanjiu* (Studies on the Township Regime under the Influence of the Tax-for-Fee Reform). Wuhan: Hubei Renmin Chubanshe.

Zweig, David. 1997. *Freeing China's Farmers: Rural Restructuring in the Reform Era*. Armonk, NY: M. E. Sharpe.

______. 2003. "To the Courts or to the Barricades: Can New Political Institutions Manage Rural Conflict?" In Elizabeth J. Perry and Mark Selden (eds.), *Chinese Society: Change, Conflict and Resistance*, second edition. New York: Routledge Curzon.

Index

Page numbers in *italics* refers to material in figures and tables.